The Allied Assault on Hitler's Channel Island Fortress

The Allied Assault on Hitler's Channel Island Fortress

The Planned Operation to Eject the Germans in 1943

John Grehan

FRONTLINE BOOKS

First published in Great Britain in 2023 by
Frontline Books
An imprint of Pen & Sword Books Limited
Yorkshire – Philadelphia

Copyright © John Grehan 2023

ISBN 978 1 39908 422 2

The right of John Grehan to be identified as
Author of this Work has been asserted by him in accordance
with the Copyright, Designs and Patents Act 1988.

A CIP catalogue record for this book is
available from the British Library

All rights reserved. No part of this book may be reproduced or
transmitted in any form or by any means, electronic or mechanical
including photocopying, recording or by any information storage and
retrieval system, without permission from the Publisher in writing.

Typeset by Mac Style
Printed in the UK by CPI Group (UK) Ltd, Croydon, CR0 4YY.

Pen & Sword Books Limited incorporates the imprints of After
the Battle, Atlas, Archaeology, Aviation, Discovery, Family History,
Fiction, History, Maritime, Military, Military Classics, Politics,
Select, Transport, True Crime, Air World, Frontline Publishing, Leo
Cooper, Remember When, Seaforth Publishing, The Praetorian Press,
Wharncliffe Local History, Wharncliffe Transport, Wharncliffe True
Crime and White Owl.

For a complete list of Pen & Sword titles please contact

PEN & SWORD BOOKS LIMITED
47 Church Street, Barnsley, South Yorkshire, S70 2AS, England
E-mail: enquiries@pen-and-sword.co.uk
Website: www.pen-and-sword.co.uk
or
PEN AND SWORD BOOKS
1950 Lawrence Rd, Havertown, PA 19083, USA
E-mail: Uspen-and-sword@casematepublishers.com
Website: www.penandswordbooks.com

Contents

Chapter 1	Early One Morning in July 1943	1
Chapter 2	'So Modest an Operation'	5
Chapter 3	Europe First	27
Chapter 4	Back to Washington	44
Chapter 5	Moscow	61
Chapter 6	Dieppe	82
Chapter 7	Husky	93
Chapter 8	'The Best Air Raid Shelter'	105
Chapter 9	Operation Constellation: The Retaking of the Channel Islands	118
Chapter 10	Operation Concertina: The Re-occupation of Alderney	136
Chapter 11	Operation Coverlet: The Re-occupation of Guernsey	151
Chapter 12	Coverlet – The Plan of Attack on Guernsey	163
Chapter 13	Operation Condor: The Re-Occupation of Jersey	177
Chapter 14	Condor – The Plan of Attack on Jersey	189
Chapter 15	Constelation Cancelled	199
Epilogue: The German Defences of the Channel Islands Today		205
Notes		210
Source Information		215
Index of People and Places		219

Chapter 1

Early One Morning in July 1943

Peter Gleeson stood waiting for his old dog Rosy to finish sniffing round the garden. It was almost three miserable years since he had been able to take her for a walk. The Germans had imposed a strict night-time curfew and only those with legitimate reasons for being abroad during the hours of darkness were permitted beyond their homes. Walking the dog was not one of them.

The situation had got worse since the British troops had retaken Alderney. What had been called a 'model' occupation had turned quite nasty. The Germans were clearly on edge and were reacting badly. But, in truth, they had little to worry about – for now anyway. It was one thing for the Brits to assault Alderney, but quite another for them to attack Guernsey or Jersey.

Almost all the inhabitants had evacuated Alderney before the Germans had invaded and only a handful had stubbornly remained. There had been rumours of terrible things on Alderney; of ill-treatment, or worse; of Russian prisoners used as slave labour overheard from half-drunk Germans talking too loudly and saying too much. It was said that no prisoner ever left Alderney – dead or alive.

It was a secret island, where the Germans could do, and did, whatever they wanted. The massive bombardment of Alderney, as well as destroying the German fortifications, must have done considerable damage to the islanders' houses and property and, as Peter looked back at his lovely old cottage, he felt for those who would return after the war to find their homes in ruin. Yet there had been scarcely 1,500 people on the island before the evacuation. Their loss was not a major one amid such a catastrophic war, and its recapture ended whatever atrocities may have been committed there.

Such a thing could not happen here, Peter reflected. There were some 25,000 islanders still left on Guernsey and 40,000 on Jersey. If the British attacked, it would be carnage. No, it could never happen here on this peaceful, if oppressed, island.

As Peter waited patiently for Rosy to finish her morning toilet – there was little else to do these days, after all – he thought he heard the sound of aero engines. Looking up he saw a feint glow to the north, the high clouds reflecting light from below, from Alderney.

Rosy poked her head out of the bush she had been investigating. The sound of the aircraft grew increasingly louder, alarmingly louder. Suddenly, he was momentarily blinded as the searchlight at the entrance to L'Ancresse Bay switched on as, one by one, were others across the island. The sky seemed lit from horizon to horizon and moments later the German guns opened fire from all around. Never had he heard such a din.

Rosy had long bolted back inside while Peter's neighbours, John and Margaret, had rushed out into their rear garden. He could see them shouting and pointing but could not hear their voices over the chattering of the anti-aircraft guns. Then it began. Explosion after explosion shook the ground. The thudding detonations and the dazzling lights overwhelmed Peter's senses, and the air was sucked from his lungs as he convulsed uncontrollably. This cannot be happening. This cannot be happening. The British are bombing their own people!

Another explosion lifted Peter into the air, flinging him into his south-facing flowerbed. Temporarily oblivious to the detonations around him, he laid there baffled, hurt, and confused. Later, Peter would later say that he had no idea how long he had remained stretched out among the marigolds and delphiniums. But he vividly recalled, as the sky began to lighten, seeing the confused mass of round white dots swirling above him.

Peter stared as German machine-guns opened fire on the paratroopers swinging helplessly below their canopies, arms flailing as their bodies shook with the impact of the German bullets. It was horrifying to watch, but he could not turn his eyes away. For the islanders the deployment of paratroopers was, if anything, far more frightening than the bombing, because it was evident that the RAF had not made a mistake – the Channel Islands were coming under a full-scale assault and the horror, death and destruction which had passed them by was now upon them.

The noise of battle, as more aircraft – Spitfire fighter-bombers and twin-engine Mosquitos – swept low over the island to attack the German howitzer batteries at Les Effards, was sickeningly disorientating. As Peter slowly regained his senses, his thoughts went first to his daughter, as any father's would. Susan lived just down Rocque Balan Lane. He had to see if she was alright.

Wobbling uncertainly, Peter picked his way past the glass that had been blown from his and next-door's windows and out onto Les Clotures Road. Gunfire thudded against his eardrums, but it seemed largely to be behind him, as if a battle had begun on L'Ancresse Common. But just as he turned down Rocque Balan Lane, Peter stopped. His daughter's house appeared as if it had been sliced in two. The easterly side of the old building stood, seemingly at a distance, unscathed. The western part had been cut down, only part of the bedroom floor protruding, defying gravity.

Similar sights were seen throughout Guernsey. It seemed that every part of the island had been struck. Huge bomb craters scarred the fields, rubble blocked the roads and bodies lay amid the ruins of houses. It was utterly incomprehensible. When the Germans approached the French coast in 1940, Britain had turned its back on the Channel Islands, abandoning them to whatever fate Hitler had in store. The reasoning, which Winston Churchill had finally had to accept, was that the only way to save the Channel Islands from becoming a battleground was by leaving them undefended and allowing the Germans to occupy the islands unopposed. As a result, for three years the islanders had endured the deadening and arbitrary impositions of the occupying forces; and, if all that was not enough, the British were now bombing them out of their homes, for the scenes across Guernsey were repeated on Jersey. What on earth had possessed the decision-makers in Whitehall to commit this outrage?

None of the above occurred, of course. When the Channel Islands were liberated and the German garrison surrendered at the end of the war, it was a peaceful, if tense, affair, and no blood was shed. But the fact that British and American military and political leaders seriously considered a massive assault upon the Channel Islands is no fiction. All it would have needed at the time was the nod of approval from Prime Minister and Minister of Defence Winston Churchill, and the attack would have been carried out, as everything had been carefully analysed and planned.

This book explains how sane, rational men, under pressure to achieve positive results, came to see the killing of British people and the destruction of their homes as acceptable collateral damage merely to strike an indeterminate, ill-defined, blow against Germany.

This is the convoluted – and admittedly protracted – story of what so nearly became one of the most controversial actions of the Second World War.

Chapter 2

'So Modest an Operation'

On 4 June 1940, as the last of the troops rescued from Dunkirk were disembarking at Dover after being chased out of France and Belgium by Hitler's blitzkrieg, Britain's new prime minister, Winston Churchill, delivered what was probably his most famous speech. He told his people the enemy would be fought on the beaches and the landing grounds, in the fields, the hills and the streets. What he also said, perhaps more significantly, was 'we shall fight in France, we shall fight on the seas and oceans, we shall fight with growing confidence and growing strength'. According to Churchill's history of the Second World War, to emphasise the point he had made in his speech, that same day he dictated a note to his military secretary, General 'Pug' Ismay:

> The completely defensive habit of mind which has ruined the French must not be allowed to ruin all our initiative. It is of the highest consequence to keep the largest numbers of German forces all along the coasts of the countries they have conquered, and we should immediately set to work to organise raiding forces on these coasts where the populations are friendly. Such forces might be composed of self-contained, thoroughly equipped units of say one thousand up to not more than ten thousand when combined. Surprise would be ensured by the fact that the destinations would be concealed until the last moment.[1]

With that simple memorandum the concept of what would eventually be known as the Commandos was conceived and, with it, Combined Operations, the body that produced a plan to attack the Channel Islands in 1943.

As it happened, Lieutenant Colonel Dudley Clark, who worked with the Chief of the Imperial General Staff, had listened to Churchill's speech and was thinking the matter over while walking home that evening.

Remembering the occasions in history when small, highly mobile forces, particularly in the Boer War, had succeeded in harassing a very much larger enemy, he felt that similar results might now be achieved by means of amphibious Commandos which, as we still had command of the sea, could carry out mobile hit and run raids across the Channel. In addition to being good for morale at home, these might provide valuable intelligence, and must also force the Germans to devote some at least of their attention and troops to coast defence over a wide area.

The next morning, following the prime minister's note to Ismay, Clark was told by the C.I.G.S., General Dill, that 'an immediate means of fostering the offensive spirit of the Army was needed', so Clark explained his ideas. Dill was impressed, submitted the idea to Churchill, and the next morning the scheme was approved.[2]

Two days later Churchill again told Ismay, 'I look to the Chiefs of Staff to propose me measures for a vigorous enterprising and ceaseless offensive against the whole German occupied coastline.'[3] The Chiefs of Staff duly responded and on 14 June appointed Lieutenant General Alan Bourne RM to the post of 'Commander of Raiding Operations on coasts in enemy occupation, and Adviser to the Chiefs of Staff on Combined Operations'. From this small beginning grew the vast organisation that, on 6 June 1944, almost exactly four years to the day after Churchill's memo, launched the greatest amphibious operation of all time.

Combined Operations and Commando raids were to play a key role in Britain's war strategy. Britain intended to mount a war of attrition by blockading enemy ports, undertaking a heavy air offensive and engaging in every form of propaganda or deception that would confuse the enemy and undermine morale. British planners did not foresee 'vast armies of infantry as in 1914-1918. The forces we employ will be armoured divisions. To supplement their operations the local partisans must be secretly armed and equipped so that at the right moment they may rise in revolt.'[4] The Commandos' part was to strike at enemy-occupied posts and positions, anywhere, at any time, tying down disproportionately large numbers of enemy troops and further weakening enemy morale while boosting that of the people in the Occupied countries. The exact wording of the directive given to Bourne was that: 'The object of the raiding operations is to harass the enemy and cause him to disperse his forces and to create material damage, particularly on the coastline from Northern Norway to the western limit of German-occupied France.'

A new body, No. 11 Independent Company, was raised on 14 June and ten days later was engaged in its first operation, codenamed *Collar*. On the night of 24/25 June, 115 men were landed on the French coast from four boats between Boulogne and the Pointe de Harbanc. Their objective, officially, was to discover the nature of the German defences and to bring back prisoners. In reality, it mattered little what they accomplished. The fact that British troops could land and attack the Germans on ground they had only recently occupied was what really counted, showing Hitler that Britain was far from beaten.

The men did, in fact, make contact with German troops. One group became embroiled in a firefight with five of the enemy, and a second group killed two German sentries at a point to the south of Le Touquet.

Though a minuscule affair in terms of the war at large, it enabled the Ministry of Information to issue a highly encouraging communique: 'Naval and military raiders, in cooperation with the RAF, carried out successful reconnaissances of the enemy coastline: landings were effected at a number of points and contacts made with German troops. Casualties were inflicted on the enemy, but no British casualties occurred, and much useful information was obtained.'[5]

There was but a little pause before the next raid was mounted, this time against Guernsey on the night of 14/15 July. As will be discussed in the next chapter, German forces had occupied the Channel Islands at the end of June and, as early as 2 July, Churchill demanded that 'plans should be studied to land secretly by night on the Islands and kill or capture the invaders. This is exactly one of the exploits for which the Commandos would be suited.'[6]

Of the three groups comprising what was codenamed Operation *Ambassador*, in which forty men of No. 3 Commando joined No. 11 Independent Company for the raid, one failed to reach land, another landed on the wrong island due to compass inaccuracies – possibly Little Sark where no Germans were to be found – while the third, which reached the correct beach on time, failed to achieve any of its objectives of killing Germans, destroying German aircraft and facilities on Guernsey airport. Heavy seas meant that the boat which landed the third group could not keep close inshore and when the men returned to the beach to reembark they had to swim some 100 yards to reach the boats. Three of the men could not swim and had to be left behind. In total, four men were captured by the Germans, with nothing tangible having been achieved.

Churchill was far from impressed with this botched affair and, two days later, Bourne, who was also trying to hold down the post of Adjutant-General of the Royal Marines, asked to be relieved of his position at the head of raiding operations. He was replaced by Admiral of the Fleet Roger Keyes, to the newly named post of Director of Combined Operations, with Bourne remaining as his deputy. This added momentum to the new force, which quickly began to take on a more definable shape. Recruits were drawn from the Army, made up almost entirely by men who had volunteered for undisclosed 'Special Duty', who underwent rigorous physical and combat training.

Bourne had struggled to find a clear direction from the War Cabinet and after being urged by Churchill to harass the enemy-occupied coasts 'ceaselessly', the prime minister changed his tune, declaring that: 'It would be most unwise to disturb the coasts of any of these countries by the kind of silly fiasco which were perpetrated at Boulogne and Guernsey. The idea of working all these coasts against us by pin-prick raids ... is one to be strictly avoided.'[7]

The Germans were equally derogatory about *Ambassador*, with a staff officer on Guernsey, Dr Maass, warning that: 'such futile enterprises were typical instances of British inefficiency and examples of what would happen should large scale landings be attempted on the Continent.'[8]

Keyes was told to plan for assaults upon the enemy with forces of between 5,000 and 10,000 men. 'If we are to have any campaign in 1941 it must be amphibious in its character', wrote Churchill, 'there certainly will be many opportunities of minor operations all of which will depend on surprise landings of lightly equipped mobile forces accustomed to work like packs of hounds.'[9] By March 1941 Keyes was ready to undertake the first Combined Operations raid of the war – against a small group of islands beyond the Arctic Circle some 900 miles from Britain.

The Lofoten Islands are situated a few miles off the coast of northern Norway and seemed an unlikely target. From there, however, the Germans obtained valuable supplies of herring and cod oil which was used to make glycerine for explosives. Also, the Germans would not suspect an attack on such a remote place and would therefore be unprepared.

The attacking force would be the recently re-designated No. 3 and No. 4 Commando. While each Commando was just 250-strong, they were to be supported by fifty-two Royal Engineers and fifty-two men from the Norwegian forces, as well as, of course, the many Royal Navy personnel and vessels.

The raiding party, of what was codenamed Operation *Claymore*, set off from Scapa Flow on 1 March, reaching the Lofoten Islands on the morning of 4 March. The small German garrisons were taken completely by surprise and by midday, their tasks having been completed, the Commandos re-embarked. Apart from the destruction of the glycerine factories and military installations (resulting in the burning of an estimated 800,000 gallons of oil and petrol) and eleven ships being sunk, the Commandos returned to the UK with 315 volunteers for the Norwegian Navy and Merchant Marine, sixty Quislings and some 228 German prisoners.[10]

The only British casualty was one British officer who accidentally shot himself in the thigh when he slipped on the frozen surface, having carelessly stuffed a .45 Colt revolver into a trouser pocket. That aside, few would doubt that the first of the twelve commando raids directed against Norway during the war was anything but a success. It was just the kind of operation Churchill wanted.

It was also in February 1941 that a scheme was devised to capture and hold Jersey and Guernsey, under the codename *Attaboy*. In a report prepared by Keyes' team following a request from Ismay, Jersey and Guernsey are referred to as islands 'A' and 'B'. It seems evident that the original intention was to recapture both islands, but this was toned down to be one in which the islands were occupied, the German garrison captured or killed, and their installations destroyed, before the British troops withdrew – all within the space of 24 hours.

Intriguingly, it was Keyes himself who saw problems with this.

The first of these was that if the approach to the islands and the withdrawal to and from the UK were to be made during the hours of darkness, then it would only be possible for the troops to remain on Island 'A' (which it must be presumed was Guernsey, the nearest of the two to England) for 4 hours and for an even shorter time on Island 'B'.

He also said that the approaches to the few beaches on which it was practicable to land troops were covered by coastal artillery batteries and what were termed Martello Towers, which were likely to have been turned into machine-gun posts. The so-called Martello Towers are actually round loophole towers built during the American War of Independence.

Keyes, wisely, was staunchly opposed to the venture, finding every possible reason not to mount the operation. His next point was that: 'Covering fire in darkness from destroyers and cruisers to silence enemy fire from batteries and strong posts is unlikely to be effective and could not be used without endangering British civilians.'

He stated that it would take a 'considerable' force to penetrate the German defences and that it was 'unlikely' that in the time available it would be possible to capture the batteries and strongpoints covering the beaches. This would mean that re-embarkation under the enemy guns would be 'costly, if not impracticable'.[11]

Keyes also observed it was inevitable that after the British troops had withdrawn, the Germans would retaliate against the civilian population, as they had in other countries, for example in Norway.

The Chiefs of Staff agreed with Keyes and, thankfully, *Attaboy* was not followed through. The subject was not dropped in its entirety, however, and Keyes was asked to look into carrying out a large raid on the islands with the limited aim of simply inflicting heavy losses on the Germans. Keyes was also against this, believing that such an operation would be difficult if not impossible to carry out and that it would be unlikely surprise could be achieved. Instead, he suggested a small operation of just 270 men to capture prisoners from whom information could be garnered. This was to be Operation *Barbaric*. Surprisingly, it was Churchill who doubted the value in such an operation, questioning whether any really useful information could be gleaned from any such prisoners. He cancelled it on his own authority.[12]

In March, Keyes asked for and received permission from the Chiefs of Staff for the assembly of a 'Striking Force' to be made immediately available for combined operations in any theatre. This resulted in all available ships and landing craft being earmarked for use by the new force.

The next combined operation in European waters was Operation *Chess*. This, though, was a small-scale affair of just seventeen men from No. 12 Commando, whose task was to carry out a reconnaissance and, if possible, capture a German soldier. However, they had been given just 1 hour ashore to accomplish this. The target for the raid was Ambleteuse, Pas-de-Calais, France.

On the night of 27/28 July 1941, the raiding party landed near Ambleteuse but was spotted almost immediately by German soldiers on the cliffs above the beach. They came under fire, which they were able, in part, to counter. After the designated hour they returned to the landing craft, still under fire, with two men being killed after reaching the vessel.

In August two further raids were mounted. The first, codenamed *Gauntlet*, was a Combined Operation not involving Commandos, which took place between 25 August and 3 September to the Norwegian island of Spitsbergen. Coal was mined there, and the intention was to destroy the mining and shipping infrastructure on Spitsbergen to deny coal to the Germans, as well as to wreck a weather station there to prevent the Germans receiving weather reports. The operation was a success, with some 2,000 Russian miners and their families being shipped to Archangel.

The second, on the night of 30/31 August, did involve Commandos. *Acid Drop* consisted of just thirty men who landed in two parties to the west of Boulogne. No Germans were encountered, and the Commandos returned to their boats after just 30 minutes.

The strength of the German forces in western Europe was such that Keyes did not believe the kind of large-scale raids envisaged by Churchill could be accomplished and instead turned his attention to the Middle East, the Mediterranean and even the Canary Islands and West Africa, with varying degrees of success.

With regards to cross-Channel operations, on the night of 27/28 September, two simultaneous raids took place involving fifty men of No. 1 Commando who landed on the French coast near Cherbourg. Both parties encountered German troops. Two men were killed and two wounded. The main aim of bringing back at least one German prisoner was not accomplished.

The very limited nature and uneven achievements of the Commandos prompted criticism from Regular Army generals who claimed that they were largely a 'waste of effort' and 'could have been better done by a unit of the Field Army'. The Army chiefs had never been very supportive of the independent nature of the Commandos, complaining that many of their best men were being lost to this seemingly exciting organisation. They believed that every division should be capable of mounting Commando-style operations, not just specially organised units, and they had already begun training regular battalions (including, incidentally, my father's battalion) at Inveraray, Scotland, in amphibious operations.

Their arguments eventually received some backing from Churchill, and no operation could thereafter be mounted from the UK without the consent of General Sir Alan Brooke, Commander-in-Chief Home Forces. In fact, the Home Forces military commanders advanced the extraordinary view, according to Captain John 'Jock' Hughes-Hallett, the naval advisor to Combined Ops Headquarters and the man who became responsible for the planning of raids, that the English south coast and the French north coast 'should be likened to a front line of two armies locked in trench warfare, with the Channel as No Man's Land between them. From this it was argued that the initiative for mounting raids should rest with the Army commanders whose areas faced a particular piece of enemy coast.'[13] Keyes' title was correspondingly changed from 'Director' to merely that of 'Advisor'.

Admiral Keyes did not like this one bit and so, on 27 October 1941, he was replaced as head of Combined Operations by Lord Louis Mountbatten, initially with the title Keyes had baulked against of 'Advisor on Combined Operations', although this was later raised to 'Chief of Combined Operations'.

Mountbatten intended to raise the raids to a much higher level. However, the first operation on his watch was one that had been organised during his predecessor's reign. Operation *Astrakan* was a mission to gather reconnaissance for a larger raid, Operation *Sunstar*, against the German gun battery at Houlgate in Normandy. The former operation involved just two pairs of canoeists. One pair was captured but the other pair landed and was able to confirm that the beach would be suitable for a larger landing. On the night of 22/23 November, therefore, 100 men of No. 9 Commando landed at Houlgate but accomplished absolutely nothing. All this indicated just how ineffectual Combined Ops had become, something that Mountbatten was determined to change.

December 1941 saw the first of Mountbatten's more ambitious enterprises. Operation *Archery* was a raid on the Norwegian islands of Vaagso and Maaloy, which included more than 500 Commandos, a cruiser and four destroyers and, for the first time, the RAF. It was a genuine combined services operation. The main purposes of *Archery* were to destroy the fish-oil production facilities as the oil was used by the Germans in the manufacture of high explosives. At the same time a diversionary raid was undertaken against the Lofoten islands by 300 men from No. 12 Commando. Both missions included Norwegian troops.

The two raids were a success, with much damage being done. They prompted the Germans to strengthen their garrisons in Norway considerably, thus reducing the number of soldiers fighting on the critical Eastern Front against the Soviet Union – precisely what Churchill had expected of the Commandos.

At the end of 1941, Brooke became Chief of the Imperial General Staff, with General Sir Bernard Paget taking over Home Forces. Just before taking up his new role, Paget was asked by the Chiefs of Staff to prepare 'a large-scale raid of some duration in the Low Countries and France' for the spring of 1942. Paget settled 'reluctantly' on Brest as the target (Operation *Sesame*), though he saw little value in such raids:

> The sole object of killing Germans is not worth of a large-scale raid since they are in good supply and of comparatively low propaganda value. The destruction of material objectives themselves must have lasting results on enemy operations or war production and the objectives themselves must not be such as can be more easily or less expensively destroyed by a) air bombardment b) naval bombardment c) minor sea or airborne raids d) local patriots.[14]

It was just such a 'minor' raid that the new year began with Operation *Curlew*, a reconnaissance mission to investigate the defences around the village of Saint-Laurent-sur-Mer in Normandy on the night of 11/12 January 1942. The fifteen men involved learned little and did not encounter any enemy troops.

Curlew's limited scale and scope smacked of the Keyes era, the stain of which Mountbatten was determined to avoid, and he was encouraged by a decision made by the Chiefs of Staff on 13 February that the policy of small raids was to be 'pressed vigorously'. Their directive to Paget, as C-in-C Home Forces, also stressed that:

> German morale and strength in the West may deteriorate at any time in the future to a degree that will permit us to establish forces on the Continent. You are, therefore, to plan and prepare for a return to the Continent to take advantage of such a situation ... You should continue your study of a major raiding operation against one of the main French ports in case it becomes desirable to carry one out ... the Advisor on Combined Operations [Mountbatten] to be consulted at all stages of the planning.[15]

Mountbatten was quick to seize this opportunity and that same month, February, he laid down plans for the most ambitious raid so far – to destroy the dockyard facilities at Saint-Nazaire in France, the only port on the Atlantic coast with a dry dock (built to accommodate the Atlantic liner SS *Normandie*) able to accommodate the largest of Germany's battleships.

At 14.00 hours on 26 March 1942, the flotilla of Royal Navy vessels left Falmouth and began its long passage to the French port. The operation involved 345 Royal Navy personnel, 257 Commandos, a four-man medical team, three liaison officers and two representatives from the press, in total 611 men. The plan was for the old destroyer *Campbeltown* to be packed with explosives and for her to be rammed into the drydock gates. The Commandos would then disembark from the destroyer and accompanying coastal craft to demolish the dock installations, searchlights, and gun emplacements. The destroyer would then be blown up, demolishing the gates and wrecking the dry dock.

Often considered the greatest raid of all, Operation *Chariot* was a resounding success. *Campbeltown* and the motor launches came under heavy fire as they entered the Loire estuary, but the destroyer was driven into the lock gates and immediately the Commandos rushed ashore. They attacked German defensive positions and destroyed the pumphouse used to pump water out of the *Normandie* Dock.

The plan had been to withdraw from the port's Mole on motor launches and transfer to destroyers waiting out at sea, but most of the small vessels had been destroyed by German gunfire. The Commandos were in a precarious situation for they were surrounded by water on three sides and German reinforcements were descending upon St Nazaire and the port. They could either surrender or attempt to escape. Being Commandos, surrender was not an option and so they tried to escape, but most did not make it.

It was not until noon that the explosives in *Campbeltown* ignited. The massive explosion ripped a huge gap through which the sea burst into the empty dry dock, taking part of the destroyer with it. The port was a scene of utter carnage; the remains of German personnel that had gone onboard *Campbeltown* were blown across the port, with some being found up to a mile away.

There was a high price to pay for the success of the raid. Out of 611 men that took part in the operation, 169 were killed and approximately 200 were captured and remained in captivity in POW camps for the duration of the war. Five Commandos did, however, manage to make their way to the Spanish border, where they travelled back home to the UK via Gibraltar.

German casualties amounted to forty-two killed and 127 personnel wounded. Such was the magnitude of the destruction the Germans were never able to use the dry dock again.

Buoyed with this great achievement, Mountbatten continued to plan and his next raid was in response to a request from the Air Ministry's Scientific Information Branch for a mission to be undertaken to seize as much instrumentation as could be carried back to England of a new machine at the German radar station at Bruneval, a small village on the French coast near Le Havre. The site was close to the cliff edge from which a path led down to an easily accessible beach. The raid was approved by Mountbatten and scheduled for late February.

Rather than launch the assault from the sea, Operation *Biting* was to see a radar specialist and 120 men of 'C' Company, 2nd Battalion The Parachute Regiment, dropped onto the cliffs close to the radar site. On the night of 27/28 February, the small force landed between 1 and 2 miles from the installation. The Paras moved swiftly towards the radar station, encountering fire from German positions in a wooded enclosure some 300 yards to the north. But the radar operators fled. Using screwdrivers, crowbars and brute force, the British team ripped out or dismantled every important component. Flashlight photographs of the mechanism were taken, and notes and hurried drawings were made.

The Paras then made their escape with all the material they could carry down to the beach for the pre-arranged rendezvous with the Royal Navy. The raid was a great success and encouraged Mountbatten to start planning another ambitious scheme, this time against the Island of

Alderney. This new plan was called Operation *Blazing* and the aim was not merely to conduct an amphibious raid on the island, but recapture and hold it.

The first formal meeting to discuss *Blazing* took place at Combined Operations Headquarters on the morning of 3 March 1942. At this Mountbatten said that the benefits of the seizure of Alderney were:

a) morale and prestige
b) the possibility of a triumph for our propaganda at the expense of that of the Germans
c) the opening of a second front though only in a very small way.[16]

The plan was for parachutists to make the initial assault, which would then be followed by the landing of other troops to complete the capture of the island. Major General Frederick Browning, General Officer Commanding of the 1st Airborne Division, insisted that the paratroopers, whom he said were 'specially skilled men difficult to replace', should be relieved as soon as possible by other troops. The paratroopers should be returned to the UK on successive nights by boat.

A suggestion was made that glider-borne troops might be used in addition to parachutists to increase the speed of the follow-up force as an alternative to arriving by sea. Browning said that if that decision was made, gliders were available. It was agreed by the fifteen senior sailors, soldiers, and airmen at the meeting that the proposition was 'attractive' and that a more detailed study should be prepared.

Meanwhile, at a further meeting on 9 March, Lieutenant Colonel Walch of the Airborne Division said that a minimum of four weeks' training would be required by his men in conjunction with the RAF for the operation, and the earliest this could begin was 1 April, meaning the troops would be ready and available for May.

As a result, an 'Outline of Operations' for *Blazing* was prepared by the Combined Operations Headquarters planning team for presentation to the Chiefs of Staff Committee. The first part of which read:

> The Germans have recently increased the fortifications of the Channel Islands with particular reference to the anti-aircraft defences. The total garrison on the Island of Alderney is now

believed to number 2,200, including a construction battalion, 640 men manning 30 light anti-aircraft and twelve heavy anti-aircraft guns, a number of coast defence gunners, signallers, R.D.F. personnel and about 500 infantry. It is believed that there are no English people on the island although it is possible there is a small working party of Islanders from Guernsey.'[17]

The stated advantages of holding the island were:

(a) A small craft base for cutting the Germans' coastal convoy route to the Atlantic ports by which they had sustained much of the U-boat campaign[18]
(b) An advance RDF station to extend the Fighter Command Coverage
(c) An emergency landing ground for aircraft
(d) A diversion which may cause withdrawal of enemy air forces from other fronts, including the withdrawal of bombers from Norway
(e) A diversion which may cause the withdrawal of military [i.e., land] forces from other fronts
(f) An opportunity for bringing enemy air forces to battle under reasonably favourable circumstances
(g) A springboard for further combined operations.

The force required for this operation was:

Naval
6 Hunt Class Destroyers
5 Infantry Assault Ships (with 4 Landing Craft, Support, and 36 Landing Craft, Assault)
8 MGBs
4 Shore based ALC
18 TLC
30 'R' Craft
4 Schuyts

Military
4 Infantry Battalions
1 Parachute Battalion
1 Commando and two troops
1 Squadron and one or two troops of army tanks
13 Bren Carriers
1 Light Battery
1 Field Company RE
1 MG Company
Signal, RAMC, and RASC detachments
10 Pioneer Sections
3 Light AA Batteries
4 Bulldozers
Some transport to follow

RAF
330 bomber sorties, including 4 squadrons for low level bombing
40 Parachute Dropping Aircraft
8 Smoke Aircraft
Fighter Wing for the protection to returning aircraft
Fighter Wing for cover over shipping in the harbour
Fighter Wing to cover the withdrawal of the shipping on D+1
4 Intruder sorties against enemy aerodromes on the night of the assault
1 anti-flak Squadron
1 close support Fighter Squadron
Fighter Sweep to anticipate the first enemy reaction
Offensive sweeps to meet the air situation as it develops
1 close support Fighter Squadron at call
RAF Servicing Commando

This meant a total of 4,800 men, thirty-six anti-aircraft guns and a company of tanks. A proportion of these forces, particularly Browning's paratroopers, would be withdrawn after the capture of the island had been completed.

After the re-occupation of the island, the only foreseeable fighter commitment would be for weekly cover of the supply convoy during the daylight period of its crossing. Support would also be needed from the RAF if the Germans were seen making preparations to retake Alderney. This support would be either to stop the enemy attack or to cover the British withdrawal if the decision was taken that Alderney could not be held against a large German assault.

The date set for the operation was 26 May 1942, with the start time of 35 minutes before nautical twilight. The main assault would go in 90 minutes later. On that day nautical twilight was at 04.22 hours; high tide was 04.52 and sunrise was at 06.02. It was expected that tactical surprise would be achieved. The operation would take place in four phases:

Phase I

A small subsidiary landing of ninety men would be made in three bays on the western end of the island. The men would shelter at the foot of the cliffs while an intense aerial bombardment of 200 or 300 aircraft would be carried out against the main German defences. This bombardment was to commence 25 minutes before nautical twilight and would last for 65 minutes. It would be followed by a low-level bombing attack of High Explosive and smoke on the area of Port Albert, which commanded the entrance to the harbour from the east. Five minutes later the parachute battalion would be dropped, supported by fighters and covered by smoke, south of the harbour bay defences. The battalion would attack those defences in the rear as soon as it had assembled. At about this time (or earlier if the light permitted), a naval bombardment would be opened against the defences of the harbour itself. The object of this bombardment was to distract the attention of the enemy's coast defence gunners from engaging the approaching assault landing craft.

Phase II

The main assault, supported by naval gunfire and fighter aircraft, would take place in the bay to the east of the harbour, with subsidiary landings close to Fort Albert. The first flight of the assault forces would include the marching personnel of three infantry battalions, a Commando, and twelve Churchill tanks, with a floating reserve of the fourth infantry battalion along with Bren gun carriers and more tanks.

Phase III

Phase III was to take effect after the capture of the island. This would see the arrival of the follow-up force and would include anti-aircraft batteries.

Phase IV

This would see the return to the UK of the assault forces not required for the garrisoning of the island.

To maintain the garrison after the capture of Alderney with food, supplies and ammunition, it was estimated that 400 tons of stores per week would be required. This would necessitate a weekly convoy of approximately twelve small coastal ships.

At a meeting at the Combined Operations Headquarters involving officers from all three branches of the armed forces on 3 March, it was proposed that in the event of the operation being a success, German prisoners and British civilians found on Alderney should be shipped to the UK on landing craft. This would give the Germans the impression that the entire raiding party had evacuated the island and the troops left to garrison Alderney should remain carefully concealed. The hope was that the Germans would deduce there was no point in attempting to re-occupy the island as the British could, at any time they chose, take it back with fatal consequences for any Germans there. The British would only reveal their presence on the island when either in a strong enough position to be able to counter any reinvasion attempts, or when Alderney was required as a springboard for further offensives.

If the Germans did consider bombing Alderney after it had been re-occupied by British troops, it was pointed out that there would be no real targets for the Luftwaffe, especially if all vessels were withdrawn from the island before daybreak each night. It was agreed, nevertheless, that light anti-aircraft guns would be set up at an early stage. Group Captain Sir Nigel Norman, who commanded the Central Landing Establishment and was in charge of the RAF's parachute operations (and who had distinguished himself in the successful parachute drop on the radar station at Bruneval), suggested the establishment of a radar station on Alderney after its capture as that would greatly improve the early detection of enemy aircraft sorties from the Continent.

The minutes of the meeting note that the proposition was 'attractive' and that intelligence should be gathered to allow outline planning to proceed, but that only the minimum number of people should be informed of the plans to ensure secrecy.

The committee met again six days later. More detailed aspects of the operation were discussed, including the timing of the withdrawal of the landing craft and of the training necessary for the parachutists. Group Captain Norman said that the longer the time allowed for preparation, the greater the chances of success, but Hughes-Hallett countered this by reminding him that the longer they waited, the fewer the hours of darkness would be as summer approached and, therefore, the greater the difficulties the surface vessels would experience.

Over the course of the succeeding days, doubts about *Blazing* came to the surface. At a meeting on 20 March, it was considered that while it was thought possible to take Alderney by surprise, especially as there was no telephone link between the island and mainland France, such a move would, most likely, put the German garrisons on the other islands in a state of heightened readiness. This would mean that any later attempt to take Guernsey and Jersey would be made much more difficult. 'It is accordingly concluded', state the minutes of the meeting, 'that assaults on the three islands must be approximately simultaneous'. Here, then, is the first mention of a large-scale attack upon Guernsey and Jersey.

After a further deliberation on 5 May 1942, the Air Officer Commanding reduced the operation to a large-scale raid, to take and hold the island for 24 hours, or longer if the situation and enemy reactions allowed. The anticipated parachute drop was abandoned, as was any form of airborne assault. Part of the reason for this was explained by one officer: 'One of the snags was that the island is only about a mile wide from the north-east side to south-west side and the prevailing wind is across that. In those days you jumped out of an aircraft with twenty men, one after the other, and the mathematics of it was that if you do that and do it perfectly you drop two or three men in the sea either before you start or at the end of the run!'[19]

The forces required for this revised operation were:

Naval
6 Hunt Class Destroyers
5 Infantry Assault Ships (5 LSC 33 ALC and 2 MLC)
8 MGBs
17 TLC
30 'R' Craft
1 Hospital Carrier

Military
6 Troops Special Service Brigade (550 All Ranks)
14 Churchill Army tanks
13 Bren Carriers
4 x 3.7-inch Howitzers
1 Field Company RE
1 troop (4 Guns) Bofors AA
1 field ambulance
RC of Signals
Services
Total Military Force 3,000 all ranks

RAF
200 to 250 Medium and Heavy Bomber Aircraft
24 Blenheim Bombers – 500 lb HE and 250 lb Smoke
14 Smoke Laying (Army Co-Operation) Blenheims
18 Long Range Coastal Fighters
8 Spitfire Wings (24 Squadrons)
12 Intruder Fighter Aircraft
24 Night Fighter Hurricanes

The four battalions of the 1st Guards Brigade Group were put on notice to move to the Isle of Wight for training. The proposed date for the attack was 26 May. As before, the operation was to begin 35 minutes before nautical twilight, with the main assault taking place 90 minutes later. This time, the operation was to be undertaken in three phases. Michael Stephen Hancock was with the Signals Section, 1st Guards Brigade:

We had a particular beach on the Isle of Wight, which had roughly the right characteristics, tarted up a bit with some little floating jetties put out so as to make it similar to where we would be landing on Alderney, and we did rehearsal landings on it.

The object of the operation was only to hold the island for about a week and the stated objects in the Chiefs of Staff approval of it included three things; one of them was in order to satisfy the clamour for a second front, which seemed a little surprising for a small scale thing such as this, but we are talking about 7,000 men, that sort of size.[20]

The revised plan was divided into two main phases:

Phase I

The first stages of Phase I were as per the first plan. But in addition to the diversionary landing on the western end of the island, intruder attacks would take place at the same time on enemy airfields either on the Channel Islands or the French coast within range. This would be followed by low-level attacks on those same airfields by fighter aircraft as soon as light permitted. The bombardment of Fort Albert and the harbour defences by the Royal Navy would also follow the same pattern as the earlier version of the operation, with the warships also engaging any enemy vessels that might be present. Air cover for the Navy ships would be provided by fighters which had taken off in the dark and formed up off the island to wait for daylight.

Phase II

As with the first incarnation of *Blazing*, the main assault, supported by naval gunfire and fighter aircraft (if disengaged from air cover of the landings) was to take place in the bay to the east of the harbour, with additional landings in the old harbour itself and close to Fort Albert. Similarly, the first flight of the assault forces would include the assaulting personnel of three infantry battalions, a Commando, fourteen Churchill tanks, and four 3.7-inch howitzers, with a floating reserve of two companies of a fourth infantry battalion, and thirteen Bren gun carriers. Continuous fighter cover for the landings would be provided as far as possible for about 90 minutes after the beginning of the assault. On completion of Phase II, the craft employed for the assault will be dispersed and camouflaged by nets from the perspective of air attacks.

The withdrawal, which was in effect Phase III, was to take place on D+1. Two alternative plans for the withdrawal were laid out, from which the Force Commanders could choose whichever one best suited the circumstances at the time.

The first of these was if the Germans on the island had been overwhelmed and enemy air activity was such that Force Commanders considered a daytime withdrawal feasible, the force would reembark in the afternoon. This would enable the return passage to England to be conducted in daylight, thus permitting fighter cover throughout part of the journey. If, however, the enemy air force was still in a strong position and the return journey would be at risk of heavy attack, the withdrawal would take place at night, the re-embarkation beginning shortly after midnight, although casualties, prisoners and a proportion of personnel could be embarked earlier. Fighter cover for the returning convoy would be provided from the UK from first light on D+1. Night fighter cover on a small scale would be provided over the island during the re-embarkation and the early stages of the journey. Whichever withdrawal was to be undertaken, it was accepted it might be the case that not all tanks or motor transport could be re-embarked, in which case those left behind would be destroyed. There was, at this stage in the planning, no further mention of Jersey or Guernsey.

All this appealed to Churchill, who was keen to encourage any of Mountbatten's schemes, however impracticable they may be. This was noted by the historian Nigel Hamilton who, regarding Mountbatten's character, wrote:

> As Chief of Combined Operations he was a master of intrigue, jealousy, and ineptitude. Like a spoilt child he toyed with men's lives with an indifference to casualties that can only be explained by his insatiable, even psychopathic ambition … a man whose mind was an abundance of brilliant and insane ideas often without coherence or consistent "doctrine". Allied to the equally undisciplined wildly

imaginative Churchill – with whom Mountbatten would often stay for weekends – the two made a formidable and dangerous pair.[21]

Brooke considered Mountbatten's visits to Chequers as 'always dangerous moments and there was no knowing what discussions he might be led into and … let us in for.'[22]

Brooke thought little of Mountbatten's military abilities, later writing that he was 'quite irresponsible'[23] and complaining that his repeated proposals to the Chiefs of Staff for raids across the Channel 'frequently wasted both his time and ours'.[24] This was repeated by one of the planners, Major General Sir John Kennedy: 'Whenever an idea, however wild, was thrown up, he [Churchill] ordered detailed examinations, or plans, or both, to be made at high speed. Our stables were so full of these unlikely starters that we were hard put to it to give the favourites the attention they deserved.'[25] This will be seen throughout this book, as the same themes and schemes were repeated tirelessly by Mountbatten.

Churchill could not accept that Britain was incapable of mounting 'so modest an operation' as the recapture of the Channel Islands and he 'thoroughly bulldozed' the General Staff and very nearly succeeded in having the plan adopted.[26] This was mainly because while this was being debated, Alan Brooke was out of London visiting various sites around the UK. In his diary he wrote: 'returned just barely in time on morning of 6 May to turn down a landing in Alderney Island as a large raid by Guards Brigade.' Such a plan, Brooke explained, was a 'fruitless venture' which would tie down a British force close to the French coast from where it could be battered relentlessly.[27] It took Brooke five days of 'difficult debate' to convince advocates of the plan to drop the scheme, which he was eventually able to do at a meeting on 11 May.

His argument was that the essential feature of the operation was the neutralisation of the coast defences by air bombardment at night, and that he did not believe 'indiscriminate' air bombardment in the night would achieve this aim, particularly as the Alderney coastline is undulating and broken.

It had been also recognised by the Chiefs of Staff that, by mid-summer, the nights were too short for an operation of this nature. Furthermore, an amphibious assault would be 'absolutely dependent' on fine weather.

Churchill, who was also at the meeting, remarked that, at present, 'we could not afford the risk of heavy casualties in our bomber force which this operation would probably entail'. He had been swayed by Brooke's determined opposition to the operation and considered the inevitable loss of aircraft a 'decisive' factor, agreeing that *Blazing* should be abandoned.

By this stage, however, the whole strategic situation had changed anyway, because the United States of America was now in the war.

Chapter 3

Europe First

The Japanese attack on Pearl Harbor, and Germany's subsequent declaration of war on the United States four days later, gave US President Franklin Roosevelt the opportunity to become actively involved in the conflict he had long wished to join. The American administration saw Germany as a far greater threat to democracy than Japan, with Roosevelt and his closest advisors believing that if the only other major democratic power still fighting Hitler, the United Kingdom, was defeated by Germany, the USA would be surrounded by hostile totalitarian regimes. Indeed, if Britain's immensely powerful Navy and its vast empire fell into German hands, the United States' very survival might be in serious jeopardy. However, after the First World War, the American people had no wish to be dragged into another European conflict. Between 1935 and 1937 Congress passed three 'Neutrality Acts' designed to keep the United States out of any potential war by making it illegal for Americans to sell or transport arms or other war materials to belligerent nations. Furthermore, a recent Gallup poll had shown that 84 per cent of Americans had answered 'No' to the question, 'Should we send our Army and Navy abroad to fight against Germany?'[1]

Despite considerable shifts in public opinion because of the increasingly dangerous international situation, Americans still hoped for peace and did not welcome the suggestion, particularly from public officials, that the United States should fight in Europe's latest war. Roosevelt, nevertheless, tried every legal means to help Britain. The Neutrality Act of 1939 lifted the ban on the sale of war materials, providing the warring nation could pay for the items on a 'cash and carry' basis. But the UK was still paying off its debt to the US from the First World War and the enormous expenditure incurred by Britain in the early part of the war against Hitler soon pushed it to the verge of bankruptcy, meaning no goods could be sold to the UK. Roosevelt got round this with the introduction of Lend-Lease, where the supplies vital to the UK's war effort could be sent to Britain immediately and be paid for at a later date.

The president also permitted his naval forces to take over much of the convoy protection duties in the Atlantic, thus releasing British warships for service elsewhere. He did this by allocating $50,000,000 of lend-lease funds for the construction of American naval and air bases in Northern Ireland and Scotland, as well as extending the US protection zone as far as Greenland. He then passed the Western Hemisphere Defense Plan No. 2, of April 21, 1941, in which the approach of any belligerent naval vessels or aircraft within 25 miles of the protection zone or the US bases would be considered an aggressive act and American commanders could attack them 'using all means at his disposal'.

Regardless of this, and the seizure of 600,000 tons of Axis- and Danish-owned shipping then lying idle in American ports and handing them over to the UK, Roosevelt still felt the need to be actively involved in the defeat of Germany and, in fact, by this time most Americans were beginning to realise that the country would have to face another war, although most still hoped to avoid it. Fortunately, the president's wishes were answered on 7 December 1941. The attack on Pearl Harbor turned public opinion in America on its head and when Germany declared war on the US in support of the Japanese on 11 December, Roosevelt knew that, at last, he could take on Hitler.

The Americans were so outraged by the Japanese attack that the embarrassing leak of Washington's war plans – the so-called 'Victory Programme' – three days earlier to the *Chicago Tribune* was immediately forgotten by the US public, indeed it probably appeared that Roosevelt had acted with great foresight in preparing for the eventuality that the US would be drawn unwillingly into the conflict.

The opening paragraph of the US Army's role in the Victory Programme, which had been compiled in September 1941, three months before the Japanese attack, made its objectives clear: 'The specific operations necessary to accomplish the defeat of the Axis Powers cannot be predicted at this time. Irrespective of the nature and scope of these operations, we must prepare to fight Germany by actually coming to grips with and defeating her ground forces and definitely breaking her will to combat.' At the time of the revelation of Roosevelt's war programme, the *Tribune*'s Chesly Manly wrote that the plans described 'a blueprint for total war on an unprecedented scale in at least two oceans and three continents, Europe, Africa, and Asia'. The Victory Programme called for a draft army of 5 million fighting troops from a total manpower of more than 10 million men in uniform, as part of a general national war mobilisation. The US, would, wrote Manly, invade Europe on the specified date of 1 July 1943 in 'the final effort to defeat the mighty German army'.[2] This would involve a United States force of 215 divisions comprising 8.7 million men.[3]

With Britain and the US now formally allies, in December 1941 Winston Churchill travelled to America to discuss future strategy with President Roosevelt. On 22 December 1941, Churchill arrived in Washington and was invited to stay with the Roosevelts over Christmas (much to Mrs Roosevelt's annoyance as her husband only informed her the day of the prime minister's arrival). The significance of the meeting between the two leaders, known officially as the Arcadia Conference, was the declaration of a policy of 'Europe First' for the direction of the war. This was defined at the conference, reiterating a decision made between the British and American Chiefs of Staff as early as February 1941. It was agreed that Germany was the predominant member of the Axis Powers, and consequently the Atlantic and European area was considered to be the 'decisive theatre'. While it was acknowledged that much had happened since February, the Joint Combined Chiefs declared their view to have remained the same: 'that Germany is still the prime enemy and her defeat is the key to victory. Once Germany is defeated, the collapse of Italy and the defeat of Japan must follow.' (At this stage it might be helpful to explain the difference between a 'joint' committee and a 'combined' one. A combined committee was one in which officers of two or more nations served together, in other words an Allied committee as distinct from a national one. A 'joint' committee, on the other hand, indicated collaboration or discussion between the military, naval and air forces of one nation. A 'joint combined' committee, therefore meant one where all the services of the nations were involved.)[4]

The course of action that would follow this agreement was to be:

1. Closing and tightening the ring round Germany.
2. Wearing down and undermining German resistance by air bombardment, blockade, subversive activities, and propaganda.
3. The continuous development of offensive action against Germany.

4. Maintaining only such positions in the Eastern theatre as will safeguard vital interests and deny Japan access to raw materials vital to her continuous war effort while concentrating on the defeat of Germany.

In the Joint Chiefs' declaration, therefore, it was 'a cardinal principle of America-British strategy that only the minimum of force necessary for the safeguarding of vital interests in other theatres should be diverted from operations against Germany'.[5]

This did not entirely suit Churchill. The threats to Britain's empire in the Middle and Far East –particularly Egypt and India – were more pressing and urgent than on the Home Front, where the fear of invasion had somewhat receded. Nevertheless, Roosevelt expected Britain and the US to launch an attack upon Hitler's so-called 'Fortress Europe' at the soonest opportunity. Equally, so did the British public and press now that America was on their side. But people did not understand, either then or after the war had been won, just how precarious a position Britain was in during the early part of 1942. Singapore, Hong Kong, Malaya and even Burma had fallen or were certain to fall to the Japanese. The pride of the British fleet, the battleship *Prince of Wales*, along with the accompanying battlecruiser *Repulse* had been sunk, and in the western theatre the disaster of Norway had been followed by reverses in Crete and North Africa, where General Rommel was earning the sobriquet 'Desert Fox' and threatening to overrun Egypt. British forces were in retreat across the globe and were in no position whatsoever to mount a major operation across the Channel.

However, it was not just the Americans pressing for an attack on mainland Europe. The General Secretary of the Communist Party of the Soviet Union, Joseph Vissarionovich Stalin, was demanding action in western Europe to lessen the pressure of the 280 German divisions that were bearing down upon Stalingrad. Russia, the prime minister was told, was losing 10,000 men a day on the Eastern Front, whilst Britain, the Soviet Ambassador mocked, was dragging its heels 'until the last button has been sown on the tunic of the last soldier'. Equally, Mackenzie King, the Canadian Prime Minister, desperately needed Canadian troops to become involved in the war to keep his politically divided nation together.

The British press, led by Lord Beaverbrook's *Daily Express*, also clamoured for Britain to help the Russians, and public gatherings across Britain demanded offensive action. When Beaverbrook delivered a speech to the Bureau of Advertising of the American Newspaper Publishers in April, he urged the United States to join Britain in striking out in support of the Soviets. 'Strike out violently', he insisted, 'strike even recklessly! ... A second front in Western Europe would provide an opportunity to bring the war to and end here and now.'

This was noted by Alan Brooke, who wrote in his diary for 16 April:

Public Opinion is shouting for the formation of a new Western Front to assist the Russians. But they have no conception of the difficulties and dangers entailed. The prospects of success are small and dependent on a mass of unknowns, whilst the chances of disaster are great and dependent on a mass of well-established facts. Should Germany be getting the best of an attack on Russia, the pressure for invasion of France will be at its strongest, and yet this is just the most dangerous set of circumstances for us.[6]

Brooke, Britain's most senior military figure, believed a premature landing in France 'could only result in the most appalling shambles which must ... reduce the chances of ultimate victory to a minimum.'

But it was the calls from the White House that were heard the loudest in Whitehall. Without US support, particularly with regards to arms, aircraft and equipment, Britain would be unable to continue its war against the Axis Powers. So, what America wanted, America got.

It had been agreed by the Joint Chiefs in December that: 'In 1943 the way may be clear for a return to the Continent, via the Scandinavian Peninsula, across the Mediterranean, from Turkey into the Balkans, or by simultaneous landings in several of the occupied countries of north-western Europe. Such operations will be the prelude to the final assault on Germany itself, and the scope of the victory programme should be such as to provide means by which they can be carried out.'[7]

As can be seen from this agreement, a landing in north-west Europe was only one of the proposed measures but, in March 1942, Harry Hopkins, Roosevelt's closest political advisor, wrote to the president with these words: 'I doubt if any single thing is any more important as getting some sort of front this summer against Germany.' This was because of the upcoming mid-term elections by which time the Americans would expect to see some positive action being taken against the enemy. Roosevelt agreed that it was 'very important ... to give this country a feeling that they are in the war' and that the Americans would soon have to start 'slugging' it out with the Germans. That same month Roosevelt wrote to Churchill asking for an attack across the Channel, declaring that: 'even though losses will doubtless be great, such losses will be compensated by at least equal German losses and by compelling the Germans to divert large forces of all kinds from the Russian front.'

As a result, on 27 March, the Commander-in-Chief Home Forces and the Commander-in-Chief Fighter Command produced a report on the possible target areas of a cross-Channel operation and submitted it to the Chiefs of Staff Committee. Their report read:

1. Our broad conclusions are as follows:
   (a) The limited object given by the Chiefs of Staff can be achieved by air action alone.
   (b) Unless German morale is broken, we do not consider that a re-entry into France with the resources at our disposal in 1942 is likely to be successful.
   (c) Should, however, circumstances force us to take military action on the Continent during 1942 we lean towards the Pas de Calais but, before coming to a final decision, we require further time to investigate other possibilities. These investigations are being pressed on as rapidly as possible.
2. We wish to draw attention to the fact that, if a combined operation is to be carried out at all this summer, a decision will have to be made without any further delay. The choice of the Pas de Calais area was dictated by the range of fighter support but opinion at C.O.H.Q. was not in favour of a landing in this area for the following reasons:
   (1) This operation would entail a direct frontal assault on the part of the coastline which was most heavily defended by the Germans. Their gun defences dominated the narrow strip of water through which our ships and craft would have to sail.

(2) The road and rail communications in this area would enable the enemy to concentrate forces very quickly.
(3) Any forces landed would have to be supplied across open beaches, exposed to the full effect of the prevailing wind in the Channel and to the greatest rise and fall of the tide.
(4) Only the most perfectly trained personnel could have a hope of succeeding against the opposition that was to be expected and it was thought that, with the little training they had had up to date, they were not fit for the task.[8]

Just a few days later, on 1 April 1942, the US Secretary for War, Henry Stimson, and the Chief of the Army Staff, General George Marshall, presented Roosevelt with a plan for an Anglo-American invasion of northern France in the spring of 1943. In what became to be known as the Marshall Memorandum, northern France was identified as 'the only place in which a powerful offensive can be prepared and executed by the United Powers in the near future. In any other locality the building up of the required forces would be much more slowly accomplished due to sea distances.' It was, Marshall continued, 'the only place where the vital air superiority over the hostile land areas preliminary to a major attack can be staged by the United Powers. This is due to the existence of a network of landing fields in England and to the fact that at no other place could massed British air power be employed for such an operation. It is the only place in which the bulk of the British ground forces can be committed to a general offensive in cooperation with United States forces.' This was, in effect, the 1941 Victory Programme (which had undergone a number of revisions during the intervening months) under a different guise.

This operation was to consist of a force of thirty American and eighteen British divisions, plus 5,800 aircraft, with a landing on broad beachheads between the French ports of Boulogne and Le Havre. Though this all sounded very exciting, it was almost laughably unrealistic. The Germans had thirty to forty divisions in western Europe, and the idea that the British and Americans could somehow transport enough troops across the Channel with the small number of landing craft likely to be available in 1943 and hold their ground against such a German force was preposterous. Brooke, particularly after his experiences during the fiasco which led to the Dunkirk evacuation in 1940, knew how insubstantial and vague such ideas were. The Americans had not begun to grasp the complexity of the logistical problems involved in such an operation, nor the strength of the existing German forces, especially with regards to tanks: 'It was not possible to take Marshall's "castles in the air" too seriously', Brooke wrote at the time. 'We were hanging on by our eyelids. Australia and India were threatened by the Japanese, we had temporarily lost control in the Indian Ocean, the Germans were threatening Persia and our oil, [General] Auchinleck was in precarious straits in the desert, and the submarine sinkings were heavy ... We were desperately short of shipping and could stage no large-scale operations.'[9] If British forces were not sent to reinforce these threatened areas and men and equipment were instead retained in the UK for operations in Europe, all these other theatres would be placed in considerable jeopardy. But the British Chiefs of Staff were obliged to pay due consideration to the American suggestion, whether they liked it or not. The entry of the US into the war had exacerbated the shipping problem. Because of America's isolationist policy, the country had not prepared for war but had, instead, focused its industrial effort to supplying Britain. All that changed after Pearl Harbor. America was at war and its armed forces demanded they received priority over materiel being sent to Britain. Shipping requirements for the Pacific theatre directly competed with those needed for the North Atlantic. But, with Washington's Victory Programme being public knowledge in the US, the Roosevelt administration had little choice but to persist with what was, in effect, announced government policy.

Marshall flew to the UK, and on 9 April met the Chiefs of Staff Committee, which since the previous month included Mountbatten who, as head of Combined Ops, was granted the temporary ranks of vice admiral, lieutenant general and air marshal, to 'reach a decision as to what the main British-American effort was to be and where it should be made'.[10] For many reasons, Marshall said, he thought that western Europe presented the most favourable theatre, and he laid great emphasis on the importance of making a decision in principle as soon as possible. This, the American general explained, was because: 'production, allocation of material, special construction, training and troop movement would have to go forward as part of a co-ordinated plan.' The British were being rushed into making a hasty decision.

Marshall continued that it was of the greatest importance that efforts were made to help the Soviet Union and that the large US army being built up and trained should be 'engaged on active operations and gain war experience'. The flow of American troops and aircraft would not reach large proportions until the autumn of 1942, but by 1943 'very considerable' US forces would be available. In fact, Marshall believed that by April 1943 there would be 1 million US troops in Britain for the operation. However, if the situation on the Russian front rapidly deteriorated, it might be possible to stage an 'Emergency Operation' on the Continent in September 1942, when some American troops would be available. Alternatively, Marshall told the Committee, if there was a sudden collapse in German morale, Anglo-British forces should be ready to exploit this with an offensive in the West.

Marshall believed that by the middle of September there would be five groups of US aircraft (400 fighters, 300 bombers and 200 transport aircraft) and two and a half infantry divisions and one armoured division in the UK.

The US Army Chief followed this by reiterating the importance of reaching a basic decision at the earliest possible date 'in order that American efforts should be co-ordinated towards a single aim and thereby mitigate the tendency to disperse forces on secondary tasks'.

On behalf of the Committee, Alan Brooke sought to constrain Marshall's enthusiasm for an assault upon the Continent, but in a positive manner. He said that they had been considering how they could help the Russians if the situation turned against them but that they were doubtful whether anything could be achieved by land operations. This of course was true, as we know from the report by the Commander-in-Chief Home Forces and the Commander-in-Chief Fighter Command examined on 27 March. On the other hand, Brooke explained, they might be able to use land forces as 'bait' to bring about an air battle on Allied terms. The RAF was keen to bring the Luftwaffe's fighters to battle to reduce the losses incurred by Bomber Command in their sorties against targets in Occupied Europe and Germany. The German fighter 'margin', as Brooke put it, was a small one and the hope was that if serious damage could be done to the fighters in the West, Hitler would have no choice but to withdraw aircraft from the East to cover the German cities, thus helping the Soviets. This would be a theme the Chiefs of Staff would return to over the coming months.

Brooke also spoke of the Commando and Combined Ops raids which were being undertaken against the Occupied coasts from Norway to the Bay of Biscay 'in order to force on the enemy a feeling of insecurity and uncertainty'. He said that English south coast ports were being developed so they could handle the great increase in traffic which would result from the maintenance of an army on the Continent. This, claimed Brooke, was bound to become known to the Germans and further increase their state of uncertainty without having to conduct any operations.

Brooke then turned to the real crux of the matter:

> If we were forced to land on the Continent this year to relieve the pressure on the Russians, we might be able to put ashore a force of some seven divisions and two armoured divisions. This force, however, [would] not [be] strong enough to maintain a bridgehead against the scale of attack which the Germans could bring against it, and it was unlikely that we could extricate the force if the Germans made a really determined effort to drive us out. The loss of this force would dangerously weaken the defence of the United Kingdom.

Though Brooke cannot have been seriously concerned about the defence of the UK as there was not the slightest possibility of a German invasion, it added weight to his argument. But Brooke then placed the idea of a cross-Channel assault into its true global perspective:

> In India and the Middle East the situation was causing us very serious concern. If the Germans decided to move down into the Mediterranean and leave the Russian front temporarily, we have insufficient forces to meet them. The whole of our effort in both theatres depended on the security of the Abadan oil. Ceylon is the lynchpin of our strategic position in the Indian Ocean theatre. In north-east India our defences are inadequate, in land forces as well as air forces. Indian divisions had been sent to Iraq, Malay, and Burma, and most meagre forces remained for the defence of India itself. The Japanese were able to operate naval forces in the Indian Ocean and might easily move four or five divisions along the Burma coast under

cover of shore-based aircraft; such a move would be most difficult to counter. The overriding restriction on our strategy was the shortage of shipping.

Mountbatten then chipped in with a review of the raids which his Combined Ops organisation had undertaken, following which he said: 'With regard to a large-scale landing on the Continent he drew attention to the great difficulties in the maintenance problem. The ports on the French coast were only small ones and to maintain a force over open beaches was extremely difficult.'

Reinforcing Brooke's words concerning shipping, Mountbatten said: 'Any operations this year on a scale larger than a raid would entail much improvisation in landing craft.' He also believed that there would be little chance of achieving surprise with a large-scale operation as the preparations for the assault were certain to be spotted by the enemy.

Air Chief Marshal Sir Charles Portal added that, from the air point of view, protecting a bridgehead would be a very considerable strain on the RAF: 'We must expect high casualties from the use of fighters in close support of land forces, which would be essential to this type of operation.' Instead, Portal said he believed that air action on its own could help the Russians by inflicting heavy losses on the Germans by compelling them to engage the British fighters at a time and place of their choosing.

Marshall closed the meeting by reiterating the need for American troops to be involved in a cross-Channel operation, explaining how he realised that 'even with good judgement, losses might be sustained and these he was ready to accept'.

The discussion was left at that but the following day, US colonels Albert C. Wedemeyer and Howard A. Craig met with their opposite numbers on the British planning staff for a detailed discussion of the strategic and logistical problems involved in the build-up to any cross-Channel operation. However, much of the day was given over to an assessment of the damage done by Japanese raids in the Indian Ocean.

Yet, as Hughes-Hallett conceded:

If the war in Western Europe was ever to be won the re-conquest of France was generally agreed to be an inevitable prelude. North-Western France was the obvious battle ground for several reasons.

Whether we liked it or not we had to maintain continuous fighter supremacy over the South-East of England to protect ourselves from German bombers and we had to maintain a large army in the United Kingdom to protect ourselves from invasion.

Yet those air and ground forces need not be employed solely in defence but could also be used to counter-attack across the Channel. 'Furthermore', continued Hughes-Hallett, 'the United Kingdom was the most convenient place in which to assemble and supply the great American Army which would be needed for an invasion, and a new front in France would threaten the Achilles heel of Germany, namely the Ruhr.'

'Against this', Hughes-Hallett warned, 'the mounting of a cross-Channel invasion offered no prospect of strategical or tactical surprise … Furthermore, the changeable weather and the strong tidal stream in the Eastern channel offered as big a threat to a small and slow-moving landing craft as did the Germans themselves.'[11]

Eventually, on 14 April, the British Chiefs of Staff accepted Marshall's proposal, agreeing that planning should begin immediately for a major offensive in Europe in 1943 and for an emergency landing, if necessary, in 1942 if the situation in Russia deteriorated significantly. The former acquired the codename *Roundup* and the 1942 emergency landing was *Sledgehammer*. The build-up of US troops in the UK for these two operations was called *Bolero*. That evening, hosting the American representatives in 10 Downing Street, Churchill declared that the 'two nations would march ahead together in a noble brotherhood of arms'.[12]

The plan for *Roundup* was taken from work that had already been done by British planners on what had been codenamed Operation *Sesame*. In this the C-in-C Home Forces was told: 'German morale and strength in the West may deteriorate at any time in the future to a degree that will permit us to establish forces on the Continent. You are, therefore, to plan and prepare for a return to the Continent to take advantage of such a situation.' He was advised that all the military resources under his command should be made available for such an operation as would be all the assault and specialist shipping in the UK apart from that needed for Mountbatten's small raids.[13]

Churchill, though, was thinking about the wider war and not just north-west Europe. He did not reject Marshall's scheme at the outset, but had other alternatives on his mind: 'The first was the descent on French North-West Africa (Morocco, Algeria, and Tunisia), which for the present was known as "Gymnast"', Churchill later wrote, though he did not voice it at the time to Marshall. 'I had a second alternative plan for which I always hankered and which I thought could be undertaken as well as the invasion of French North Africa. This was "Jupiter" – namely, the liberation of Northern Norway.'[14] This penchant Churchill had for mounting peripheral operations had led to the disastrous Dardanelles campaign in the First World War and it flew directly in the face of Marshall's insistence on focussing on what he termed 'the main project – offensive operations on the Continent'.

The day after the Chiefs of Staff had agreed to the American proposal, 15 April, Brooke had lunch with Marshall, after which he recorded his opinion of the US general:

> He is, I should think, a good general at raising armies … but his strategical ability does not impress me at all. In fact, in many respects he is a very dangerous man … Marshall has started the European offensive plan and is going one hundred per cent all out on it. It is a clever move which fits in with present political opinion and desire to help Russia. It is popular with all military men who are fretting for an offensive policy. But, and this is a very large "but", his plan does not go beyond landing on the far coast … I asked him this afternoon – Do we go west, south or east after landing? He had not begun to think of it.[15]

Brooke continued his condemnation of Marshall's lack of detailed planning. He was amazed to discover that the head of the American Army had not studied any of the strategic implications of a cross-Channel operation. Marshall believed that the main difficulty would be the landing of the troops on the enemy-held coast. Brooke knew that the real struggle would come after the troops were ashore as the Germans would be able to reinforce their forces on the coast far quicker than the Allied troops could be ferried across the Channel. 'I asked him to imagine that his landing had been safely carried out, and asked him what his plans would then be … I found that he had not begun to consider any form of plan of action or … to visualise the problems that would face an army after landing.'[16]

In all fairness to Marshall, he had no experience of amphibious warfare. Up to this point in time, as a general rule, when American troops had been sent to overseas theatres they had been able to land on friendly shores and organise for battle with little interference from the enemy. The Navy's contribution to such tasks was in escorting convoys to the theatre of operations and securing the lines of communications to support the Army in the field. The few real amphibious landings had been very limited in scope, usually little more than river crossings or raids. In point of fact, US forces had never conducted a combat amphibious operation prior to 1942.[17]

Brooke tried to explain to Marshall, without success, that until the Mediterranean was opened again to Allied ships, the crippling dearth of shipping would not be alleviated. Brooke also told Marshall that if the Soviets 'cracked up', Hitler could concentrate the bulk of his forces in France which would make an invasion impossible and place any Allied troops who had established a foothold on the Continent in serious trouble. 'Our only hope', said Brooke, 'would be to operate in [North] Africa'. Despite his condemnation of Marshall's strategic vision, Brooke found him to be charming and dignified and, from his diary, it is clear he believed Marshall was a trustworthy individual. Though their ideas would continue to clash, they held each other in mutual high regard.

Knowing full well that he had failed to fully convince the British with his cross-Channel offensive plan, Marshall returned to Washington to press on regardless with *Bolero*, presenting Roosevelt with what was, in reality, an ultimatum: 'If the "Bolero" project is not to be our primary consideration', he told the president, 'I would recommend its complete abandonment. We must remember that this operation for 1942 depends primarily upon British forces and not our own. They have far more at stake than do we and are accepting very grave hazards to which our own risks are not comparable. They have accepted the "Bolero" project with a firm understanding that it would be the primary objective of the United States. If such is not to be the case, the British should be formally notified that the recent London agreement must be cancelled.' Roosevelt, of course, had no choice but to back Marshall or abandon his declared strategy, which was, naturally, out of the question.

Having received the president's confirmation of his commitment to *Bolero*, and with the emergency operation *Sledgehammer* still a possibility, it was important for Marshall to move as many ground divisions and supporting units to the UK as possible before September. Shipping was the constraining factor. Ships were needed from the shipyards to transport troops across the Atlantic, but landing craft were also required from the ship builders to mount the operation across the Channel. In terms of priorities, assault vessels stood tenth on the American shipbuilding list.[18] There was no easy solution to this problem of competing demands – and it would eventually be Britain's route out of a cross-Channel operation in either 1942 or 1943.

The early shipping movements from America were scheduled firstly to create an air force and secondly, a ground force in the UK in time for offensive operations on the Continent in 1942 or 1943. The most critical item in the planning of all the invasion operations was the provision of landing craft. The idea of using large numbers of specially constructed craft for landing operations was so new that no generally accepted doctrine had been developed. The Army knew very little about landing craft and, during the first years of the war, the Navy was urging other types of construction, with the result that landing craft requirements were not determined until it was too late for *Sledgehammer*. But so insistent was Marshall that if it was determined an emergency landing was necessary in September, 'it will be carried out with whatever personnel and equipment is actually available at the time.' It was this kind of reckless thinking which terrified Brooke and the British Chiefs of Staff.

The issue of landing craft was raised with Roosevelt on 14 May by General Somervell and Vice Admiral Frederick J. Horne, Vice Chief of Naval Operations. The president was informed of the approximate number of landing craft that could be made available by 15 September 1942 and by April 1943. With an estimated force of from three to four American divisions in the United Kingdom by September, the landing craft estimated as being available could carry assault elements to a total of 21,000 men, 3,000 vehicles, and 300 tanks; far below the number envisaged in the *Sledgehammer* plan. The plans for *Roundup* called for an assault force of approximately 77,000 men, 18,000 vehicles, and 2,250 tanks, which meant the Americans would have to build some 765 landing and assault craft of several types by the spring of 1943. Construction in time would be physically possible only if such vessels were given precedence over all other items in the War Department's production programme. Roosevelt's answer was: 'work must be gotten under way as quickly as possible.'[19] As a result, production of landing craft was given 'Priority A' classification.

Another thorny problem faced the US and British leaders – that of command. It had been understood that a British officer would command all the forces engaged in *Sledgehammer*, but no decision had been reached regarding *Roundup*, which would be composed predominantly of American troops and equipment. This would soon be settled in favour of General Dwight Eisenhower, who was initially given command of the US forces in the European Theatre, but a few months later would attain the title of 'Supreme' commander. Eisenhower's first active command, however, would not be in Europe, as will shortly be seen.

The US policy of merely holding the Japanese while focussing the main Allied endeavour on Europe proved impossible to maintain. Throughout the early months of 1942, the Japanese continued to advance across the Pacific region. By the end of March 1942, the Japanese had conquered Malaya, the Netherlands East Indies, most of the islands to the north and east of Papua New Guinea, and had occupied the main coastal centres of Lae and Madang on the New Guinea mainland. The Island of Corregidor, which guarded Manila Bay, had become the final refuge of the American and Filipino forces. Their valiant last stand ceased on 6 May, bringing organised Allied resistance in the Philippines to an end. Three weeks later the British and Indian forces in Burma were driven out of the country, with the Japanese reaching the border with India. Australia was also under threat; a Japanese bombing raid was mounted on Darwin resulting in the largest single attack ever mounted by a foreign power on Australia. The advance of the Japanese Navy through the Indian Ocean was also a major concern. With transit through the Mediterranean hazardous at best, Britain's shipping routes to Egypt and India skirted round South Africa and then passed the Vichy French Island of Madagascar. If the Japanese Navy was able to occupy bases in Madagascar from where it could severe Britain's communications with Cairo and Delhi, then the whole of North Africa and the Indian sub-continent would be at the mercy of the Axis Powers.[20]

All these areas needed urgent attention and reinforcement from the UK. Until the Pacific theatre could be stabilised there could be no thought of launching huge assault forces across the Channel. A large force was despatched to seize Madagascar from the French in May, which included landing craft and British battalions trained in amphibious warfare, reducing still further the UK's capacity to mount an operation across the Channel. Marshall's plan was clearly unworkable, at least for the foreseeable future.

Nevertheless, Mountbatten was advised by the Combined Commanders on 6 May that: 'The policy of large scale raids should be intensified.' Following this, two days later, he was 'invited' to 'initiate the preparation of the best plan possible for a major raid on the French coast within the area of fighter protection. The raid should be planned to take place about the middle of July.' It would prove to be a costly disaster.

Chapter 4

Back to Washington

In the first quarter of 1942, oil tankers with a combined capacity of more than 600,000 tons were lost to German U-boats and in May and June of that year, German submarines sunk in excess of a 1.5 million tons, taking the total for the first half of 1942 to more than 4 million tons of shipping. As a result, Marshall's targets for the mass transportation to the UK of US troops across the Atlantic under *Bolero* were behind schedule almost before the operation began.

The danger posed by the Japanese fleet in the Pacific led to the withdrawal of the major warships of the British Eastern Fleet to the African coast. This prompted fears that India was about to be lost to the Japanese and Churchill begged Roosevelt for help, particularly in the form of aircraft. At the same time, Australia, worried about an imminent invasion, asked for the return of the troops it had sent to the Middle East or, alternatively, an increase in the number of American troops or aircraft stationed in the Antipodes.

In the midst of all these troubles, the Chiefs of Staff Committee was, nevertheless, obliged to examine proposals for cross-Channel expeditions to appease the Americans, urged on by Churchill and his protégé Mountbatten. Churchill described the raid on St Nazaire in March 1942 as a 'brilliant and heroic exploit' and pressed Mountbatten to 'turn the south coast of England from a bastion of defence into a springboard of attack … your whole attention is to be concentrated on the offensive.'[1] Mountbatten had, in all fairness, endeavoured to do this, having tried to convince Brooke and his fellow Committee members to undertake a number of other operations without success, including *Blazing*, as well as one on Bayonne, and another on the Adour Estuary in south-western France (Operation *Myrmidon*).

Undeterred, Mountbatten and his team devised what was probably the most unrealistic of all his impracticable ideas, although it was certainly the most glamourous. In recognition of the stated objective to 'Make

Germany continuously employ her air forces in active operations and to cause protracted air fighting in the west, in an area advantageous to ourselves, in order to reduce German air support available for the Eastern Front as early as possible,' the astonishing Operation *Imperator* was put on the table in March 1942 and is examined below.[2]

There were, in the meantime, other smaller raids. On the night of 10/11 January, Operation *Curlew* had been attempted with the aim of discovering the layout of the German defences in the area around the little French village of St Laurent-sur-Mer which, on D-Day in June 1944, would be the centre of *Omaha* beach. Bad weather resulted in the raid being aborted mid-Channel, but the raid was mounted the following night, with the fifteen-strong party wading ashore in freezing conditions then through snow as the men moved inland. Little was achieved.

Operation 'J V' was a Commando raid against shipping in Boulogne on the night of 11/12 April 1942 and was carried out by two men of No. 6 Commando. The men paddled a two-man canoe into Boulogne harbour, planted a limpet mine on a German tanker and withdrew unseen.

This was followed by Operation *Bristle* which took place on the night of 3/4 June. The target of the raid was a German radar site at Sainte-Cécile Plage between Boulogne and Le Touquet. The raiding force, which was again provided by No. 6 Commando, was defeated by the strong German defences. During the return voyage, at around dawn, the naval force was attacked by German fighter aircraft that damaged two motor launches and one MGB, killing one commando and two naval personnel and wounding another.[3]

These, though, were mere sideshows and did not lead to the air battle against Luftwaffe fighters that the British planners believed would offer the most benefit both to Bomber Command and the Soviets. The area where Fighter Command could be most effective was, obviously, that part of the Continent closest to the UK, i.e., the Pas-de-Calais. The intention was, therefore, for Combined Ops to establish a bridgehead in that region 'through which there would pass a raiding force which would carry out operations calculated to seriously damage German prestige and so to force the Germans to reinforce France or bring back forces from the coast.' To this 'General Definition of the Intention' was added 'the operation must so be conducted that it cannot effectively be represented as a major military defeat'.

The Chiefs of Staff, therefore, ordered plans from Mountbatten's team for an operation in July that would consist of a raiding force of from two to four divisions and a period for the raid of from one to four weeks. Despite opposition to such a raid, a 'direct order' had been received, and Mountbatten's Headquarters' planners sat down to work something out on that scale: Operation *Imperator*. The reason for this insistence by the Chiefs of Staff might have been to stop the Americans pushing for the far more dangerous aims of *Sledgehammer*, as it was clearly stated that if a large raid was undertaken in July, it would be impossible to mount *Sledgehammer* in September. Though this is mere speculation, it may be that the planners at Combined Headquarters wrote up *Imperator* with their tongues stuck firmly in their cheeks; their plan was to land a force of sixty Valentine tanks which would race down to Paris and destroy the German military headquarters at the Hotel Crillon on the Place de la Concorde and then rush back to the coast, re-embark and sail back to the UK![4]

The first part of *Imperator* would be the establishment of a bridgehead in the Pas-de-Calais region. Inevitably, the size of the operation would be limited by the number of landing craft available. This was eighty Landing Craft, Tank; 120 Landing Craft, Assault; eighty Landing Craft, Mechanised; and 120 'R' boats. There was also the possibility of using airborne forces in the widest meaning of the term. The bridgehead force that could be carried in that number of craft was 6,600 men.

It was agreed that the mouth of the River Somme presented the most attractive area for the bridgehead. In the preamble to *Imperator*, the topography in this region was described as 'tank country', in that the beaches on the whole were extremely flat and behind them the land consisted of open rolling downs presenting very few obstacles to armoured vehicles. To the flanks of this area the country was either heavily canalised or else it was swampy near the coast and intersected by rivers.

It was also agreed that in order to achieve greater surprise, the raiding force of tanks should re-embark at another place. It was proposed that they should return via Rouen, where serious military damage could be inflicted on enemy positions and then re-embark at Dieppe. Because Fighter Command would be engaging the Luftwaffe over the bridgehead area, not to mention the distances involved, it would only be possible for the RAF to provide fighter cover for the raiding force in the form of two or three squadrons along the roads leading to the re-embarkation point.

In a meeting on 18 May, further details were discussed. It was laid down that the entire operation would take place over the course of three to four days and that the bridgehead would be held for that length of time to deceive the Germans into believing the tanks were going to return there. The enemy would think that they could cut off the tanks and annihilate them, thus gaining a morale-boosting victory – one 'vital to his military prestige'. The withdrawal of the raiding force through a second, and totally different, port, would take place at exactly the same time as the evacuation of the bridgehead.

A 'Rough Plan' was written up in which it was confirmed that the bridgehead would be established at the mouth of the Somme and as soon as this foothold was gained, the raiding tanks would be landed and immediately head for Paris. It was essential that the tanks reached the French capital before nightfall on D-Day.

The landing was broken down more precisely as follows, based on Z = nautical twilight on 4 August 1942:

Z = the infantry of two brigades is landed; all landings to be completed by Z+60 hours
Z+90 = 20 tanks land
Z+90 = 2 battalions of reserve infantry brigade (that which will hold the bridgehead) land
Z+120 = 20 tanks land
Z+120 = remainder reserve infantry brigade land
Z+120/180 = 28 carriers/armoured cars land for the infantry of the raiding party
Z+150 = 20 tanks land
Z+210 = landing complete
Z+270 = raiding for leaves for Paris

Throughout the above period, heavy, continuous air cover would be needed of fighters from two or three Wings.

At dawn on D+1 the raiding force would head straight for Rouen and do as much damage as possible to the shipyards there. On D+2, the tanks would drive to the selected point at or near Dieppe to re-embark. The Somme bridgehead would then be withdrawn.

It was stated it could be taken for granted that the initial surprise, not to say astonishment, of the Germans would put them off balance and that such a state of affairs might continue throughout this fast-moving operation.

The conclusions drawn were that the plan should prove, bizarrely, 'feasible and prudent' and that 'its accomplishment would also achieve objects of lasting importance in obliging the enemy to strengthen his forces in occupied territories.' However, objections were raised by Brooke (of course), who was against the inland element of the operation, i.e., the raid on Paris, as it would have no bearing on the main objective of any such activity, that of bringing about an air battle with the German Air Force. It was also opposed by Leigh-Mallory, who said that the tanks with their accompanying petrol lorries and infantry vehicles would be at the mercy of the German Air Force in an area where they could not be protected by Fighter Command. Equally, both the bridgehead and the embarkation point were at such a distance from the English airfields that fighter cover would be limited. But then, as a direct alternative to *Sledgehammer*, a revised *Imperator* plan was put forward by Leigh-Mallory, who wrote that having 'thrown a spanner in the works' to stop *Imperator*, felt he should try to come up with some alternative idea.

In the *Sledgehammer* scheme, Leigh-Mallory explained, a force of two armoured and six infantry divisions was to be employed, and the holding of a perimeter of 35 miles exclusive of Calais but inclusive of Boulogne was envisaged, indeed, the operation involved the capture of Boulogne itself. *Sledgehammer* suffered from two major defects, the first of which was that it was doubtful that Boulogne, as a port, was capable of maintaining such a large force, and secondly that it was of limited duration, which would mean a great deal of materiel would have to be left behind when the Allied force withdrew, as had happened at Dunkirk.

The report detailing Leigh-Mallory's new plan was again to assault and capture Boulogne, but this time to take the high ground surrounding the town and turn it into a fortress with strong landward and air defences and hold it permanently. 'We have many examples in this war', ran the new report, 'of the difficulty capturing such an area if powerfully fortified, and strongly held'. Tobruk was cited as an example of this, as were towns and villages in Russia which had been turned into small fortresses and held against powerful attacks. The report continued:

Such an action on our part would deprive the Germans of a port which is in constant use by their ships ... and their shipping route going eastwards from Le Havre would be lost.

We could render the maintenance of the German army opposing us in the Boulogne area difficult by destroying important points in the railway and canal systems – by raids by our armoured forces, and by a vigorous air offensive against both road and railway communications ... It is unlikely that the Germans would be able to eject us from the Boulogne area without bringing a number of high grade divisions from Russia ... To hold Boulogne would give us a jumping off place when we were ready for more extensive operations.

In addition, of course, would be the constant wish to engage the Luftwaffe in costly battles close to England. It was even suggested that Folkestone could be used as the supply port which might tempt the Luftwaffe into attacking it, enabling the RAF's fighters to pounce on them.

The final advantage of the new plan was that the port of Boulogne was capable of supplying the force required, the latter being far less than that required for *Sledgehammer*.

If the revised plan was rejected, the Deputy Chief of Combined Operations proposed yet another scheme similar to the original *Imperator*. In this, a bridgehead would be established in the Le Touquet-Etaples area where, it was claimed, there was 'plenty' of good cover for tanks and stores. He suggested the bridgehead should be held for approximately a week, during which time a series of raids could be carried out by an armoured force within range of their fuel capacities. The objective of the raids would be to destroy power stations and important communications networks such as railways. This region was also close enough to England to bring about the much-desired aerial battles with the Luftwaffe under advantageous circumstances. Such raids, it was hoped, would prompt the French Resistance to extend its activities, to which end the plan was endorsed by SOE.

On 25 May, Mountbatten submitted his assessment of the various ideas put forward for *Imperator* to the Secretary of the Chiefs of Staff Committee. In total, he looked at just three of the various schemes that had been drawn up. The first of these was another new plan for *Imperator* and involved a raid on the German Air Force Sector Control Station at St Omer in the Pas-de-Calais. Regarded by the Combined Ops Headquarters staff as 'hazardous but feasible', this was to be an attack in which the infantry of two divisions, one parachute brigade, and one armoured brigade group, accompanied by anti-aircraft and field artillery, with two army tank battalions, would land, advance to St Omer, destroy the Luftwaffe station, and withdraw in the space of four days.

The second was a plan prepared by the *Sledgehammer* force commanders. In this operation, two infantry and one armoured division would capture and hold Boulogne for three weeks, but if the armoured division was not included, the operation could be limited to fourteen days. The third was the tank dash to Paris. One of the advantages with this version was that it could be achieved with substantially smaller forces than the other two projects. The date had, by then, slipped away and whichever one was adopted, it could not take place before the second week of August.

Of the three, it was the original tank raid on Paris which Mountbatten considered the one to fall most easily within the existing capabilities of the Allies. But Mountbatten repeated that whichever plan was adopted, it would have to be the principal Allied effort in the European theatre in 1942. The view was that the losses in men and equipment would be high and such losses could not be made good in time for *Sledgehammer* in September.

It was the inability of the RAF to give protection to the tank raiding force which finally saw *Imperator* dropped, and the proposed holding of Boulogne was not taken any further. This meant that *Sledgehammer* was still on the table, which seriously worried Brooke and his colleagues on the Chiefs of Staff Committee. Somehow, the Americans had to be dissuaded from pursuing this disastrous scheme, and it was Mountbatten who was handed this unenviable task.

Mountbatten travelled to Washington in early June in advance of the second of the summits between Churchill and Roosevelt at Washington. Prior to his departure for the American capital, Churchill had sent a note to Roosevelt, the gist of which was that at the meeting between the Chiefs of Staff Committee, Britain had given no commitment to undertake an operation in Europe but had simply discussed the current state of plans and preparations, though was holding out the possibility of more definite statements after the talks scheduled to take place between the Allied leaders in Washington.

Mountbatten presented Roosevelt and Hopkins with the British case against *Sledgehammer*, the principal point being that the small number of landing craft available meant the operation would be so limited, the Germans forces in France would not have to withdraw ground forces from the Russian front to deal with it.

Roosevelt suggested postponing *Sledgehammer* by a few weeks when more landing craft might be available. This, though, would mean an operation in late autumn, leaving little time to seize a port before the winter weather disrupted supplies and reinforcements crossing the Channel. As far as Mountbatten was concerned, it was 'out of the question' to supply troops over the beaches in winter.

If *Sledgehammer* was impracticable, then the feasibility of *Roundup* was clearly also in question. Mountbatten must have put his point across well, as Roosevelt said that he 'did not wish to send a million soldiers to England and find, possibly, that a complete collapse of Russia had made a frontal attack on France impossible.' Preparations for *Sledgehammer* would continue quietly in the background, just in case the situation demanded some form of emergency offensive in Europe but only on that basis. Certainly, a vast amount of planning effort was put in by all three of the UK's armed forces during the spring of 1942 to allow for any eventuality.[5]

It may be recalled one of the main strategic aims of the Joint Chiefs at the Arcadia Conference was that of 'Closing and tightening the ring round Germany'. The 'main object' of this strategy was 'to strengthen this ring, and close the gaps in it, by sustaining the Russian front, by arming and supporting Turkey, by increasing our strength in the Middle East, and by gaining possession of the whole North African coast'. If Britain was to hold onto its eastern empire, its lifeline through the Mediterranean and the Suez Canal had to be kept open. The key stations along this vital route were Gibraltar, Malta, Cyprus, and Alexandria. With Axis forces operating in Italy and North Africa and the French holding North-West Africa, this umbilical cord was in grave danger of being cut. While British planners were content to remain on the defensive and maintain their war of attrition, the Mediterranean theatre was the one place where offensive action was deemed essential. This was put into words by Foreign Secretary, Anthony Eden: '[It is] ... in North Africa that our fighting must be done. Nowhere else could Britain get to grips with the enemy on land. We could not foresee when a landing in Europe would be practicable again, but our sea-power, using exterior lines, made it possible to build up our strength in Egypt and the Western Desert. This was the theatre where the army must prove itself.'[6] There were also other considerations, as one historian has written:

> In a war won principally by Russia and the United States, British interests were certain to receive short shrift; British armies must therefore produce results while their effort could still be appreciated ... It was also perfectly understandable that whatever effort was expended should be made to serve those British interests that her allies were unlikely to protect ... Well might British strategists ask themselves: Why make enormous sacrifices elsewhere if that meant losing the Empire? Would America or Russia be the least bit grateful if Britain sacrificed her imperial efforts to their strategic conceptions?[7]

At the same time, Roosevelt needed to make something happen, and quickly, and that could only happen with full British support. He was also well aware of Britain's need to occupy all of North Africa to secure its route through the Mediterranean. So, he proposed that it might be wise to divert perhaps six American divisions – the number due to be sent to Britain in the summer and early autumn – to the Middle East or to operations in French North Africa. The president told Marshall to look into the matter in advance of the second meeting with Churchill in Washington.

Churchill and his small party, which included Brooke and Ismay, flew by flying boat from Scotland late on the evening of 17 June, arriving in Washington in the early evening of the following day. The purpose of the trip to what was called the Second Washington Conference, was to reach a decision on Allied operations for 1942-43 based on realities and not pipedreams. The Americans still wanted to see large-scale and immediate action, as laid down by their War Plans Division of the War Department General Staff:

> Time is of the essence and the longer we delay effective offensive operations against the Axis, the more difficult will become the attainment of victory ... we will be confronted in the not distant

future by a Germany strongly entrenched economically, supported by newly acquired sources of vital supplies and industries, with her military forces operating on interior lines, and in a position of hegemony in Europe, which will be comparatively easy to defend and maintain.[8]

There was no disagreement on the great assault upon Germany which would one day have to take place but, as we have seen, the British saw this haste as hugely dangerous, arguing against undertaking an operation 'for the sake of action at any price which ended in disaster and gave the enemy an opportunity for glorification at our discomfiture'.[9]

But Churchill need not have worried, Mountbatten had done his job well. Mountbatten's offensive spirit was much appreciated by the Americans (and being a member of the British royalty was highly respected by Roosevelt) and if he said that an operation was not possible, then clearly it was not possible. It was, therefore, to discuss arrangements for an attack upon North Africa (previously planned as Operation *Gymnast*) that the British leaders sat down with their US counterparts on 19 June at the British Embassy. As requested by Roosevelt, Marshall and his team had drawn up a plan envisaging an American force 220,000 strong, which included including six divisions and twenty-four squadrons of aircraft.

Marshall, however, was not in favour of such an operation. Though he had drawn up plans as requested by his Commander-in-Chief, the president, he continued to oppose the scheme as it meant that the build-up of US troops in Britain would be delayed and that, therefore, an attack in western Europe would be pushed further into the distance. On the day Churchill arrived in the United States, Marshall submitted a lengthy memorandum entitled 'Brief in defense of BOLERO'.

Against this background, the talks between the heads of the various services of the two nations proceeded as arranged. Both parties agreed that the principle determining factor was the situation in Russia. Against this uncertain backdrop, the British team outlined a number of possible cross-Channel operations they had considered:[10]

(a) A landing in the Pas de Calais area. A maximum of about six divisions could be employed but it was not thought that this force would be sufficient to divert appreciable German land forces from the Eastern Front. Subsequent maintenance of the force through the ports of Calais and Boulogne would be difficult. Purely air operations over the Continent had not achieved the hoped-for air battles and a six divisional landing within range of fighter air cover seemed unlikely to achieve important results.

(b) Establishment of a bridgehead at Cherbourg or the Brest salient. A bridgehead on the Brest salient had advantages in that it possessed good ports and a sufficiency of space. Brooke said he had studied this terrain after Dunkirk and had found the front through Rennes to be approximately 150 kilometres and would require a force of some 15 divisions. It was, however, a possibility worth further careful study.

(c) Large Raids. Further raids on a large scale had been planned, including a raid to last two or three days, by one armoured division and one infantry division, but the difficulties of landing in the Pas de Calais area would necessitate this raid taking place further to the westward on the out-skirts of the area covered by fighter protection. In general, the policy of raids was proving successful in holding down considerable German forces in France.

(d) Operations in Northern Norway. Consideration had been given to the possibility of a landing in northern Norway aimed at freeing the northern convoy route from attack by German aircraft. It had been thought that this might be undertaken by sailing a convoy containing troops and diverting it at a suitable moment to the northern Norwegian coast. Maintenance of the force, however, would be difficult north of Narvik and this front would require three divisions with an additional division and a half in reserve, which was more than could be put in the normal 35 ships of a Russian convoy. Operations in conjunction with the Russians from Murmansk had also been considered but the Germans themselves appeared to be launching an attack against this front. Any operation aimed at relieving the threat to the northern convoy route should take place almost at once as the dangerous period was during the short nights of summer.

Brooke, on behalf of the British party, followed this up by describing its views on future operations in the Far East and Pacific theatres, and other spheres. Finally, the agenda for the remainder of the conference was decided upon. This was to include discussing the practicalities of a cross-Channel operation in either the Pas-de-Calais region, or Brest, or on an Atlantic port such as Bordeaux, in which case in might be hoped that assistance would possibly be given by the Vichy French; agreeing the command structure for any such Continental offensive; and alternatives to an invasion of the Continent – which in British terms meant French North Africa.

Marshall, for his part, was determined to set out his stall from the beginning, listing all the reasons why he was against an expedition to North Africa. He said that any such operation would 'thin out' naval concentrations in other theatres, meaning the Americans would therefore not have the resources to help the British in the Middle East. Marshall also pointed out that the British and American economies were at full stretch and opening another front would inevitably weaken other areas, with unforeseeable consequences. But most especially in Marshall's view, it would seriously slow down the *Bolero* plans.

Thus ended the first day's discussions. The two sides were still a long way apart.

The talks resumed the next day in the Combined Chiefs of Staff Building, with Admiral 'Ernie' King, Commander-in-Chief, United States Fleet, declaring his opposition to a North Africa operation: 'An entry into N.W. Africa would open a ninth front with all the increase in overheads and escort and transportation problems involved therein ... By putting all our efforts into *Bolero* we were concentrating to the maximum on one front.' King also said that such a large operation would involve a great deal of transport and naval shipping to the determent of the Pacific campaign.

Marshall, predictably, was quick to follow up King:

> Large scale operations on the Continent in 1943 would clearly not be possible unless all efforts were concentrated now on their preparation. If we changed our plan now, and opened up another front, we should probably achieve nothing ... To defeat the Germans, we must have overwhelming power, and Northwest Europe was the only front on which this overwhelming superiority was logistically possible. It was, therefore, sound strategy to concentrate on this front

and divert minimum forces only to the other fronts. From a military point of view, therefore, there seemed no other logical course than to drive through with the *Bolero* plan.

While the soldiers, sailors and airmen haggled over strategy, the two political leaders were discussing a project on which there was both unanimity of purpose and the closest of collaboration – the creation of a nuclear weapon. Only after they had confirmed their mutual cooperation on the nuclear programme did Churchill and Roosevelt consider future joint policy, on which there was also full agreement on an attack across the Channel in 1943, but not for any major operations in 1942. Churchill began this element of the talks by declaring that the British were making 'arrangements' for a landing of six or eight divisions across the Channel in September, as the Americans had wished. But, Churchill continued, 'no responsible British military authority' had so far been able to make a plan for September 1942 'which had any chance of success'. He therefore asked the president if his military staffs had been able to devise a purposeful plan, knowing full well from his briefings with Brooke that the Americans had no real idea what to do other that simply land and fight.

Pretending, it must be assumed, to show real interest in an American plan, the prime minister asked what the objectives of the plan were; what forces would be employed; at what points would they strike and what landing craft and shipping were available? He also asked who the officer was that was prepared to command the enterprise, and what British forces and assistance would be required?

If, Churchill maintained, a plan could be found that offered 'a reasonable prospect of success', he would be glad to agree to it:

> His Majesty's Government will certainly welcome it and will share to the full with their American comrades the risks and sacrifices. This remains our settled and agreed policy.
>
> But if a plan could not be found that offered a good chance of establishing a permanent lodgement on the Continent, the British Government was opposed to undertaking the operation at all, on the grounds that it "would not help the Russians whatever their plight, would compromise and expose to Nazi vengeance the French

population involved and would gravely delay the main operation in 1943."[11]

Just before setting off for Washington, Churchill had written a note to Ismay on *Roundup* in 1943, telling him to find a means of making it happen. In this extraordinary document, Churchill envisaged six 'heavy' disembarkations and at least another six smaller feints to 'mystify' the Germans. This would disperse the German Air Force and minimise the immediate opposition to the landings. The landings should be as far afield as Denmark, Holland, Belgian, the Pas-de-Calais, the Cotentin Peninsula, Brest, St Nazaire and at the mouth of the Gironde.

He accepted that casualties among the first waves would be heavy, but he expected the French people would be 'roused' into action, 'deranging the enemy's communications and spreading the fighting over the widest possible areas'. Amid this upheaval the second waves would land with large numbers of tanks and motorised brigades to exploit selected points where breakthroughs had been achieved. The Allied air forces would operate from captured coastal airfields and at least four major ports would be seized. It was a wild, and typically impractical, Churchillian scheme. It also meant that Brooke was now fighting on two fronts, against both Churchill and Marshall.

Back at the conference, Brooke then turned to the subject of the so-called 'sacrifice' operation on the Continent in 1942 to relieve pressure on Russia if the Soviet situation took a sudden turn for the worse. Brooke explained that this question had been exhaustively examined by the British Chiefs of Staff, but they had not been able to discover any 'worthwhile' objective:

> The Germans had about 25 divisions in France now, but with the landing craft available this autumn not more than six divisions at the most could be transported across the Channel from England. It was doubtful if the Germans would bring back large air forces to deal with such a landing. Even if the landing force gained a bridgehead, we should not have sufficient additional forces available to follow up since the number of divisions that could be provided with the necessary services for mobile operations was at present limited.

Major General Eisenhower believed that there was a possibility at least of securing a bridgehead and holding it which would 'certainly' oblige the Germans to bring back air forces to 'deal with the situation'.

What perhaps was not fully appreciated by most other than Brooke, was that the mere presence of large numbers of US troops and aircraft in Britain and the Mediterranean was of enormous help to the Soviets. Nearly half of Hitler's air force and around a quarter of his ground forces were guarding and garrisoning western Europe and the Mediterranean. Hitler knew he was in a life and death struggle with Stalin and that if he did not defeat the Soviets quickly, he faced certain disaster. Even if Britain and America undertook a major incursion into western Europe, Hitler could not risk reducing his fighting strength on the Eastern Front.

Other aspects of the war, apart from the central issue of offensive action against Germany, were also discussed. These included the actions deemed necessary to hold back the Japanese in the Pacific, the supply of aircraft to the various theatres and of the measures to be undertaken to minimise the shipping losses from German U-boats. Also, in a bid to ease British concerns over the Middle East and, no doubt to demonstrate that the US was listening to its Allies, Marshall offered up his proposal of sending to the British army in Egypt 300 M4 tanks and 100 self-propelled 105-mm guns and 150 men specially qualified to work with tanks and self-propelled artillery, as well as 4,000 Air Corps personnel. This movement would involve no direct conflict with the *Bolero* schedules. He also offered to make available, in the United Kingdom, instructors and equipment from the 1st Armored Division to train British troops in the use of the American equipment sent to the Middle East.[12]

All this apart, it was, of course, with Churchill and Roosevelt that the final decisions would be taken on Allied strategy in the coming months. They were presented with a summary of the joint discussions for their consideration. The report advised against any considerable operation in the Atlantic theatre in 1942 unless it became necessary or 'an exceptionally favourable opportunity presented itself'. They advised further study of possible operations in western Europe given such a contingency – against Brest, the Channel Islands, or northern Norway. As to the comparative merits of these operations, they concluded: 'In our view each would be accompanied by certain hazards that would be justified only by reasons that were compelling in nature. Any of these plans, however, would be preferable to undertaking *Gymnast*, especially from the standpoint of dispersing base organization, lines of sea communication, and air strength.'

This was not the first time that official reference had been made to mounting an operation against the Channel Islands. The subject had been raised by Mountbatten on his visit to Washington earlier in the month. But now it had been put on record at the highest level of government that the Channel Islands were a legitimate target for an Allied offensive.

On 21 June, Churchill and Marshall presented their cases to the president at a long, heated meeting at the White House, also attended by Hopkins, Brooke, and Ismay. Following this, Ismay drafted a revised version of the Combined Chiefs of Staff plans for offensive operations for 1942-43:

1. Plans and preparations for operations on the continent of Europe in 1943 on as large a scale as possible are to be pushed forward with all speed and energy. It is, however, essential that the United States and Great Britain should be prepared to act offensively in 1942.
2. Operations in Western Europe in 1942 would, if successful, yield greater political and strategic gains than operations in any other theatre. Plans and preparations for the operations in this theatre are to be pressed forward with all possible speed, energy, and ingenuity. The most resolute efforts must be made to overcome the obvious dangers and difficulties of the enterprise. If a sound and sensible plan can be contrived, we should not hesitate to give effect to it. If on the other hand detailed examination shows that despite all efforts, success is improbable, we must be ready with an alternative.
3. Provided that political conditions are favourable, the best alternative in 1942 is Operation GYMNAST. Accordingly, the plans for this operation should be completed in all details as soon as possible. The forces to be employed in GYMNAST would in the main be found from BOLERO units which had not yet left the United States.[13]

Item number 3 was unacceptable to the Americans and the second sentence was changed in the final draft to read: 'The possibilities of operation GYMNAST will be explored carefully and conscientiously, and plans will be completed in all details as soon as possible.' To Marshall, *Gymnast* was nothing more than one of many *possible* operations.

As it transpired, an operation which would have a very considerable effect on Allied plans was close to implementation. It was called Operation *Rutter* – and it came just at the right time for Churchill after it was announced on 9 May that the Soviet Foreign Minister was coming to London.

Churchill demanded something to present to Vyacheslav Molotov and, four days later, Mountbatten presented his outline plan for a large raid against Dieppe, which would involve just one infantry division plus supporting troops. This was sufficiently limited in scale that Brooke could, albeit reluctantly, agree to and big enough for Churchill to be able to show that Britain was taking the Kremlin's appeals for help seriously.

Chapter 5

Moscow

With the American and British Chiefs of Staff still unable to agree on strategy – the British persisting on the occupation of French North Africa and the Americans demanding a cross-Channel attack – there was real danger that the Allies simply did not have the capacity to function as a military coalition. It was up to the men at the very top to break the deadlock or see the alliance fall apart before it had really begun.

Roosevelt sent Marshall back to London in the middle of July 1942, along with Admiral King and Harry Hopkins, to sort out Allied policy. The president instructed his team to finalise plans for the rest of 1942 and 'tentatively' outline Allied strategy for 1943. He told them that Britain and the US must concentrate their forces and avoid dispersion, and that American ground troops *must* be sent into action against the Germans in 1942, in whichever theatre offered the strongest possibility of this happening. This was a crucial instruction, and the one that probably brought the Americans round to accepting the British North Africa proposal. Brooke simply would not be budged. An invasion of northern France at that stage of the war would be a disaster and the Americans would simply have to accept this fact

Roosevelt still wanted to see *Sledgehammer* take place in 1943, and Marshall and his team were told that the operation was of such extreme importance that its adoption should be promoted 'with the utmost vigour'. But, being a politician, Roosevelt was a pragmatist. So, he told Marshall et al, 'If *Sledgehammer* is finally and definitely out of the picture, I want you to consider the world situation as it exists at that time and determine upon another place for US troops to fight in 1942.'

It was with these instructions in mind, on 20 July, that Marshall met the British Chiefs of Staff. The latter had also received a brief from their own political and military leader, Prime Minister Churchill, who also wanted a decision to be made, one way or the other. It is clear from his note to the Chiefs of Staff that, just like Roosevelt, he wanted a solution to be found, regardless of what decisions were made.[1]

From the outset it was evident that the American delegation was still intent on trying to bring the British round to agree on a cross-Channel operation in September. Brooke had to restate all the previous arguments against this. He said that with the forces available by early autumn, they would not be able to maintain a bridgehead on the Continent throughout the winter. The only, and inevitable, result would be the loss of the six divisions that had been landed.

The meetings continued on the 21st. The American team handed across a written memorandum in which they maintained their adherence to an attack on the Cherbourg salient 'as the preliminary move to a general attack in 1943'. Brooke decided to talk to Churchill, who told him to present the American proposal to the War Cabinet. This he did, and the Cabinet was unanimously opposed to it.

The Cabinet broke up and Brooke went for lunch, during which he received a note informing him that the Chiefs of Staff were to meet the prime minister at 15.00 hours at No. 10. When they arrived, they were told that Roosevelt had cabled Churchill to say that 'the Western Front in 1942 was off', and that he would try and convince his Chiefs of Staff to adopt an operation against French North Africa.

Marshall's team still remined unconvinced, noting that:

> Nothing developed [in the discussions] which changed our considered opinion that Great Britain is the only area from which the combined strength of the United Nations can be brought to bear against our principal enemy – Germany, so that no avoidable reduction in our preparation for ROUNDUP should be considered as long as there remains any reasonable possibility of its successful execution. A Russian collapse this Fall or a termination of the present campaign leaving Russia relatively impotent and incapable of offensive action would, however, make the objective of a continental operation in 1943 impossible of attainment. In this event the United Nations are forced to a defensive, encircling line of action against Germany for the coming year unless a crack-up in German morale, of which there is no present indication, should occur unexpectedly. Combined operations against the West and Northwest Coasts of

Africa for the purpose indicated above is the logical line of action in this alternative.[2]

In simple terms, if an attack across the Channel was definitely out of the question for the autumn of 1942, then an operation to invade French North Africa was, as Roosevelt had urged, a realistic alternative.

They confirmed this on the 24th, declaring that they would accept an expedition to French North Africa but that planning for *Roundup* would continue with an execution date of 1 July 1943, as per their Victory Programme. At the same time, they begrudgingly acknowledged that *Sledgehammer* was 'not to be undertaken as a scheduled operation'. But Marshall and King wanted it placed on record that a commitment in North Africa meant that in all probability an attack across the Channel would not be possible in 1943. They wanted to demonstrate that it was the British who had forced the Allies to abandon the offensive in the European theatre, apart from air operations. However, not wishing to give up *Roundup* entirely, Marshall and King asked that a final decision on a return to the Continent in 1943 be left until 15 September 1942, by which time the situation in Russia might have swung decisively in the Soviets' favour, making a cross-Channel operation more practicable. This was agreed, and Brooke did not want it to be seen that the British had committed themselves to a purely defensive stance in north-west Europe and at the next Combined Chiefs of Staff meeting, the American statement was modified to read: 'that the organization, planning, and training for eventual entry in the Continent should continue so that this operation can be staged should a marked deterioration in German military strength become apparent, and the resources of the United Nations, available after meeting other commitments, so permit.' This in turn was agreed upon by the Americans.

The following day, 25 July, the Combined Chiefs gave the operation for the invasion of French North Africa the codename *Torch* and took up arrangements for command and for staff planning. When informed that an agreement had finally been arrived at, Roosevelt declared he was 'delighted' and the Allies could now move 'full speed ahead'. Should there be any doubt, Roosevelt told his staff 'very definitely',[3] that he, as Commander-in-Chief, had made the decision that *Torch* would be undertaken at the earliest possible date. He considered that this operation was 'now our principal objective and the assembling of means to carry it out should take precedence over other operations'.

While Churchill and Brooke had managed to persuade the Americans to adopt *Torch*, they knew they still had to do something to appease the Russians, the press and, it seemed, just about everybody else, with an attack into northern Europe. In reality, Stalin knew full well that the UK was in no position to mount a second front on the Continent in 1942. His aim was merely to extort supplies of every type from the British; and his policy worked perfectly. In August 1941 Britain gifted the Soviets more than 200 Hawker Hurricane fighters and thereafter put all supplies sent to Russia on a lend-lease basis, but without the preconditions the US had placed upon the goods send to Britain.[4] But no matter how generous the Allies were, it was never enough to please Stalin, who found that the more he complained the more the West gave. He refused the offer of two divisions of British troops – he had men enough – but continued to demand a second front to keep goods flowing into the Soviet Union.

Churchill, whose mental health (and indeed his physical health – he survived a mild heart attack during this period) was often in question, was suffering severely during this period. Anything which might ease the pressure on him would be more than welcome. He was quick, therefore, to pick up on any suggestion which might help his situation. One such that appealed to him was Operation *Blazing* and he had very nearly been 'bulldozed' by Mountbatten and the Chiefs of Staff into adopting the plan while Brooke was temporarily out of London. As we now know, Brooke was able to put a stop to Mountbatten's scheme.

Nevertheless, there was no doubt that in either 1943 or 1944, Allied forces would reinvade Europe and there was universal agreement that any operation of this kind would have to include the early capture of a port to allow supplies and reinforcements to be landed quickly. An attack upon the port of Dieppe, in conformity with the instructions of the Combined Commanders on 6 May, would be an ideal practice for such an operation and would actually prove a tough test for the assaulting troops. The Dieppe area, the Ministry of Information explained:

> is made up of high cliffs, mostly un-scalable, broken here and there by narrow clefts or by the mouths of rivers. At the foot of the cliffs

lie stony and inhospitable beaches ... To land at low water on these beaches is very difficult and dangerous because of the rocks in the sea's bed and the angle of the shore itself, which makes the task of beaching a landing craft and taking it away a matter of the greatest skill and judgment. The cliffs behind the beaches are not numerous and those which exist are, for the most part, narrow and very easily defended. Men moving up them to the attack are at the mercy of defenders in position at their top, who can destroy the attackers with the greatest ease as they clamber laboriously upwards.[5]

To satisfy the needs of the Canadians and Americans, the bulk of the raiding force would come from the 2nd Canadian Division based in England, accompanied by a number of US Rangers. The Royal Navy would provide the transport across the Channel and British Army Commandos would be used to assault the flanking artillery batteries. The scale of the operation, it was hoped, would be large enough to appease all the concerned parties, as well as give an accurate example of what a large cross-Channel raid would involve. It was a typically British compromise.

With Brooke and Churchill actually agreeing on a plan of action for once, the Chiefs of Staff were more than happy, if not considerably relieved, and despite many questions still remaining unresolved at that stage, the operation was given the go-ahead.

Mountbatten had wanted to use the highly trained Royal Marine Division, supported by Army Commandos. However, he was told instead he could have one of the Canadian divisions which was kicking its heels in England. This was the final piece of the jigsaw. It would be the largest cross-Channel of the raid of the war and would surely satisfy all those who demanded action.

The practicalities of mounting a raid on Dieppe were first investigated by the Target Committee of Combined Operations Headquarters in early April 1942, the task of devising an operational plan being handed to its Planning Staff under the general direction of Hughes-Hallett. From an early stage the idea of a frontal assault was rejected. Instead, it was proposed that a landing at brigade strength, supported by tanks, would be made on each flank – one at Quiberville, some 6 miles to the west of Dieppe, and at Oriel-sur-Mer, about double the distance to the east. A third brigade would be held as a floating reserve to reinforce either flank, or to land at Dieppe as the flanking brigades approached the town.

On 30 March, the Chiefs of Staff gave their approval of the plan and the new Commander-in-Chief, Home Forces, Lieutenant General Bernard Montgomery, was nominated as the senior Army officer for the raid. But Montgomery was far from impressed with the military plan. In particular, he believed that the distance the flanking forces had to travel was too great for the RAF to be able to maintain aerial superiority, which was essential if the attack was to succeed. Instead, Montgomery said that Dieppe should be taken frontally in a dawn attack with two smaller landings either side to seize the cliffs overlooking Dieppe.

These competing assessments were appraised by the Chiefs of Staff, who broadly supported Montgomery's view, reasoning that the element of surprise would be lost once the flanking attacks landed, thus allowing the defenders in Dieppe time to prepare for the eventual assault. The time taken by the flanking forces to reach Dieppe – especially with regards to the western approach, where two streams would have to be crossed potentially impeding the tanks – would also enable the Germans to call up reinforcements, and delays in the capture of Dieppe would compromise the time/tidal constraints imposed upon the Navy. As a result, the decision was made to mount a frontal assault (Scheme A) preceded by flank attacks at Puits and Pourville, while at the same time parachute and glider-borne troops would be used to capture the batteries at Berneval and Varengeville-sur-Mer. The assault would be preceded by an air bombardment of 'maximum intensity' by 150 high-level bombers, four squadrons of low-level bombers and no less than sixty squadrons of fighter planes to provide aerial support for the flotilla of boats and troops during the raid itself. The raid would take place between two tides, i.e., 12 hours, during daylight. A modified version of this plan was given the green light by the prime minister and the Chiefs of Staff under the codename 'Rutter'.

While the main reasons for mounting a large-scale assault upon Occupied France were primarily political, the troops were given sixteen specific objectives from which items had to be collected or which had to be captured and destroyed. These included capturing the post office to obtain records of telephone subscribers; releasing French prisoners from the local jail; and even collecting samples of French bread! These may at first sight be trivial, but, as will be learned, two of the other objectives were of considerable importance.

On 5 June a modification to the plan was introduced in which it was decided to abandon the high-level bombing of Dieppe on air and military grounds. 'The Air Force Commander [Air Vice-Marshal T. Leigh-Mallory] was of the opinion that the bombing of the port itself during the night prior to the assault would not be the most profitable way to use bombers and might only result in putting the enemy on alert'. Similarly, Major General J.H. Roberts, the Military Commander, took the view that the destruction of large numbers of houses and the setting of a considerable portion of the town on fire through bombing would probably prevent the tanks from operating in streets chocked with debris. There was also a disinclination to bomb the homes and businesses of innocent French civilians.[6]

As an alternative to high-level bombing, Leigh-Mallory proposed diversionary bombing attacks should be made on Boulogne and the nearby airfields at Abbeville-Drucat and Crécy. This would have two advantages; firstly, the diversionary attacks would occupy the attention of the German radar network and secondly, it would put the two closest Luftwaffe airfields out of action.

It was also agreed that fighters should attack the beach defences and the high ground on either side of Dieppe and that the German Divisional Headquarters at Arques-la-Bataille should be bombed. The bombardment was now to be limited to the 4-inch guns of six destroyers and the 250 lb bombs of Hurricane fighter-bombers. A force of Motor Gun Boats was to operate off Boulogne in the early stages of the raid to give the impression that the assault would take place there instead of at Dieppe.

The troops were moved to the Isle of Wight and a period of intensive training followed. When the men were considered sufficiently trained, a full-scale exercise, *Yukon I*, was carried out. It was not a success. Many of the Landing Craft, Tanks, were late reaching the beach, some of the troops were landed at the wrong beach and in broad daylight, liaison between the Royal Engineers and the infantry was defective, and progress inland by the troops was very slow.

Mountbatten ordered a repeat exercise, *Yukon II*, for 23 June, to iron out these problems, with the idea of carrying out the operation at the first favourable date after 24 June. The period when astronomical and tidal conditions were favourable was limited to some five or six days twice a month,[7] and it had been accepted that settled fair weather for a period of at least 48 hours was necessary for the operation. Unfortunately, the weather proved uniformly unfavourable for the airborne troops, though not consistently so for the beach landings, and on 5 July the operation was further postponed and the plan again altered. Owing to the changed states of the tides, troops would now have to be re-embarked 3 hours later than originally arranged. This necessitated 3 hours longer air cover and, in the opinion of the Military Commander, might give the enemy the opportunity to organise infantry and artillery opposition on a scale which might prejudice the re-embarkation. The Force Commanders therefore informed the Chief of Combined Operations that in their view, the operation had a diminishing chance of success as each day passed and should not be carried out in its original form on the date proposed (7 July). They were accordingly instructed to consider a modified plan whereby the operation would take place on one tide only.

The landing was now to be made as near low water as possible and to be completed or nearly completed by the next high water, 6 hours later. Though on the one hand this 'one tide' plan had the advantage of increasing the intensity of air support by shortening the time during which cover would have to be given, on the other hand, it tended to complicate the task of removing the German barges in Dieppe harbour, which was one of the operation's objectives. The great raid was becoming smaller with the passing of every week.

If this was bad news for the assaulting forces, then worse was to come. The public debate concerning a second front had not gone unnoticed across the Channel. In the months leading up to Operation *Rutter*, the Germans had made significant improvements to their coastal defences and large numbers of reinforcements had been drafted-in, some even being transferred from the Russian Front, to protect the French ports. On 20 July, the Joint Intelligence Sub-committee had informed the Chiefs of Staff that 'all ports are especially strongly defended. Defence of the coast will pivot on ports which will probably be converted into quasi-fortresses with all-round defence.'[8]

From the transcripts of German communications, intercepted and translated at the Government Code and Cypher School at Bletchley Park,

Churchill was aware that Panzer units and crack SS Divisions had been moved to the coastal zone. In particular, the 10th Panzer Division – a battle-hardened formation at full strength in both men and machines – had been moved to Amiens, less than 40 miles from Dieppe. The Panzer Division's forward detachment was just 14 kilometres (8.5 miles, or less than an hour's drive) south of Dieppe! Just to make matters worse, the 302nd Division, which held Dieppe, was reinforced in July and again in August to bring its strength up to three battalions, totalling 3,500 men.

Little of this information was passed down to the officers responsible for conducting the raid, who were told that the town was occupied by 'low-category troops amounting to one battalion, with 500 divisional or regimental troops in support, making no more than fourteen hundred men.' What is more, the German defenders were 'second rate' and were likely to include older men aged 40-45.[9] They were not told the truth.

Such, then, was the situation as the troops moved down to their embarkation points for the biggest cross-Channel raid of the war so far.

The invasion flotilla assembled in the Solent at the beginning of July and, on the 2nd of the month, the men of the Second Infantry Division, a contingent of US Rangers and the 14th Canadian (Calgary) Tank Regiment were loaded on board. Operation *Rutter* would commence that night.

Then things started to go wrong. Adverse weather delayed the sailing of the flotilla. Day after day the troops waited on the weather reports when, on the morning of 7 July, the Luftwaffe came by. A flight of four Focke-Wulf 190s, each armed with machine-guns, 20mm cannon and a single high-explosive 500 kg bomb, attacked the exposed vessels.

Two Landing Ships, Infantry (L.S.I.) – HMS Princess Astrid and HMS Princess Josephine Charlotte – then lying in Yarmouth Roads, Isle of Wight, with troops embarked ready for the operation – were hit, the latter being severely damaged.

Hurried attempts were made to find alternative transports but by then it was too late. The tides had become unfavourable. There was also every possibility that the German pilots had reported seeing a considerable build-up of shipping which, in light of concerns that the British might be about to launch a large-scale raid upon the French coast, would have further alerted the Germans to the possibility of an attack. The generals were left with no choice: operation was impractical and had also probably been compromised. The commanding officers had no alternative, *Rutter* had to be cancelled.

It was, in fact, Admiral Sir William James at Portsmouth who had the final decision on whether the *Rutter* ships should sail, and it was he who cancelled the operation on 7 July. The troops were stood down and allowed to continue with their duties and training as before.

The cancellation of *Rutter* did not help Churchill, nor the ambitious Mountbatten, at all. In April, Mountbatten had spoken confidently of mounting a sizeable raid once a month up to and including August, with smaller scale operations interspersed every couple of weeks. Altogether twenty-five raids had been proposed. But, apart from Bruneval and St Nazaire, there had been nothing for him to boast of. There was to be a descent on a house on the seafront at Ostend which was used by the Luftwaffe as a convalescent home for injured pilots. Then, there was to be another raid in April to the Adour Estuary in south-west France, the aim of which was 'the destruction of an important explosives factory at the mouth of the River Adour and the severing of the rail connection from France to Spain which is vulnerable in this area'. Operation *Myrmidon*, as mentioned previously, involved approximately 3,000 Commandos and Marines with a regiment of tanks and a motorised battalion.[10]

This force set sail in the transport ships *Queen Emma* and *Princess Beatrix* and spent a month sailing off the French coast disguised as Spanish merchant ships. On 5 April the ships approached the mouth of the estuary to carry out the landing. However, amid bad weather they encountered a sandbar they had not expected and which they could not cross; the raid was called off and the ships returned to the UK. The operation, Hughes-Hallett admitted, achieved absolutely nothing.

Operation *Abercromby*, the final raid in April, was for a reconnaissance around the village of Hardelot near Boulogne, with the aims being to capture prisoners and damage the German defences. After one postponement, the troops landed and encountered some resistance and in his report on the raid, Lord Lovat of No. 4 Commando, wrote that they were lucky to have got away unscathed.

The next raid to be proposed was *Biting* which, as we know, bit the dust. Operation *Barricade* saw eleven men of No. 62 Commando attack a suspected coast-watching radar station north-west of Pointe de Saire, to the south of Barfleur. Unfortunately, they landed at the wrong place but, nevertheless, they encountered a German patrol and a firefight broke in which at least three of the enemy were killed. The Commandos returned without loss.[11]

The next was *Aimwell*, which was yet another proposal to seize Alderney, this time as the platform for an operation to attack Cherbourg (Operation *Gabriel*). The latter was to be similar in scope to *Rutter*, the troops occupying the port and doing as much damage and killing or capturing as many Germans as they could in the time allowed. It was to be carried out in the latter half of September 1942.

According to Mountbatten's preamble to *Aimwell*, the Chiefs of Staff had given their approval for three major raids in 1942 (one of those had been *Rutter*) and Mountbatten was looking at how he could find another target. He listed the likely places: Dunkirk, Calais, Cap Gris-Nez, Boulogne, Abbeville aerodrome, Le Havre, the Channel Islands and St Nazaire. He stated that the majority of these sites were well defended with strong coast defences and to raid them would require more landing craft than was then available. The only three he considered practical targets were, therefore, Abbeville aerodrome, St Nazaire, and the Channel Islands by which he meant Alderney. He then dismissed St Nazaire because the shipping required to go that far would probably not be available. This left just two. A raid on the aerodrome at Abbeville Mountbatten had been described as 'complex', so, by a process of elimination, Alderney was the place he believed a major operation could succeed. Why he thought this would be approved after *Blazing* had been turned down just a few months earlier is a mystery. Nevertheless, he pressed on with a full appraisal, adding that from Alderney the German coastal shipping route to the Biscay U-boat bases could be cut. It was also known that the French rail network did not have the capacity to keep the U-boats fully supplied and that they relied upon the coastal deliveries.

Alderney was the nearest of the Channel Islands to the UK, most of its civilian population had already been evacuated and, being the smallest of the three main islands, its capture would require the least effort. The island would be seized and held for 48 hours, the entire garrison of 2,500 would be killed or captured and its defences would be demolished. Learning something from the rejection of *Blazing*, Mountbatten accepted that holding the island permanently might prove too costly. He also acknowledged that the capture of Alderney was likely to result in the Germans strengthening their defences on the Cotentin Peninsula, making a subsequent attack there more difficult.

The forces required were, as might be expected, not dissimilar to those of *Blazing*, with the assault wave consisting of seven Commandos, one paratroop battalion, one squadron of Army tanks (twenty machines) and four bulldozers. A floating reserve of one infantry brigade, thirteen Bren gun carriers, and one battery and two troops of light anti-aircraft guns, and one 3.7-inch howitzer battery (six guns). The follow-up force would be the remainder of the Commandos, a Royal Artillery field regiment, and ancillary units. Additional forces would be required to hold the island for the designated period.[12]

What is interesting is that Mountbatten accepts that the Germans might well have strengthened the fortifications on Alderney since his team last examined them for *Blazing*, yet the forces supposedly required to take the island were slightly smaller.

Again, six destroyers would be required, along with the gunboat *Locust*, nine landing ships, 117 landing craft of different sorts, plus eight Motor Gun Boats.

The air forces required were 400 sorties from heavy night bombers, i.e., Bomber Command, for the preliminary bombardment and two day squadrons of bombers i.e. USAAF to support the assault landings. Intruder fighter sorties would be needed to attack enemy airfields on the French mainland, and three 'anti-flak' squadrons to supress the German batteries on Alderney during the assault, plus fighter protection for the support bombers and cover for the assault convoy, landings and the withdrawal, should that take place in daylight.

Mountbatten said that the night bombing would be directed across the whole of the island, but with two aiming points, one at the centre of the island, just east of St Anne, and another further east, midway between an imaginary line drawn from Saye Bay to Longy Bay. The day bomber attacks would focus upon the harbour, the Fort Albert area, and around Fort Tourgis.

The actual attack was detailed under what Mountbatten called 'Sequence of Operations'. In this, the 400 night bomber sorties would be 'concentrated in time and space to overwhelm the anti-aircraft defences and produce the greatest morale effect'. At the same time the intruder attacks would take place on the Luftwaffe aerodromes. The two day bomber squadrons, with fighter escort, would begin their attack at Zero Hour, which would be approximately 1 hour after nautical twilight and would last for 5 minutes. The anti-flak squadrons would then swoop in, their attack lasting for a further 5 minutes. The fighters providing the protection for the convoy and the landings would be airborne from first light.

The paratroopers would be dropped in the southern part of the island between Zero Hour+45 minutes to Z+60. Forty aircraft would be required, involving Whitley bombers from Bomber Command and Army Cooperation Command. Eight Bristol Blenheims would also deploy smoke to screen the paratroop drop.

Some 3,000 men of the Commandos, together with the tanks and a light anti-aircraft battery, would land in three waves on three different beaches. The primary task of the first wave was to secure the landing beaches by establishing a beachhead and overcoming any enemy defensive positions which could bring fire to bear on the beach. This would enable the second wave to land unopposed at Z+45 minutes and attack 'limited' objectives. To 'distract' the Germans' attention from the main landings, small detachments would be put ashore along the southern coast of the island at Z Hour.

The third wave, which would include the tanks, the howitzers, and the anti-aircraft batteries, would land at either Saline Bay or the harbour at Z+90 minutes and would push through to take the rest of the island, capturing or destroying the garrison. Surprisingly, the report acknowledged that it might not prove possible to capture Fort Albert in the first two days of the operation and that the plan therefore did not depend on seizing the harbour.

Zero Hour for the assault was to be 10 minutes after sunrise. Group 1, of two Commandos, would be put ashore from eighteen Landing Craft, Assault and ten Landing Craft, Personnel, in Saline Bay; Group 2 (one Commando) would be landed from 9 LCA and six LCP; and Group 3 (also one Commando) would also land from 9 LCA and six LCP in Corblets Bay.

Neither *Aimwell* nor its extension, *Gabriel*, survived the scrutiny of the Chiefs of Staff for all the reasons that had been stated time and time again.[13]

One Combined Ops raid which did get beyond the planning stage was Operation *Backchat*, in which sixty men of No. 12 Commando were to land on the French coast at Anse de St Martin on the north-west corner of the Cotentin Peninsula and, as usual, kill or capture as many German soldiers as possible. The plan received approval and was scheduled to be undertaken between 21 and 24 July. However, *Backchat* was delayed due to the weather and was gradually forgotten about.

With the months slipping away and no other major cross-Channel raids on the table for 1942, Mountbatten did not want to lose the one big operation which had received backing from the Committee. With this in mind, *Rutter* was not entirely abandoned, with Mountbatten able to gain Brooke's acceptance that, as so much thought and planning had gone into *Rutter*, if there was to be any further consideration given to an attack upon the French coast, re-mounting it would be the easiest, quickest and most cost-effective option of all those that had been suggested.

Whatever would be decided, there would be limited involvement from either Brooke or Churchill as they were shortly afterwards on their way to Cairo, where General Auchinleck was not displaying the effective ambition that the prime minister sought against Rommel's Afrika Korps. From there the two men and their advisory teams were to fly to Moscow. All that followed, therefore, happened while the senior political and military leaders were out of the UK. Mountbatten saw this as his chance and, on 12 July, he asked the Chiefs of Staff to consider mounting an operation to replace *Rutter*.

The senior military commander for *Rutter* had been General Montgomery, but he had been sent to Cairo to take charge of the Eighth Army. Similarly, the Naval Force Commander for *Rutter*, Rear Admiral Baillie-Grohman, had also been moved on to another posting. *Rutter*'s Air Force commander, Air Vice Marshal Trafford Leigh-Mallory, was only interested in bringing the Luftwaffe to battle at a time and place of his choosing, and if that meant Dieppe, then that was fine with him.

The posting of Montgomery to Egypt left Major General 'Ham' Roberts as the Army man responsible for remounting *Rutter*, if such a decision was made. He was not keen on this without a full reappraisal. Montgomery had also made his opposition known, stating that: 'If another raid was mounted, the objective should be anywhere but Dieppe because of German foreknowledge.'[14]

There matters seem to have stood, with *Rutter* suspended but not having been dropped and with keen support from Mountbatten and Hughes-Hallett, indifference from Leigh-Mallory, and opposition by Roberts. As for Brooke and Churchill, they had other matters in mind as they were preparing for their visit to Cairo at the end of the month. Both would be out of the country when the raid on Dieppe took place.

It has been stated by numerous historians that there is no direct evidence pointing to who authorised the operation against Dieppe to go ahead,[15] and this is the great mystery of the Dieppe raid which has led to conspiracy theories and claims of hidden motives. There was in place a strict protocol to be followed whenever an operation was proposed. Yet this procedure does not appear to have been undertaken with the re-mounting of *Rutter*. The raid is scarcely referred to in Brooke's diaries and, in Churchill's version of events, he states that 'extra-ordinary steps were taken to ensure secrecy. For this reason no records were kept.'[16] This is patent nonsense. No records were kept by the Chiefs of Staff, nor the Cabinet Office? Does this mean that there were fears of a leak at the very top of government or the military? Obviously not, because the records of the other major and minor operations were kept. This was a very thin smoke screen Churchill deployed and can be safely swept aside, as the following memorandum of 14 July demonstrates, just two days after Mountbatten had asked permission from the Chiefs of Staff to re-launch the raid on Dieppe:

> 'The Chiefs of Staff have directed that if possible, an emergency operation is to be carried out during August to fill the gap caused by the cancellation of *Rutter*. But as *Rutter* had been cancelled, the new operation needed a new name. It was called *Jubilee*.
>
> In order to cut down training requirements, the same forces will so far as possible be employed, and the planning of the new operation has to be entrusted to the Force Commanders from the outset.
>
> The locality and form of the new operation are being chosen so as to ensure that the training of individuals of lower formations will be as similar as possible to that which was given for *Rutter*.
>
> 'Owing to the appointment of Rear Admiral, Combined Operations [Baillie-Grohman] as Rear Admiral Expeditionary Force and, owing to the dispersal of the Senior Officers on his staff,

the Naval Staff for Operation *Jubilee* is being provided by Combined Operations Headquarters. The Force Commanders and their staffs for *Jubilee* will be working for the next fortnight on the second floor, and these rooms are not to be used for other purposes."[17]

It was merely the case that there were no other operations planned for 1942 and as Dieppe had already been sanctioned, it made sense to see if the tide and weather conditions might prove favourable for a raid on Dieppe before the unpredictable weather of autumn put an end to any such enterprises. It is quite clear that Churchill knew full-well about the re-launching of *Rutter* and was pleased to be able to demonstrate to Molotov and Stalin that he was sincere in his determination to help the Soviets.

This had been emphasised in a confidential *aide-mémoir* drawn up by the Chiefs of Staff that Churchill had handed to Molotov during his visit to London in June. It stated that the British Government 'shall continue our policy of raids against selected points on the Continent. These raids will increase in size and scope as the summer goes on. By this means we are preventing the Germans from transferring any of their 33 Divisions in Western Europe to their Eastern Front and keeping them constantly on the alert, never knowing at what point the next attack may come.'[18]

Following up on this, according to a memorandum from General Andrew McNaughton, the commander of the First Canadian Army in Britain: 'It appears that Stalin had cabled the Prime Minister asking what was being done to distract the Germans by raiding. The Prime Minister had been very pleased to be able to reply indicating action was in hand and in consequence he had approved the highest priority in preparation for J[ubilee].'[19]

A further indication that the re-mounting of *Rutter* had received full approval can be seen from the fact that when Brooke arrived in Cairo on 30 July ahead of the prime minister, he discussed the raid with Montgomery.[20] So, paper trail or not, that the raid on Dieppe was to be reinstated was known by all senior figures. How could the Canadians commit more than 6,000 men, the RAF supply nearly seventy squadrons or the Royal Navy in excess of 200 vessels to an operation just on Mountbatten's word or that of a mere captain, Hughes-Hallett? Indeed, the official account states unequivocally: 'The Chiefs of Staff, however, after careful consideration approved the operation.' The only conclusion that can be drawn from all this is that authorisation was granted verbally and because *Rutter* had already gone through the rigorous assessment only a few weeks previously, there was no need to go back and waste valuable time repeating what had already been done before.

The troops taking part in *Jubilee* would be the same ones as before and, as with *Rutter*, the main force would sail from the Solent with other ships from Littlehampton and Newhaven joining the flotilla at sea.

By early August the plan had assumed its final shape. There were to be four flank attacks launched at nautical twilight, followed half an hour later by the assault on Dieppe. The Naval Force consisted of 237 vessels, including eight destroyers, twenty-four Landing Craft, Tanks, seventy-four Landing Craft, Personnel, and sixty Landing Craft, Assault. A total of more than 6,000 troops would be involved from No. 2 Canadian Division, Nos. 2, 4, and 6 (Army) Commandos and 'A' Commando Royal Marines. There were also fifty men from the US 1st Rangers. The RAF would deploy sixty squadron of fighters, five of bombers and two of fighter-bombers.

The principal flanking attacks were instructed to capture the 'Goebbels' Battery near Berneval and the 'Hess' battery near Varengeville. The inner flank attacks were designed to take another battery – 'Rommel' – and attack in the rear the east headland above Dieppe.

The direct assault upon the town would see troops land on the main beaches, who would then take and hold the town. The east and west headlands were to be heavily bombed, as was the battery on the east cliff and the two batteries behind the town, and immediately after aircraft were to throw smoke screens over the two headlands. Fighters armed with cannon were to co-operate with the attacks on the Berneval and Varengeville batteries and were also to shoot-up the defences along the front at Dieppe. Meanwhile, the destroyers would provide a covering bombardment. The gunboat *Locust* and other craft carrying the Marines were to enter Dieppe harbour, cut out the landing barges, trawlers and any other naval vessels, and demolish naval installations and harbour works.

All this was laid out in the official documentation relating to *Jubilee*. But there were other objectives which were only referred to obliquely in official documents. Some have claimed that these objectives were the real reason why the raid on Dieppe had to be carried out – and so important were these they could not be committed to paper. In truth, there were numerous reasons for mounting *Jubilee*, not the least of which was because after his visit to Cairo, Churchill was scheduled to fly to Moscow.

Churchill arrived in Russia on 12 August ahead of Brooke and others. He sat down with Stalin that evening, accompanied by Roosevelt's representative, Averell Harriman, who the following year was appointed United States Ambassador to the Soviet Union. Churchill opened the meeting with the main subject to be discussed: the Second Front. He told the Soviet leader that the British and American governments did not believe they could undertake a major operation in 1942. September was the last month in which such an enterprise could be considered and there were simply not enough weeks left to arrange an operation of the scale necessary to have any impact on German troop dispositions. Stalin's demeanour gradually hardened as he listened to Churchill's explanation, but the prime minister endeavoured to lift Stalin's mood by discussing what he described as 'a very great' operation in 1943. He told Stalin that for this operation, a million American troops were scheduled to reach the UK in the spring of 1943, which would make a total expeditionary force of twenty-seven divisions, to which the British would add a further twenty-one divisions.

Churchill continued to explain that there were lots of reasons why a second front in 1942 was out of the question, with one of the major problems being a shortage of landing craft. The vessels currently available could carry no more than six divisions across the Channel and maintain them there, but such a force would soon be overwhelmed by the superior numbers of German forces in France. Nevertheless, landing craft were being built in large numbers in both the US and the UK and Churchill claimed that for every one division that could be carried this year, 1942, it would be possible next year to carry eight or ten times that number.

Stalin was unimpressed. Was it really the case, he asked, that Churchill was unwilling to sacrifice a mere six divisions to help the Red Army? Churchill confirmed that was indeed so. Such a landing, said Churchill, would be more harmful than helpful, as the troops, tanks and ships that would inevitably be lost would have a serious impact on the Allies' ability to mount a decisive campaign in 1943.

Stalin, according to Churchill, was becoming restless: 'A man who was not prepared to take risks could not win a war.' Why, he wanted to know, were the British so afraid of the Germans?

It was then that Churchill pulled his rabbit out of his hat or, to be more accurate, a map of the Mediterranean and North Africa out of his briefcase. What, Churchill asked Stalin, constituted a Second Front? Was it an operation mounted across the English Channel, or was it an attack on any point occupied by the Germans? The prime minister explained that France was not the only place where the Allies could have a major impact upon Hitler's already stretched resources, as he launched into his description of the hoped-for assault upon French North Africa.

Stalin's attention had at last been drawn, as he listened to Churchill's portrayal of the operation which, if all went to plan, would take place by the end of October 1942. Churchill said that: 'If we could end the year in possession of North Africa, we could threaten the belly of Hitler's Europe.' To illustrate his point, Churchill drew a sketch of a crocodile, demonstrating how, with the help of the drawing, 'it was our intention to attack the soft belly of the crocodile'.[21]

Stalin quickly grasped the advantages of Operation *Torch*, recognising it would hit Rommel 'in the back', would 'overawe' Spain and keep it out of the war, and would expose Italy's southern flank. After 4 hours of talks it seemed that Stalin's confidence in the Western democracies had been somewhat bolstered and the beginnings of a firm relationship between Churchill and Stalin had been established.

If Churchill believed he had won Stalin round to the idea of a Second Front in North-West Africa, he was quickly disabused when the two leaders met again the following evening. Stalin said many 'disagreeable things' in a very uncomfortable 2 hours for Churchill with the Soviet leader. The prime minister was handed a paper, as was Harriman for onward transmission to Roosevelt, which was uncompromising in its language:

> As the result of an exchange of views in Moscow which took place on August 12th of this year, I ascertained that the Prime Minister of Great Britain, Mr. Churchill, considered the organization of a second front in Europe in 1942 to be impossible

> As is well known, the organization of a second front in Europe in 1942 ... had as its object the withdrawal of German forces from Eastern front to the West ... It is easy to grasp that the refusal of [the] Government of Great Britain to create a second front in 1942 in Europe inflicts a moral blow to the whole of Soviet public opinion, which calculated on the creation of a second front ... [and] will undoubtedly lead to a deterioration of the military situation of England and all remaining allies.[22]

As it was late in the evening, Churchill said that he would respond the following day. His reply, drawn up with Brooke and Alexander Cadogan, Permanent Under-Secretary at the Foreign Office, read, in part:

> 'The best Second Front in 1942 and the only large-scale operation possible from the Atlantic is "Torch". If this can be effected in October it will give more aid to Russia than any other plan. It also prepares the way for 1943 ... Compared with "Torch" the attack with 6 or 8 Anglo-American divisions on the Cherbourg Peninsula and the Channel Islands would be a hazardous and futile operation.
>
> The Germans have enough troops in the West to block us in this narrow peninsula with fortified lines and would concentrate all their air forces in the West upon it. In the opinion of all the British naval, military and air authorities the operation could only end in disaster.
>
> Even if the lodgement were made, it would not bring a single division back from Russia. It would also be far more a running sore for us than for the enemy and would use up wastefully and wantonly the key men and the landing craft required for real action in 1943. This is our settled view.[23]

Instead, Churchill used and exaggerated the scale of the impending Dieppe raid to help demonstrate to Stalin that British troops were not sitting on their hands waiting for the Soviets to defeat Hitler. 'In order to make Germany anxious about an attack across the Channel,' he told Stalin, 'there will be a more serious raid in August, although the weather might upset it. It will be a reconnaissance in force. Some 8,000 men with 50 tanks will be landed. They will stay a night and a day, kill as many Germans as possible and take prisoners. They will then withdraw.'[24]

As can be seen, an operation against the Channel Islands was still colouring the thoughts of Churchill and Brooke, even though Brooke had dismissed Mountbatten's proposal just a few weeks earlier. As it happened, the raid on Dieppe had already taken place while he was en route to Moscow and, as Brooke had predicted, it was a ghastly disaster.

Chapter 6

Dieppe

The 237 ships, boats and landing craft left England's south coast at the end of a warm and sunny late summer's day. They were to form up in the Channel as if they were a normal convoy of civilian vessels to avoid alerting the enemy. Strict radio silence was to be enforced, other than in exceptional circumstances, until the troops actually began landing on 'Red' and 'White' beaches. Only shaded stern lights were to be displayed. The vessels carried 298 officers and 4,663 enlisted men of the Canadian Army, 1,005 officers and other ranks of No. 3 and No. 4 Commando and the Royal Marine Commandos, eighteen members of No. 10 (Inter-Allied) Commando, fifty US Rangers and a handful of other, more clandestine, individuals, making a total of 6,100 of all ranks.

Lieutenant F. Royal was an official Canadian photographic officer on board Landing Craft, Tank No. 11: 'When we got into the Channel, I could see the assault landing craft and the tank landing craft in front of us, on the sides and behind us. We travelled in convoy through the night. The sea was absolutely calm. There was not a cloud in the sky and by the light of new moon I was able to distinguish the dark shapes of the other craft around us.'[1]

As the flotilla approached the French coast another group of vessels was also heading towards Dieppe. A German convoy, sailing through the Channel from Boulogne to Dieppe, was on a collision course with the flotilla. The convoy's presence was detected by a radar station on Beachy Head, East Sussex, at 01.24 hours. The officer at Beachy Head immediately informed Admiral Sir William James at Portsmouth, who relayed the warning to Hughes-Hallett, *Jubilee's* Naval Force Commander on the destroyer *Calpe*, just minutes later. The flotilla, however, continued serenely upon its original heading. Further warnings were sent from Portsmouth, but Hughes-Hallett took no evasive action.

Predictably, at 03.47 hours, the German convoy made contact with the assault flotilla, as a starshell exploded high above the most easterly group of the invasion force, Group 5, and gunfire blazed out across the water. Three minutes later the Port Commandant at Dieppe was informed that the German convoy had engaged enemy ships.

Group 5 consisted of twenty-three Landing Craft Personnel (Light), also known as Eurekas or R boats, carrying No. 3 Commando, whose task it was to assault the Berneval battery in what was codenamed Operation *Flodden*. They were escorted by a steam gunboat, a motor launch, and a flak landing craft. The German convoy they encountered consisted of five small freighters escorted by three minesweepers or armed trawlers.

Sub-Lieutenant D.J. Lewis, Royal Canadian Naval Volunteer Reserve, was on the Eureka closest to the enemy, just behind the steam gunboat, when the fight began: 'a starshell went up on the starboard hand and lit the whole fleet in a horrible quivering semi-daylight. Our boat was leading the starboard [sic port] column. It was immediately enveloped in the hottest tracer fire I have ever seen. The air was filled with the whine of ricochets and the bangs of exploding shells, while after every burst of the streaking balls of fire came the clatter of Oerlikons.'[2]

Outnumbered and outgunned, and with no means of illuminating the enemy vessels, the British boats were severely handicapped. In the encounter the British escort vessels were seriously damaged and one of the German boats was a total loss. But, more importantly, the landing craft carrying No. 3 Commando, along with a contingent of US Army Rangers, were completely scattered, some of them being damaged.

Though Lieutenant Colonel Durnford-Slater had orders that if any of his LCPs were sunk, he was to carry out his 'allotted tasks with reduced numbers', he had no idea where most of his boats had gone. In consultation with Commodore Wybud, he decided that a daylight assault on a well-defended position with the few boats still with the group was impracticable and he relayed this to General Roberts on the headquarters ship off Dieppe. As a result, it was agreed to abandon Operation *Flodden*.

Unaware that the operation had been called off, the Commandos on eight of the landing craft pressed on towards the French coast determined to carry on with their mission against the Berneval battery, with the rest of Group 5 turning back to England. This was just the first of the many disasters that were to be played out that fateful day.

Goebbels Battery was situated to the north of Berneval-le-Grand. An independent strongpoint (*Stützpunkt*), it was separate from Dieppe and its defences. The first troops to land on either of the 'Yellow' beaches were part of a detachment of No. 3 Commando under Major Peter Young, whose men were landed dry shod on Yellow Beach 2 as their landing craft beached on the high tide 5 minutes ahead of schedule. Though Young had just two other officers and seventeen Commandos with him he was determined to carry out the attack on the 'Goebbels' Battery as planned.

The big guns of the German battery had begun firing on the main assault force heading for Dieppe and Young knew it was vitally important that he tried to silence the guns with the tiny force he had with him.

They moved straight through a wood and towards Berneval itself. Young knew that it would be futile to try to assault the battery with the few men he had with him and that the best he could do was to harass the battery as much as possible to prevent it from inflicting serious damage on the attacking forces. When they reached the village, they tried to set up firing positions overlooking the battery. They considered setting up a Bren gun in the bell tower of the church, but found that it did not have a staircase. Some of the locals suggested that the Commandos went through an orchard to a cornfield where they would have a clear line of sight to the battery. The Commandos managed to get to a position within 200 yards of the battery. Young split his men into three small groups, directing them to cut telephone wires to disrupt communications and to fire on the battery for as long as their limited quantity of ammunition lasted in a bid to distract the enemy gunners: 'Once we were in among the crops I formed the men into two lines in extended order, with a good distance between each man and with the second line firing between the intervals in the first line. We now opened a hot fire at the smoke and flashes around the gun positions. Groups of riflemen were firing at us from the battery position, but they were not marksmen.'[3]

The big German guns did try to shell the Commandos, but were unable to counter their fire, being unable to sufficiently depress their barrels.

Unaware that Operation *Flodden* had been called off, a further six boats,[4] reached Yellow Beach 1 under covering fire from the motor launch *ML 346*. The boats touched down 20 minutes late. 'Expecting that the enemy would be sitting waiting for us, we were very surprised and relieved to land without a shot being fired at us. We made haste to get off the beach but were held up while the wire was being cut,' recalled one of the commandos. 'While this was being done, Jerry began firing from the cliffs, and although our passage through the wire was slow because of the mines, nobody, so far as I know, was hit, in spite of terrific firing overhead. Once on top, we went forward until we were stopped by very heavy machine-gun fire from the front.'

Among those that landed were the men the from the 1st US Ranger Battalion, becoming the first American troops to set foot on mainland Europe in the Second World War. One of their number, Second Lieutenant Edward Loustalot, had the unlooked-for distinction of being the first US soldier of the war to be killed on European soil, after dying attempting to silence an enemy machine gun. There were also five men of the fifteen-strong French detachment of No. 10 (1A) Commando. Most of these chose to wear their blue Marine uniforms and their 'France' shoulder insignia.

About 35 minutes after the first boat had reached Yellow 1, the last boat arrived, bringing the number of men who landed on this beach to 120. But, as the boat pulled away from the beach, it was sunk by enemy gunfire.

Though the Commandos did advance about half a kilometre inland almost level with the Goebbels Battery and succeeded in knocking out one German machine-gun position, the odds were stacked against the attackers. Not only did the German defenders outnumber the small force put ashore, but they were soon powerfully reinforced.

It was very evident that there was no chance of taking the battery with the Commandos pinned down at the foot of the cliffs. Consequently, at 07.00 hours, it was decided to abandon the attack upon the battery and try to save as many men as possible.

But, having reached the beach, they found the sea empty; the Navy, having had no communication with the Commandos, thought that they had all perished and none of the LCPs returned to Yellow 1.

The stranded Commandos came under fire from the cliffs above and were taking heavy casualties. Twenty or so took refuge in a cave where they were safe for a while, though acutely conscious that the Germans would soon be upon them. By 10.00 the Germans were on the beach and advancing down it, taking prisoners. Having no more ammunition, the senior officer in the cave ordered the men to break their weapons and surrender. Two officers and eighty men were taken prisoner, many of whom were wounded. All the men who had landed on Yellow 1 had been killed or captured, apart from two who had managed to swim out to boats and were saved.

Remarkably, all the men that had landed on Yellow 2 were taken off the beach, with just one man wounded by a mine. Young and Lieutenant Anthony Ruxton were the last men away, these two grabbing lifelines as the boat moved away, being pulled along for about 300 yards before they were hauled on board.

Over to the west of Dieppe, the other large coastal battery, 'Hess' Battery, near Varengeville, was the target of No. 4 Commando. As with the Goebbels Battery, the one near Varengeville was also an independent *Stützpunkt*, of six 150mm guns in a concrete emplacement just over half a mile inland from the coastal cliffs. Intelligence reports had estimated there were around 200 men at the battery, with a further two infantry companies in support nearby. The emplacement was surrounded by concrete defences, landmines, concealed defensive machine-gun posts and layers of barbed wire, and was also protected from air attack by an anti-aircraft gun emplacement.

No. 4 Commando was led by Acting Lieutenant Colonel Lord Lovat with a much smaller force of 252 men compared with the 400-plus who had started out from England under Durnford-Slater, though their task was no less formidable. The operation was codenamed *Cauldron*, and the orders Lovat had received were straightforward: Take the battery 'with all possible speed'.

Lovat's plan was a simple as his orders had been. He intended to split his Commando into two groups to land on Orange 1 and 2. Group 1 was to engage the battery positions from the front with mortars, light machine-guns and small arms fire, while Group 2 would make a wide sweep to a position behind the battery, and on a prearranged signal, assault the battery from the rear.

Lovat's operation went almost exactly to plan. The Commandos overran the battery and destroyed the German guns. In what has been called a 'classic' Commando action, Lovat had achieved all his objectives and he was rightfully proud of what had been achieved, but what the twenty-fourth Chief of the Clan Fraser did not know was that his operation was the only truly successful one. On the other beaches, *Jubilee* had already become an unmitigated disaster.

During the planning for *Rutter/Jubilee*, Jock Hughes-Hallett had emphasised the importance of the inner flank attack upon Puys (or Puits) – Blue Beach – as he later explained: 'It had always been realised that unless the east headland which overlooks the town and port of Dieppe was captured, the frontal assault on the town, on which the whole operation chiefly depended, would probably fail.'5

Near this eastern headland there were numerous objectives, notably the 'Rommel' four-gun battery, barracks, gas works and various gun sites. Such was the importance of taking these positions just two days before *Jubilee* sailed, Hughes-Hallett sent a letter about this to Mountbatten, in which he stated that if any of the LSIs carrying the troops to land at Blue beach were sunk, the operation should be aborted. These positions were to be attacked by troops of the Royal Regiment of Canada.

The narrow beach by the tiny hamlet of Puys is situated between rising cliffs with a seawall some 10 to 12 feet high running between the two cliffs. At normal high-water mark the beach between the cliffs is only some 75 yards wide. In 1942 the seawall was topped with barbed wire. There were only two exits through the seawall from the beach and these were also heavily wired.

Due to mistakes in the dark, at 04.40 hours, 5 minutes after the Canadians were supposed to have been disembarking onto the beach, the column of boats was still 2 miles out. As the craft were preparing for the final run in, the Germans fired flares over the approaches to Dieppe harbour, 'wrenching aide the cloak of dawn' and exposing the whole of the Blue Beach assault force.

With no aerial bombardment, the Royals only hope of success had been if they could land undiscovered in the dark and take the German positions by surprise. All that had now gone. *Jubilee* was now certain to fail. However well or bravely the attackers performed, from that moment on to continue was 'an act of sheer sacrificial defiance'. The entire operation should have been called off. But there was no mechanism for the various vessels to be withdrawn. The first wave landed 17 minutes late and the Germans were at their posts, waiting.

Captain G.A. Browne, the artillery Forward Observation Officer, witnessed the destruction of the Royals: 'In five minutes time they were changed from an assaulting battalion on the offensive to something less than two companies on the defensive being hammered by fire which they could not locate.'6

Some 20 minutes behind the first wave, the second reached the shoreline. Rather than reinforcing the attack, these extra troops merely added to the growing list of casualties.

One small party of the Royals from the first wave did manage to get off the beach, but became cut off from the rest of the regiment and were compelled to surrender.

Scarcely any of the Royals escaped from Blue Beach, with 464 of the 556 who set off from England being either killed or captured. With 200 of these being killed, the regiment suffered not only the highest fatal casualty rate of any unit on the raid, but also the highest of any Commonwealth or American unit, per proportion of forces engaged, during the Second World War.

The South Saskatchewan Regiment, numbering 523 officers and men under Lieutenant Colonel Dollard Merritt, touched down unopposed at 04.52 on Green Beach just 2 minutes late, though further to the west than planned. The arrangements were that 'B' Company would clear the town of the enemy while 'A' Company mounted the eastern heights to attack the coastal batteries and the 'Freya' radar station, one of the raid's key, and, as mentioned earlier, highly secret objectives.

The Canadians had to mount the seawall using scaling-ladders, the first men up using wire-cutters to cut through the barbed-wire which topped the wall. Once through the gap, those companies whose objectives lay to the east had to turn left and dash through the silent streets of Pourville to the bridge over the River Scie, which led to the road leading to eastern ridge towards Dieppe. But before they could reach the bridge, the Germans awoke, quite literally, to the danger they were in. From that point onwards, the attack on Pourville became a bloodbath.

The secret mission to break into the German radar station, undertaken by a radar expert, Jack Nissenthall, was a partial success. Though unable to force his way into the radar station, he was able to cut its eight telephone wires. This mean that the German operators, unable to communicate through the secure land line, had to use open radio which was picked up by listening stations on the other side of the Channel, resulting in much useful information being gathered.

The main assault was to be delivered against the sea front of Dieppe itself, over Red and White beaches. It was here that fifty-two Churchill tanks of the 14th Canadian Tank Battalion (the Calgary Regiment) were to land to break into the town in support of the Royal Hamilton Light Infantry and the Essex Scottish Regiment. The story of failure on the other beaches was repeated here.

The German weapon positions were set in caves in both headlands, with guns that could be brought out to fire and then pulled back in, and most of the weapons on the promenade were sited in concrete pillboxes, casemates, and bunkers. The Germans had even constructed underground bunkers on the promenade covered with grass and completely invisible from the air. The actual front of Dieppe from the Casino to the harbour mole inclusive, was also held in strength with well-armed German army and air personnel.

The troops landed with little loss, but their troubles then developed rapidly, because instead of advancing quickly while the enemy was still taking cover from the aerial and naval bombardment, they remained under the shelter of the sea wall, thus losing precious moments. When they started to advance the Germans had recovered and opened heavy fire.

The murderous enfilade fire from guns concealed in the east cliff face was much greater than had been anticipated. These guns were 'impossible to detect even at close range until they fired,' reported Lieutenant-Commander McMullen, 'and ... could not easily be silenced by our own fire. This enfilade fire made the capture and retention of the beaches almost impossible and was therefore the main cause of the failure to press on through Dieppe and attain objectives laid down in the plan.'

Another factor was the vast depth of wire between the seawall and the buildings lining the far side of the promenade from where the Germans were firing directly at the attackers. Until they could get to the buildings and silence the enemy, the attackers were going to suffer more and more casualties. The men of the Essex Scottish tried to blast a way through the wire with a Bangalore torpedo, but it only cut halfway through the 6-feet-deep entanglement. Only two small parties reached the town itself, achieving practically nothing.

The regiment of tanks, of which much was expected, was possibly the greatest disappointment of the raid. Due to the ferocity of the enemy fire, only twenty-eight were landed, with every one of them being later damaged, destroyed abandoned. A small number did manage to climb off the beach onto the promenade, but found heavy concrete roadblocks barring the streets leading into the town which they could not overcome. Only two members of the tank crews who landed managed to get away and return to the UK, the remainder were either killed or taken prisoner

Though General Roberts sent in all his reserves and the Royal Marine Commandos, none were able to achieve a significant breakthrough and by 09.00 hours it had become clear to him and Hughes-Hallett that the troops ashore were in difficulties. It was not for another 90 minutes, however, that the order to withdraw was signalled to the men on the beaches.

The original intention, had the raid gone according to plan, was to take most of the troops off the beaches in tank and personnel landing craft. However, Hughes-Hallett decided that such was the volume of enemy fire, he could not risk sending in those larger craft. This meant abandoning any tanks that might still be serviceable and left the recovery of the troops to the Landing Craft, Assault and the Motor Landing Craft. Few reached the beaches.

At Green Beach only 353 returned to the UK from the 523 that had disembarked just a few hours earlier. On the main Red and White beaches, little more than 400 were rescued under conditions of the greatest difficulty, the crews of the landing craft showing complete contempt for danger in their efforts to save as many men as they could.

At 12.40 Hughes-Hallett moved in close to the beaches in *Calpe* for a final personal inspection. With protection from a Landing Craft, Assault on each bow, *Calpe* steered for the eastern end of Red Beach, opening fire with her 4-inch guns. At just under a mile from the shore she came under heavy fire and as no troops could be seen on the beach, *Calpe* retired behind the smoke screen. It appeared impossible to bring off any more troops, but before finally abandoning the attempt, Hughes-Hallett wanted to make one more effort at rescuing at least some more men from the Dieppe beaches. It was at this time, however, that Roberts received a signal saying the remainder of the troops ashore were surrendering. This was the inauspicious end to Mountbatten's super-raid.

There is no question that the raid was a failure in almost every respect. Of the 6,086 men that landed in France, a total of 3,623, constituting almost

60 percent, were either killed, wounded, and or taken prisoner. In terms of equipment lost, the Germans listed: 29 Churchill Tanks, 7 Scout Cars, 1 Jeep, 1 Personnel Truck, 1,300 Rifles, 170 Machine Guns (Bren and Sten), 42 Boys Anti-Tank Rifles, 70 light Mortars, 60 Heavy Mortars, and vast quantities of ammunition, explosives and clothing.

Even the long sought for great battle with the Luftwaffe was disappointing, with the RAF losing ninety-six aircraft to the Luftwaffe's forty-eight. The Royal Navy lost thirty-three landing craft plus one destroyer, and seventy-five men killed or died of wounds, with a further 269 missing or captured.

Generalmajor William Hasse offered a German perspective on why the raid failed: 'The British completely miscalculated the strength of the German defences and tried to overcome them by landing the main body of their forces, particularly the tanks, right in front of Dieppe. They persisted with this plan though they knew the strength of the defences, concrete constructions, anti-tank walls, machine-gun positions etc. We know this from their [captured] maps.' One element that was not fully appreciated was the German heavy mortars. It was estimated that these mortars accounted for approximately 32 per cent of the Allied casualties.[7]

It was not long before the purpose of the raid was called into question. Among these were the comments from the Principal Landing Officer, Major Brian McCool, after his surrender. During his two-day interrogation, a German officer asked: 'It was too big for a raid and too small for an invasion. What was it?' To which McCool replied: 'if you can tell me the answer, I would be grateful'.

This view was soon to be repeated in the Allied press as more details about the raid became known: 'Now the truth is known, we do not believe public opinion in Canada will be satisfied with the official explanation that the raid on Dieppe was instrumental in obtaining crucial information on the defensive organization of the enemy. If the expedition's only goal was to survey coastal defences, one wonders why the same result could not have been achieved with a smaller deployment of troops.'[8]

The raid did produce one discernible benefit; it demonstrated in the starkest terms to the Americans that a full-scale invasion of the Continent was not possible in the immediate future with the troops and shipping available in the UK. Operation *Torch*, which was due to be launched against French North Africa in November, had swallowed up more than

100,000 troops and, even more critically, some 500 transport and assault craft.

It might reasonably be assumed that there would be no further discussion regarding large cross-Channel raids, especially as Mountbatten had been handed a key role in *Torch*. Part of his Combined Ops Headquarters team was placed under Eisenhower's command and Mountbatten himself was put at the general's disposal. But he still retained his seat on the Chiefs of Staff Committee and, shaking off the Dieppe fiasco as a new year approached his team began to draw up plans for 1943 – and those plans included the Channel Islands yet again.

Chapter 7

Husky

One of the unspoken aims of Roosevelt's policy in the war was to ensure that, at its end, the United States would be the dominate economic world power. This would mean loosening Britain's grip on its far-flung empire. After the First World War, President Wilson had sought a similar goal with his 'Fourteen Points', three of the first five of which were aimed (indirectly) at the United Kingdom. These covered freedom of the seas, which previously Britannia ruled; free trade between countries – Britain, of course, controlled trade with its colonies; and that 'colonial claims over land and regions will be fair'. Despite these being agreed, Britain had, in fact, extended its empire during the inter-war period.

Thus, when Churchill argued forcefully for action in the Mediterranean which would help the UK retain its hold on its colonies, the Americans, who wanted to see an end to Britain's empire, were far from willing to help. There was even a suspicion that by eliminating or reducing French and Italian influence in the region, Britain's position in the Mediterranean would be strengthened.[1] As one historian has described it, the Americans were 'sensitive, indeed severely so, to every hint of a diversion in the direction of what they regarded as British imperial interests'.[2] It was against this backdrop that Churchill and Roosevelt and their respective teams met at Casablanca in French Morocco for ten days in January 1943.

In reviewing the war situation as it stood at the beginning of 1943 on the first day of the conference, Brooke observed that 'Italy was becoming more and more shaky; and if she collapsed, Germany would not only have to bolster up Italy by sending troops into the country but would also have to replace the numerous Italian divisions in Yugoslavia and in Greece. Alternatively, she would have to withdraw altogether from the Balkans and Italy, and leave it open to the Allies.'[3] There were, therefore, strong reasons for pushing Italy to the brink by invading the country from North Africa.

All indications showed that Germany's manpower was failing, Brooke said, and that she was also suffering from oil shortages, a situation which would only get worse. Taking all these factors into account, 'it seemed at least possible that the precarious internal situation of Germany might make it possible to achieve a final victory in the European theatre before the end of 1943'. The question before the Combined Chiefs of Staff was the best method, or methods, of bringing that victory about.

Brooke said that apart from doing everything to bolster the Soviet Union, which was engaging with the bulk of the German forces, the means by which the Western Allies could strike at Germany was by amphibious operations which, of course, included an invasion of the Continent. 'The possession of sea power,' continued Brooke, enables us to threaten the enemy at several points and thereby compel him to disperse his forces. Once committed to a point of entry, however, the enemy would be able to concentrate his forces against us, and it was therefore necessary to choose this point of entry with the greatest care at the place where the enemy was least able to concentrate large forces.'

Determined not to be drawn into a premature cross-Channel offensive, Brooke wanted to present the invasion of Europe through Italy as a viable operation and one which offered the best chance of success. 'As a point of re-entry to the Continent,' Brooke said, 'France had great advantages. In the first place the sea-crossing was short, and we had better facilities for giving air support to our invasion. On the other hand, the German defences in this area were most strong and Germany's power of concentrating against us was greatest.' He said that a recent study had shown that the east-west communications across the Continent enabled Germany to move seven divisions simultaneously from the Russian front to the west in about twelve to fourteen days. The north-south communications on the Continent were not nearly so good. Not more than one division at a time could be moved from the north to the Mediterranean front. The Italian railways were also close to the coast and vulnerable to interruption from the sea. 'From this point of view,' Brooke argued, 'the southern front seemed to offer better prospects for amphibious operations.'

Brooke then praised the Americans and complemented them on their organisation and cooperation in *Torch*, indicating that a similar operation against Italy was likely to produce the same satisfactory results. The invasion of French North Africa had begun on 8 November 1942 with landings in Algeria and Morocco against only limited opposition, the French colonial forces soon laying down their arms. But Hitler responded swiftly, airlifting troops into Tunis and shipping tanks and heavy equipment across the Mediterranean. The British and Americans now had a fight on their hands. Though the battle for Tunisia was ongoing, and would continue until May, the Allies had a far greater number of troops, tanks, and artillery, as well as, rather belatedly, virtual control of the sea, and their victory was inevitable. *Torch* also achieved the Allies' long-term aim of drawing German troops and aircraft from other areas, of which more than 300,000 of the former and over 300 of the latter were eventually lost to Hitler. All of this, and what had happened at Dieppe, demonstrated just how correct the British had been in their strategic assessment.

Brooke ended his opening talk at Casablanca with a summation of the above: 'The British Chiefs of Staff felt that we should first expand the bomber offensive against the Axis to the maximum and that operations in the Mediterranean offered the best chance of compelling Germany to disperse her resources. With this end in view, we should take as our immediate objective the knocking out of Italy.'

The estimate of the British Chiefs of Staff was that by August 1943 there would be some thirteen British and nine US divisions available for cross-Channel operations, even allowing for operations in the Mediterranean theatre. The problem remained, however, of a shortage of shipping. Requirements for landing craft to be made available for operations in Burma and the Mediterranean meant limited numbers available for cross-Channel assaults.

Sir Charles Portal then spoke about the situation in the air:

The present state of the German air force is critical. The stamina of the air crews is decreasing; the crews lack interest and are less determined, and their training is deteriorating. One explanation for this is that training units and personnel are being used for combat purposes because of a shortage of aircraft. He felt that there is no depth behind the German front line of aircraft. The British Intelligence Service is of the opinion that if the United Nations can keep Germany fighting with aircraft, they will suffer losses from which they cannot recover.

Far better for the Allies, then, to mount only limited operations in the Channel where the Luftwaffe would be drawn into battle on the RAF's and the USAAF's terms (or as Portal put it: 'to meet them while they are attempting to stop our amphibian operations') until the point was reached when the German aircraft would not pose a serious obstacle to an invading force.

Astonishingly, regardless of the obvious success of *Torch*, Marshall still clung to his old theme: 'The United States Chiefs of Staff are concerned as to whether operations in the Mediterranean area would bring advantages commensurate with the risks involved,' he said. 'The [US] Joint Chiefs of Staff are inclined to look favourably on an operation from the United Kingdom because of the strong air support that can be furnished from that base as well as the relative ease with which it can be supplied from the United States.'

However, Mountbatten made the point that the training of crews to operate landing craft and of the troops to use them was a slow process, so the number of craft available for operations could not be speedily increased, which limited the scope of any cross-Channel enterprises. Surprisingly, US General Mark Clarke who, as the Commanding General, Army Forces in the European Theatre of Operations, had been given the job of examining the feasibility of a cross-Channel invasion, agreed with Mountbatten. This would not have pleased Marshall, particularly as he had appointed Clarke to come up with plans for a cross-Channel operation, not to oppose such a move. Clarke compounded this by also agreeing with the British that 'operations in the Mediterranean could be mounted more efficiently' than across the Channel, explaining that 'the troops in North Africa have had experience in landing operations, and that there will be an excess number of troops available for the operation once the Axis has been forced out of Tunisia, and finally that training will be more effective if undertaken in close contact with the enemy.' In his diary, Brooke wrote that it had been 'a very long and laborious day'.

At 10.00 hours the next day, 15 January, Marshall briefed Roosevelt on the discussions of day one. He told the President that the British Chiefs of Staff believed the Allies should expand the bombing effort against the Axis Powers and that operations in the Mediterranean offered the best chance of compelling Germany to disperse her air resources. The British were 'extremely fearful of any direct action against the Continent until a decided crack in the German efficiency and morale has become apparent'. Instead, the British favoured an attack against Sicily as the first move against the Italian mainland.

Marshall, of course, told Roosevelt that any further actions in the Mediterranean would jeopardise the *Bolero* schedule which, in turn, would put back the eventual re-invasion of Europe through northern France.

That same day, the Combined Chiefs of Staff resumed their meeting. Reading the minutes of the meeting, it can be seen how Brooke presented his case. At the same time as saying he was in favour of shutting down operations in North Africa as soon as possible to concentrate on the Channel, he also presented the case against such a move.

He began, though, by looking at the possible invasion areas:

a) The Calais-Boulogne area which, although heavily defended, was within fighter cover of the UK
b) Cherbourg Peninsula, which could be seized by a comparatively small force
c) Brest Peninsula, which was a more worthwhile objective, but would require a much larger force, say, at least fifteen divisions, to hold the 150 kilometres of front.

He explained that it would not be possible to begin any of these operations until the early autumn, when it was calculated there would be between twenty-one and twenty-three divisions available. This meant there would be no help in relieving the pressure on the Soviets until then and there was no point in undertaking any operations on a small scale as they would have little more than a local effect.

Brooke then set out the alternatives:

The Mediterranean offered many choices: Sardinia, Sicily, Crete, and the Dodecanese. Our amphibious power enabled us to threaten all these points simultaneously and thereby cause the Germans to disperse their forces. Unless they were to risk the loss of these islands, they would be compelled to reinforce them as well as the coasts of Italy, Greece, and France. If Italy could be knocked out, Germany would be involved in large new commitments in an attempt to bolster her up and replacing Italian troops in the Balkans. Other German satellites might also fall out.

Concluding, he said: 'our best policy would be to threaten Germany everywhere in the Mediterranean, to try to knock out Italy, and to bring in Turkey on our side.'

It is interesting to note how, gradually, the British Chiefs of Staff had managed to steer the focus of the Allied effort away from the invasion of northern France over the months since Marshall had first travelled to London to urge action against the Continent in 1942. Almost a year on, no such operation had taken place and it seemed unlikely that anything would happen in 1943.

Brooke continued, stating that one of the great advantages of adopting the Mediterranean policy was that a larger force of heavy bombers could be built up in the UK for the attack on Germany than if the bomber force was deployed in support of an invasion of France.

Of course, the American delegation was opposed to this, with Admiral King saying that if the Allies concentrated more troops in the Mediterranean to carry out an attack upon Italy, the more likely Germany was to move into Spain in order to cut the Allied line of communications through the Strait of Gibraltar. That was a preposterous suggestion. With Hitler's forces already stretched to the limit, there was not the slightest possibility of the Germans being able to find the extra troops required to occupy a large country like Spain. But this indicated how desperate the Americans were to find reasons to stop further operations in the Mediterranean and concentrate on the Channel.

After stating all the reasons why Hitler would not invade Spain, Sir Charles Portal effectively ended the Mediterranean versus northern Europe debate by stating: 'The total coastline of Sicily was about 500 miles, and it was anticipated that some 7 to 8 enemy divisions would be defending the island. This compared very favourably with the coastline of Northern France, which was the same length, more strongly fortified and would be defended, by 15 divisions.'

He ended by saying:

It would be much more advantageous for the Germans if we built up against France and left the Mediterranean alone. They would then be able to withdraw large numbers of air forces from the Mediterranean and reinforce the Russian Front, relying on the strong defences of Northern France to resist an invasion. On the other hand, if we kept the Mediterranean active, they would be compelled to keep large air forces there the whole time. This was of the greatest importance since Germany's main shortages were air forces and oil.

Sir Dudley Pound chipped in with an additional reason for selecting the Mediterranean: 'Once the North African Coast had been cleared, even without having Sicily in our possession, it would be possible to run a convoy of thirty ships once every ten days through the Mediterranean, in substitution for the present shipping to the Middle East, Persian Gulf and India, which moved via the Cape. This would effect a saving of some 225 ships.'

As shipping capacity was always an issue, this final point, it would seem from the recorded minutes of the meeting, silenced the Americans round the table. The discussion then centred around which points in southern Europe, other than Sicily, would be the most likely to achieve the desired results mentioned above. There was none.

On the 16th the Combined Chiefs returned to their discussions, with Marshall, yet again, objecting to the British proposals. He opened the discussion by asking the British delegation how they thought they could defeat Germany if they were so reluctant to re-invade northern France? He said that the aim of the Western Allies was to do everything they could to take pressure off the Soviets, and that 'any method of accomplishing this other than on the Continent is a deviation from the basic plan'.

He then listed five issues that he had with the British Mediterranean plan. One of these was that the loss of landing craft in an amphibious assault upon Sicily would, according to Eisenhower's estimates, result in a loss rate of between 50 and 75 per cent. This would have an extremely detrimental effect on the timing of any cross-Channel operation. His final point was: 'Was an operation against Sicily merely a means towards an end or an end in itself? Is it to be a part of an integrated plan to win the war or simply taking advantage of an opportunity?' Obviously, Marshall thought it was the British taking the latter.

Admiral King and General Arnold reinforced Marshall's words, both questioning how attacking Sicily/Italy could have any real bearing on what was happening in Russia, and, as Arnold asked, what 'relation such an attack would have to the whole strategic conception'. Evidently, the Americans had decided overnight that this would be the central theme of their opposition to the British aim of further operations in the Mediterranean theatre. It was important, Marshall reiterated 'that we now reorient ourselves and decide what the "main plot" is to be. Every diversion or side issue from the main plot acts as a "suction pump."'

Brooke fought back, saying something that the Americans would not have wanted to hear. The only country, or collection of countries, capable of employing land armies large enough to seriously challenge the Germans was the Soviet Union, not the United States. 'Any effort of the other allies must necessarily be so small as to be unimportant in the over-all picture.'

The Americas were not to be diverted from their main goal of a cross-Channel operation in 1943, arguing that Allied air power was the key factor. While the British planners doubted that any foothold gained on the Continent could be held against the weight of forces the Germans could bring to bear, the Americans believed that a bridgehead on the French coast would be protected by the Allied air forces, which were gaining in strength every month. Any cross-Channel operations that brought the Luftwaffe into battle with the fighters of the RAF should be encouraged, as this would speed up the decline of German air strength and advance the date when the re-invasion of the Continent could begin.

Unimpressed, Brooke stuck to his guns:

> The Germans still have sufficient strength to overwhelm us on the ground and perhaps hem us in with wire or concrete to such an extent that any expansion of the bridgehead would be extremely difficult. Moreover, we cannot undertake any operation in Northern France until very late in the summer of 1943. Since, therefore, we cannot go into the Continent in force until Germany weakens, we should try to make the Germans disperse their forces as much as possible. This can be accomplished by attacking the German allies, Italy in particular.

He repeated his contention that if Italy was knocked out of the war, Germany would be forced to occupy that country with a considerable number of divisions and, in addition, would be compelled to replace Italian divisions in other Axis-occupied countries such as Yugoslavia and Greece. Brooke said that at the same time as operations against Sicily were being undertaken, there must be a continued build-up of the Allied forces in the UK trained and ready to undertake the final action of the war as soon as Germany showed definite signs of weakness.

The British delegation reiterated its reasoning of the previous day, with Pound adding that by opening the Mediterranean route from the oilfields of the Arabian Gulf, fewer tankers would be needed to cross the perilous North Atlantic, where high numbers of ships were lost each month to German U-boats.

Determined not to be deflected from their main aim, the Americas persisted in pushing forward the attack across the Channel. King made the point that once British and US forces were established in France, American troops could be sent there directly from America without the need for trans-shipment in the UK. He also remarked that the German U-boat problem might be largely solved by capturing the Brest Peninsula and with it the U-boat bases there. Both sides were digging in.

Mountbatten then spoke of the number of landing craft available for amphibious operations. While the Americans spoke of more than twenty divisions being available to launch an offensive from the UK by mid-September, the reality was that there would only be landing craft to carry four brigade groups across the Channel in the first wave.

This seemed to have tipped the balance, as Arnold voiced what Marshall must have feared, that it was clear the earliest practical date for the re-invasion of northern France was the spring of 1944. One can only wonder if Brooke's sigh of relief was heard across the table. With evident misgivings, the Americans agreed to look at the invasion of Sicily, Operation *Husky*.

Brooke went to bed early, exhausted. He wrote that night in his diary: 'all matters have to be carefully explained and reexplained [to the Americans] before they can be absorbed. And finally, the counter-arguments put forward [by them] often show that even then the true conception has not been grasped and the process has to be started again.'[4]

It was the same story the next day, with all that had been agreed the previous day seemingly having been forgotten. Marshall again stressed that the agreed policy had been to defeat Germany directly, not indirectly through the Mediterranean. King, on the other hand, was totally opposed to the major proportion of the US war effort being focussed on Europe and he wanted a re-adjustment of resources in favour of the war against Japan.

The British had to come up with an arrangement which the Americans could agree to, and, after another morning session on the 18th, where both sides were just as far apart as ever, Brooke and Washington-based Field Marshal Sir John Dill, the Senior British Representative on the Combined Chiefs of Staff, compiled a paper which was presented to the Americans and to Churchill that same afternoon. The main points of this were:

> We shall concentrate on the defeat of Germany first which will be followed by the defeat of Japan.
>
> Our efforts in defeating Germany will be concerned first with efforts to force them to withdraw ground and air forces from the Russian front. This will be accomplished by operations from North Africa by which Southern Europe, the Dodecanese Islands, Greece, Crete, Sardinia, and Sicily will all be threatened, thus forcing Germany to deploy her forces to meet each threat. The actual operation decided upon is the capture of Sicily.
>
> At the same time, we shall go on with preparing forces and assembling landing craft in England for a thrust across the Channel in the event that the German strength in France decreases, either through withdrawal of her troops or because of an internal collapse.

Much to Brooke's surprise, the entire paper, which included details concerning logistical help for China and Russia, and the continuing bombing campaign against the Third Reich, was accepted with few alterations. At last, a plan of operations for *Husky* could be drawn up, and the tone of Brooke's notes in his diary change. He described the Americans as 'charming people to work with' and 'as a team they are friendliness itself'.

The 19th was set aside for discussions on the U-boat war and the bomber offensive, leaving Friday 22 January free for *Husky*, and it was on that day the Channel Islands were mentioned for the first time at this conference. Even though *Husky* was to be a combined operation, the senior command positions were to be held by Eisenhower, General Alexander (Britain's Commander-in-Chief, Middle East), and Admiral Cunningham (Commander-in-Chief, Mediterranean). There was no place for Mountbatten other than in the preparation of landing craft and the training of crews and troops in their use.

Nevertheless, a diversionary action in northern Europe was agreed as being important. To this end, the following was stated: 'The US Chiefs of Staff considered it most desirable that any operation of the type mentioned in paragraph 2 (a) of the paper, e.g., against the Channel Islands, should be coordinated in time with *Husky*.' Paragraph 2 (a) read: 'Raids with the primary object of provoking a major air battle and causing the enemy loss.' To enable such an operation, it was 'most desirable for the Channel Assault Force to be kept in being for cross-channel operations this summer.'

On the 23rd, at a meeting with the Combined Chiefs and Roosevelt, the president asked about operations against the Brest Peninsula and the Cherbourg Peninsula, as well as the Channel Islands. Mountbatten informed him that the operation against the Channel Islands, as decided the previous day, would be timed to coincide with *Husky*.

There it was. Mountbatten had been given his chance to mount an operation against the Channel Islands – authorised at the highest level; and as soon as the conference at Casablanca was over the following day, the 24th, he set his staff to work.

As it happened, at the same time these discussions were in progress, another plan for an attack upon the Channel Islands was being considered in London. On 1 February 1943 a paper was presented to the Chief Planners outlining a scheme to kill or capture the entire German garrison of Sark using airborne forces and/or one Commando delivered by sea.[5] The operation, codenamed *Bunbury*, was to take place towards the end of March (later changed to April) and would be undertaken on one night during the hours of darkness. The objectives of the raid were spelt out as follows:

(a) To destroy the German garrison on Great and Little Sark.
(b) To implement the Prime Minister's decision that raids are to be carried out.
(c) To obtain information of the defences of the Channel Islands.
(d) To harass the German high command and pin down troops.
(e) To give battle experience to troops of the Airborne Division.
(f) To gain operational experience in the use of Landing Craft, Infantry.

The operational plan estimated the German garrison to number around 300, armed with nothing heavier than light machine guns and a few mobile 3.7 cm flak guns.

There were objections to the raid from both the Royal Navy and RAF. The Navy was concerned with the safety of their boats during the withdrawal as by then the German forces on the other islands and the mainland would have been alerted. The RAF explained that there was no really suitable dropping zone on Sark. The only 'reasonable' DZ was in the open fields to the east of the Seigneurie, which measured approximately 600 yards by 150 yards. Even so, that area included twenty-five fields, and the assembly of the force and the collection of armaments containers would not be a quick operation. Given that there was no ideal DZ and the small size of Great Sark (no paratroopers could be dropped on Little Sark) the RAF declared that it was confident all the troops could be landed on Sark but 'no particular part of the island could be specified'. Similar difficulties were envisaged if gliders were to be used, as there was no obvious place for flare path to be laid out.

Various attack plans were considered. One was a 'swamp' attack, in that the paratroopers would land all over the island in force and overwhelm the enemy with the weapons they carried as they landed. Another was a 'normal' attack in which the paras would form up before moving against the Germans. The third, and preferred, plan, was for 400 paratroopers and 500 commandos, who would be able to deliver both the swamp attack (paratroopers) and the normal attack (commandos).

However, objections were raised on the grounds that such a raid would only serve to raise the level of preparedness of the garrisons on the other islands and cause the Germans to improve their defences in the Cherbourg area, thus compromising *Hadrian* and its prequal, *Constellation*, both of which will be examined next. Mountbatten had greater schemes in mind than minor operations against tiny Sark.

Chapter 8

'The Best Air Raid Shelter'

It was back on 12 June 1940 that when the British War Cabinet met to discuss the pressing problem of what to do about the Channel Islands. Following the evacuation of the bulk of the British Expeditionary Force from Dunkirk less than two weeks earlier, and the impending collapse of resistance in France, the position of the Channel Islands had become perilous in the extreme. The Chiefs of Staff Committee had been asked to provide an assessment of the strategic importance of the Channel Islands as matters stood at the time, and it was this report that Winston Churchill and his five-man cabinet discussed that Wednesday morning.

Among the fifteen points noted by the Chiefs of Staff Committee, a few are of considerable significance. These read:

Strategic position of the Islands. There are three main islands located as follows:

1. Distance from the French coast, 10-30 miles
2. Distance from Portland, 60-90 miles
3. Distance from Dieppe, 130-160 miles

Should the Germans succeed in occupying the whole north coast of France, the Channel Islands could evidently not be held by us for long; but under these conditions they would no longer be of value to the enemy who would have many better mainland harbours and aerodromes available. On the other hand, it is inconceivable that the Germans would occupy the adjacent mainland and leave the Islands untouched.

There are aerodromes on both Jersey and Guernsey [there was also one on Alderney that opened in 1935] … In addition, there are many sheltered bays with sandy beaches suitable for the landing of troop-carrying planes. The harbours of the Islands will give complete shelter only to light craft.

Possession of the Islands would give Germany air, and possibly M.T.B. bases which might be used for the development of an attack on our lines of communication ... the Western Approaches and our southern coastline, or on Eire. The establishment of any such bases would, however, necessitate the provision of strong defences against attack by sea or air and to establish these a seaborne expedition would be required. Moreover, the enemy's line of communication would be extremely hazardous ...

If the enemy should decide on the occupation of the Islands, he could in existing circumstances, land an overwhelming force in troop-carrying aircraft, and there is little we could do to interfere with his initial action. He might also be able to transport troops into fast motorboats. Once in occupation, however, the difficulties of maintenance, though not insuperable, would make his position precarious. It is doubtful therefore if Germany would think it worthwhile to attempt the occupation of the Islands. Germany might well attempt a raid, however, with the objects of a) destroying the [telephone] cable to France; b) striking a blow at our prestige by the temporary occupation of British territory.

The COS then looked at the military forces existing on the islands. On the outbreak of war, the Militia were embodied both in Jersey and Guernsey (the smaller islands of Alderney, Sark and Herm are dependencies of Guernsey). The Guernsey Militia, however, was disbanded in January 1940. This left the following forces in the islands:

Guernsey and Alderney District
The 341st M.G. Training Centre (1,500 men) is located in Alderney This force, combined with the RAF personnel at the training school in Guernsey, is adequate for the protection of the [telephone] cable and the defence of the Islands against minor raids.

Jersey District
The only defence in this Island consist of some 150 men of the Jersey Militia, who have a proportion of Lewis guns and some

250 rifles. There is also a party of 50 naval ratings at the Fleet Air Arm aerodrome. These latter are only partially trained and may be removed. A local Defence Force against parachutists is being formed some 500 strong, but rifles will not be available locally for more than half this number. There are also small detachments of Royal Engineers in Guernsey and Jersey, and one Army Technical School, for boys in Jersey

There are no coast defences or AA guns in the Islands and no considered appreciation for defence is believed to exist.

Acts are about to be passed which will ender all male inhabitants liable for military service; those of suitable age and fit for service overseas, in the ranks of United Kingdom military forces, and older men and those unfit for service abroad in units for local defence.

The COS offered a number of alternative courses of action that the UK could undertake:

a) To provide the full scale of defence required to prevent the capture of the Islands. With the forces at present at our disposal this is clearly out of the question.
b) To provide forces from the United Kingdom to secure the Islands against minor raids; but in no circumstances to involve ourselves in a commitment to reinforce the garrison; we should, therefore, be prepared to evacuate them ultimately.
c) To limit the defence of the islands to local resources. Existing resources are not at present sufficient to defend the island against minor raids. This course would not ensure the safety of the cable and would not afford a reasonable measure of protection to the local inhabitants.
d) To demilitarize the Islands. This might have unfortunate repercussions on the French. We might be accused of exposing the French Northern flank to a further scale of attack from bases in these Islands. This would no longer apply if the German advance reached a position on the mainland adjacent to the Islands.

In addition, the evacuation of the civil population of approximately 100,000 must be considered.

If civilians were to be evacuated, it would have to be done quickly, before the Germans were fully established on the French coast, as the evacuation of large numbers of people under heavy air attack could not be contemplated.[1]

The conclusions drawn were that the 'Channel Islands are not of any major strategic importance to either ourselves or to the enemy'. Equally, on strategic grounds, attempting to hold the Channel Islands against a determined effort by the Germans would 'not be justified at the expense of our commitments elsewhere'.

In addition, the following factors weighed heavily against any attempt to hold the islands:

1. The difficulties of maintaining supply lines from England, which would be subject to disruption by German sea and air attacks.
2. The likelihood that British garrisons would ultimately have to surrender the islands due to lack of supplies and the propaganda this would provide Germany.
3. Maintaining garrisons on the islands would tie up manpower needed for the war effort, manpower which could be better employed defending England.
4. The likelihood that actively defending the islands would result in German military attacks, causing significant loss of civilian life.[2]

However, as the UK was obligated to provide for the reasonable security of the islands, the Chiefs of Staff felt that, despite the enormous drain it would have on shipping, it was the UK's duty to provide for the voluntary evacuation of at least some of the population. This last point was clarified by stating that free and voluntary evacuation should be made available to all women and children. This was later extended to include men of military age and then opened to all who wished to leave.

Though initially it was proposed that, as 'a certain measure of defence should be provided for the two main islands,' one battalion of infantry should be sent to both Jersey and Guernsey, the situation in France was deteriorating by the hour. The very same day as the COS meeting, news reached London of the fate of the 51st (Highland) Division, which had withdrawn from defending the Maginot Line to the Channel coast. The 51st had been unable to march north to Dunkirk and had instead reached

Saint-Valery-en-Caux, where it had become trapped with its back to the sea and been obliged to surrender. The decision to send two battalions to the Channel Islands made at the meeting in the morning of the 12th had, by early evening, become highly questionable. Though the proposal was adopted by the War Cabinet, on the 13th the idea was dropped and, as the islands could not be defended by the limited forces at hand, there was little point in maintaining any military presence. The COS recommended, therefore, that the islands be demilitarised and preparations put in hand for the destruction of facilities which might be of value to the enemy.

The list of recommendations included:

i) That all regular troops should be withdrawn from the Islands.
ii) That the local forces which remain should be given the role of internal security (including anti-sabotage) only.
iii) That preparation for destruction of the facilities which might be of value to the enemy, and which he could not equally well obtain on the mainland, (e.g., oil stocks) should be made to be carried out in case of invasion.
(iv) That as the Islands will have been demilitarized it will be unnecessary and undesirable to evacuate women and children, and that the Minister of Home Security should be so informed.
(v) That orders should be issued to the Lieutenant-Governors not to defend the Islands in the event of enemy invasion by sea or air ... We consider that effect should be given to these recommendations immediately the aerodromes are no longer required.

The demilitarising of the Channel Islands was discussed at a War Cabinet meeting on 19 June. Churchill was not in favour, arguing that 'it ought to be possible, by the use of our sea power, to prevent the invasion of the Islands by the enemy and that, if there was a chance of offering a successful resistance, we ought not to avoid giving him battle there'. The Vice-Chief of Naval Staff pointed out, however, that the material necessary for the defence of the islands was not available. All the anti-aircraft guns and fighter aircraft available were needed for the defence of the UK. Furthermore, he added: 'The Islands were too far away from our shores and too near enemy-occupied bases at Brest and Cherbourg for an effective use of naval forces to prevent invasion by sea.' There was really no practicable way Britain could defend the islands.

The decision to demilitarise was announced to the Channel Islanders on the 19th, with the people of Jersey reading in the *Evening Post* that day: 'The island is not to be defended; it is to be completely demilitarised and declared an undefended zone.' The *Evening Press* in Guernsey, likewise, informed the islanders of the demilitarisation and instructed all people to hand in their firearms.

A 'military expert' wrote in *The Star*:

'The Government's decision to demilitarize the islands need surprise nobody familiar with the map. The German occupation of Northern France has deprived the islands of any strategic value they might ever have had. In peacetime the garrison of the whole group consisted of no more than a single regiment. Since the islands are of no strategic use to Great Britain – or for that matter to Germany – there was no further need for their continued fortification which might only have exposed the inhabitants to unnecessary danger from German bombardment.

The *Star*'s correspondent continued: 'The demilitarisation, it was pointed out in London last night is, somewhat analogous to declaring Paris an open city.

'There need be no fear, military experts declared, of the Germans taking advantage from the British decision to quit. The Nazis could no more hold positions on the islands than we could defend them.' How wrong those military experts would prove to be!

The Channel Islanders received official notification of the demilitarisation from King George VI on 24 June. His 'letter of assurance' was published in the Royal Square in Jersey and was posted in the parish church notices:

For strategic reasons it has been found necessary to withdraw the Armed Forces from the Channel Islands.

I deeply regret this necessity and I wish to assure My people in the Islands that, in taking this decision, My Government has not been unmindful of their position. It is in their interests that this step should be taken in present circumstances …

How true this was became all too apparent on 28 June. At around 18.45 hours that evening, German bombers appeared over both St Helier and St Peter Port. Targeting the two harbours with bombs and machine-guns, the Germans struck dock facilities as well as nearby buildings. The heaviest attack was delivered against St Peter Port. In what has been called 'The blackest day Guernsey had ever seen', thirty-four people were killed and a further thirty-three injured. The destruction was considerable, as resident Bill Green observed: 'Forty-nine vehicles were burnt out or seriously damaged. Bomb craters were everywhere … The whole of the front … suffered considerable damage, there was hardly an unbroken window to be seen.'[3] The town itself was targeted, and railway sheds, hotels and other areas of the island were hit by stray bombs.

'Bombs were dropped at La Rocque … the planes sweeping over roads with machine-guns blazing,' recalled Jersey's *Evening Post* reporter Leslie P. Sinel. 'Houses were wrecked at South Hill, stores were set on fire in Commercial Buildings and hundreds of panes of glass were shattered in the Weighbridge vicinity, stained-glass windows in the Town Church being damaged.'[4] Doctor Averell Darling was the Resident Medical Officer on duty in Jersey General Hospital: 'As I got there the first victim arrived. He had a great hole blown in the side of his chest and he died within a matter of moments. Fifty per cent of those who were admitted to the hospital and who died were killed by bombs. The other half died from machine gun bullets.'[5]

Altogether, the casualty count across the two islands totalled more than 145 people. It appears that of the nine Heinkel He 111 bombers of 1/Gruppe Kampfgeschwader 55, only six attacked the islands, with the other three remaining in reserve.[6] The maximum bomb load of the He 111 was 2,000 kg. The most that could have been dropped on either island was, therefore, 6,000 kg, or approximately 6 tons. These numbers are to be borne in mind when reading the following chapters of this book.

Two days later, on 30 June, German aircraft, having encountered no resistance to their flights over the islands, landed at Guernsey airport and formally accepted the surrender of the island. Jersey followed suit on 2 July, marking the start of almost five years of occupation.

To ensure the safety of the Channel Islanders, as soon as it was known in London that the Germans had landed in Guernsey, the British Foreign Office asked the American Ambassador in London, Joseph P. Kennedy, to pass the following official message via the United States Embassy in Berlin to the German Government that evening: 'The evacuation of all military personnel and equipment from the Channel Islands was completed some days ago. The Islands are therefore demilitarised and cannot be considered in any way as a legitimate target for bombardment. A public announcement to this effect was made on the evening of June 28th.'

This was an important message as the initial plan the Germans had drawn up for the capture of the Channel Islands – Operation Green Arrow (*Grüne Pfeil*) – called for the German Air Force to deliver a preliminary aerial bombardment, and for Stuka dive-bombers to support the assault landings which would be undertaken by six infantry battalions and a detachment of German marines. Fortunately, the Islanders were saved this punishment. The demilitarisation of the Channel Islands, though bitterly resented by some, meant the islands and the islanders would never know the full horrors of war.

The islanders and the Germans learned to live with each other. In what was described as 'a model occupation', the existing local governments of the bailiwicks of Jersey and Guernsey were allowed to continue to function, though under strict rules imposed by the Germans. There was both collaboration with the occupiers, in that more than half of the population worked for the Germans, and some minor acts of resistance. In reality, it was hard to find work not related to the occupation and difficult to conduct any clandestine operations in small islands with large German garrisons.

Hitler was delighted to have seized British territory, and was determined to hold onto the Channel Islands, whatever the cost. Throughout the rest of 1940 and early 1941, as the UK fought for its survival during the Battle of Britain and the Blitz, there was no possibility of British forces being in a position to contemplate re-taking the Channel Islands. But in the summer of 1941, with the RAF having moved onto the offensive and with the majority of German troops and aircraft being transferred to the Eastern Front in preparation for the invasion of the Soviet Union, Hitler was concerned with the security of the Channel Islands.

The more Hitler thought about them, the greater became his fears that Britain would try to reclaim the islands while most of his forces were in Russia. After studying the state of the islands' fortifications and the strength of the garrisons in early June 1941, he issued instructions to improve every element of the islands' defences. Then, on 19 July, in 'Directive No. 33', he ordered that: 'In the west and north all three elements of the Wehrmacht [the army, the navy and the air force] must be prepared to withstand possible English attacks throughout the Channel Islands.' It marked the start of a huge building and armaments programme.

Prior to this, work had already begun on strengthening the islands' defences, this being undertaken by German Army and Navy construction units. These were mainly units of company strength taken from Construction Battalions, Bridge Construction Battalions, Fortress Construction Battalions, and Railway Construction Battalions These units arrived in March 1941 and stayed for 3-6 months, after which elements of the Organisation Todt (OT), a civil and military engineering organisation, began to arrive. From that point onwards it was OT which took control of the building programme. Dr Fritz Todt visited all three main islands and concluded that the work would be divided into six parts:[7]

1) 319 *Infanteriedivision* whose role would be that of tactical reconnaissance.
2) Individual troopers would be responsible for the construction of normal field works, i.e. trenches and weapon pits, etc.
3) The Division's engineers were to handle the laying of land mines and distribution of flame-throwers.
4) The Construction Battalion would build those works which were more elaborate than the field type but which were not intended to withstand a prolonged bombardment. The wall of such buildings would have a maximum thickness of one metre.
5) The Organization Todt would provide the labour for all building in the heavy construction program covering buildings with walls above metre thick, quarrying, tunnelling, the construction of roads and railways, organizing transport, unloading ships and the supervision of civilian construction firms.

 To the OT, Jersey was named JAKOB (with GUSTAV and ADOLF for Guernsey and Alderney).
6) The job of the Fortress Engineer Headquarters Construction Battalion was to oversee the heavy construction program, carry out the mounting of heavy guns, some tunnelling, and to supervise the OT.

Among the first and easiest actions to be taken was the immediate reinforcement of the garrisons, with an additional infantry regiment to be sent to both Jersey and Guernsey. More, and heavier, artillery pieces were to be shipped to the islands, some forty-two in total, and greater protection for the defending troops, in the form of bunkers and casemates, were to be built. In addition, there were casemated coastal guns, personnel shelters, searchlight bunkers and anti-tank guns enfilading the beaches, plus 'resistance nests' at key points across the islands. Hitler ordered that obstacles should be set up on all open spaces where parachutists or gliders might land and that at least 200 strongpoints should be formed in both Jersey and Guernsey.

The existing fortifications of the islands were incorporated into the German defensive systems. This was particularly the case with Alderney where, because of its position close to Britain's traditional enemy, France, a harbour had been created during the mid-1800s for the Royal Navy. To defend the harbour a series of thirteen forts had been built and it was these, in differing states of repair, which were first used by the German garrison and improved by OT. Alderney would become the most heavily fortified, for its size, of all three main islands with, in addition to these thirteen strong points, twelve resistance nests, five coastal batteries, twenty-two anti-aircraft batteries and three defence lines. The larger Guernsey was almost equally as well fortified, with fourteen coastal batteries and thirty-three anti-aircraft gun sites.

By early November 1941 considerable amounts of stores and personnel had begun to arrive on the islands, and the fortification programme was soon to be underway. The Germans transported more than 16,000 slave workers, mostly Ukrainians, to the Channel Islands to build the fortifications, as well as paid foreign labour recruited from occupied parts of Europe, including French, Belgian, and Dutch workers. In 1941 hundreds of unemployed French Algerians and Moroccans were handed to the Germans by the Vichy government and sent to Jersey. Around 2,000 Spaniards who had taken refuge in France after the Spanish Civil War and who had since been interned, were also handed over for forced labour, as were 1,000 French Jews.[8]

On 15 December 1941 Hitler issued the order for the construction of the Atlantic Wall, of which the Channel Islands were an important part, and on 20 October 1942 he gave instructions for the fortification of the islands:

1. Operations on a larger scale against the territories we occupy in the West are, as before, unlikely. Under pressure of the situation in the East, however, or for reason of politics or propaganda, small-scale operations at the moment may be anticipated, particularly an attempt to regain possession of the Channel Islands, which are important to us for the protection of sea communications.
2. Counter-measures in the islands must ensure that any English attack fails before a landing is achieved, whether it is attempted by sea, by air or both together. The possibility of advantage being taken of bad visibility to effect a surprise landing must be borne in mind. Emergency measures for strengthening the defence have already been ordered, and all branches of the forces stationed in the islands, except the Air Force, are placed under the orders of the commandant of the islands.
3. With regard to the permanent fortification of the islands, to convert them into an impregnable fortress (which must be pressed forward with the utmost speed) I give the following orders:
    (a) The High Command of the Army is responsible for the fortifications as a whole and will, in the overall programme, incorporate construction for the Air Force and the Navy. The strength of the fortifications and the order in which they are erected will be based on the principles and practical knowledge gained from building the Western wall.
    (b) For the Army: it is important to provide a close network of emplacements, well concealed, and giving flanking fields of fire. The emplacements must be sufficient for guns of a size capable of piercing armour plate 100 mm thick, to defend against tanks which may attempt to land. There must be ample accommodation for stores and ammunition, for mobile diversion parties and for armoured cars.
    (c) For the Navy: one heavy battery on the islands and two on the French coast to safeguard the sea approaches
    (d) For the Air Force: strong points must be created with searchlights and sufficient space to accommodate such AA units as are needed to protect all important constructions.
    (e) Foreign labour, especially Russians and Spaniards but also Frenchmen, may be used for the building work.

4. Another order will follow for the deportation to the continent of all Englishmen who are not natives of the islands, i.e. not born there.
5. Progress reports to be sent to me on the first day of each month, to the C-in-C of the Army and directed to the Supreme Command of the Armed Forces (OKW) – Staff of the Führer, Division L.

Construction work in the Channel Islands peaked in April 1943. Coastlines were ringed with resistance nests and strong points, all of which were protected by minefields, as were potential landing beaches. Eventually, a staggering 67,000 mines were laid on Jersey, 54,000 on Guernsey, 37,000 on Alderney and 4,500 on Sark.[9] Quite justifiably, each of the three main islands were given the description *Festung* – fortress. One-twelfth of all the concrete and steel used in the construction, such as it was, of Hitler's proposed Atlantic Wall[10] which stretched 2,687km from northern Norway to the Franco-Spanish border was used in the building of the fortifications of Guernsey, Jersey and Alderney, which together have a coastline of only around 150km.

Just as Hitler had ordered, those British people not born on the islands were deported to the mainland and were interred in prisoner of war camps in Germany. This totalled some 2,300 men, women, and children.

All this was meant to deter the Allies from any attempt at retaking the Channel Islands, as Hitler himself was recorded as saying in July 1942: 'If the British had continued to hold these islands, fortifying them and constructing aerodromes on them, they could have been a veritable thorn in our flesh. As it is, we now have firmly established ourselves there, and with the fortifications we have constructed, and the permanent garrison of a whole division, we have ensured against the possibility of the islands ever falling again into the hands of the British.'[11]

Britain had chosen to demilitarise the islands to save them from destruction, and the vast defences sent out a clear signal – if the UK was ever to attempt to recapture them the consequences for the islanders would be immeasurable, as had been witnessed during the bombing attack of 28 June 1940.

But, apart from the few Commando raids and a number of small sorties by the RAF, the islands were never subjected to a major assault by the British or Allied forces, prompting one German solder, Kurt

Spangenburg, a non-commissioned officer in a machine-gun battalion posted to Guernsey in 1940, to remark: 'because the civilian population lived here the British never made a bombing attack. I always said the Channel Islands were the best air raid shelter in Europe.'[12]

Chapter 9

Operation Constellation: The Retaking of the Channel Islands

The Allies' major effort in the West in 1943 was to be Operation *Husky*, giving it priority of men, equipment, and shipping, over all other schemes in the Western theatre. It was within that setting that Mountbatten had to garner the resources to continue his cross-Channel raids and, as the scale of operations had generally increased enormously since the Americans had joined the war, his pin-pick raids were of decreasing importance. He needed Combined Ops to be having a greater impact if he was to continue to be invited to sit at the high table. He was also keen to undertake some spectacular operation to keep his mentor, Churchill, happy and possibly to redeem some of his prestige after the Dieppe debacle.

A further inducement was the decision to appoint a 'Supreme' Commander who would be responsible 'for all United Nations for the invasion of the Continent from the United Kingdom'. It was also made clear that the appointee would be an American. Evidently, such a person would be stepping on Mountbatten's toes, and so the relationship between the two had to be spelt out: 'Should small-scale operations, such as the Channel Islands, be considered desirable by the British Chiefs of Staff separately from a larger Channel operation, they will be dealt with by the Chief of Combined Operations, United Kingdom. If such an operation is connected with a larger Channel operation he will work under the Supreme Commander's direction.'[1]

If Mountbatten was to continue to be involved at the highest levels, he needed Combined Ops to be undertaking high profile operations, not raids against the Channel Islands if such a move was now considered 'small scale'. So, on 9 October 1942, Mountbatten's team came up with a plan to rival *Roundup*, and was in fact promoted as an alternative; Operation *Arabian*, a plan to capture and hold the Brittany Peninsula.

Operation Constellation: The Retaking of the Channel Islands 119

Mountbatten offered two possible courses of action. The first was a limited operation with two objectives:

Objective A. To eliminate the German U-boat bases within the Brittany Peninsula, so improving the conditions under which we are waging the Battle of the Atlantic.
Objective B. To secure a foothold on the Continent which can be held until the time is ripe for larger operations, thus securing the use of the major ports in Brittany through which US forces could pass direct.

The second, as an alternative to *Roundup*, had just one objective:

Objective C. To secure Brittany as the bridgehead of a continuous operation to clear the enemy from France and the Low Countries.

Mountbatten pointed out that even if Brest, Lorient, St Nazaire and Nantes were eliminated as U-boat bases, the Germans would still be able to berth all their U-boats in the Biscay ports. But, if Allied forces were established in Brittany, they would be able to attack the German submarines in their passage to and from their Biscayan bases.

As regards Objective B, Mountbatten wrote: 'There is a great advantage in securing a bridgehead through which US forces could pass direct onto the Continent without passing through Great Britain.'

Mountbatten saw Objective C in two stages. The first was in securing bridgeheads around ports and airfields behind which the invasion force could be built up. The second was after the Allies had been firmly established on the mainland, the operations to liberate the occupied territories in the West could begin.

Mountbatten then produced a 'for and against' list comparing the advantages of *Arabian* verses *Roundup*:

Phase I

Roundup
The three assault areas are widely separated, in order to bring on air battles in the Pas-de-Calais area where conditions are most favourable to us, and at the same time secure major ports in the Havre-Cherbourg area. The bridgehead will therefore be long and vulnerable.

Arabian
Brittany offers major ports within a much shorter bridgehead but the capacity of the ports requires examination.

Phase II

The centre of the bridgehead in Rouen, which is more or less centrally placed in relation to the three possible objectives of of this phase, which are:
Paris 64 miles, Antwerp 200 miles, Atlantic ports 2-300 miles. Further, the capture of Paris offers a great deal of control over the rest of France and largely cuts off the Atlantic ports from Germany.

The centre of the bridge-head would be Rennes, which is further from these objectives, e.g., Paris 200 miles, Antwerp 400 miles, although some of the Atlantic ports are included within the bridgehead, i.e., Bordeaux.

Mountbatten concluded that: 'In general, the naval effort involved in an expedition to Brittany would be greater but not much greater than for an expedition further east (i.e., Boulogne or Le Havre) and should be within our resources. The difficulty of the approach to the beaches during the assault phase is largely, perhaps completely, off-set by the probability that beaches sheltered from the weather can be used during the build-up.'

He also added that the port defences in both areas were known to be strong, as were beach defences from the Cotentin Peninsula eastwards, whereas they were comparatively light on the Brittany coast. In addition, Mountbatten gauged the speed and capacity of the likely enemy response to the invasion. Again, he saw an advantage in landing in Brittany, claiming that the Germans would not be able to concentrate their forces

Operation Constellation: The Retaking of the Channel Islands 121

to counter the Allied assault as quickly in Brittany as they would in the Cherbourg-Boulogne area.

He did accept that the greater distances involved would mean the RAF would be unable to provide as much protection – only a quarter – in the *Arabia* area compared with *Roundup*. Against this, he estimated that the Luftwaffe would take one day longer to arrive at the Brittany airfields.

In a 'Summary of Conclusions' drawn up by the Planning Staff, it was stated that an operation against Brittany had the advantage of meeting weaker beach defences and that the rate of arrival of enemy reinforcements would be slightly slower and could be interrupted more easily. On the other hand, the fighter cover for the assaulting forces would be far weaker; the maximum force which could be maintained through the Brittany ports after three months of operations was unlikely to exceed twenty-five divisions, unlike the thirty or more through the Dieppe/Cherbourg area. Finally, a landing in the Brittany area would place the Allied troops further from Paris. The decision arrived at by the Joint Planning Staff of the Chiefs of Staff was, consequently, that a direct assault on the Brittany Peninsula unaccompanied by major assaults elsewhere should not receive any further consideration.

It was back to the drawing board for Mountbatten and his team, who, never short of ideas, came up with another raid which might have been seen as quite a triumph. This was Operation *Witticism* (originally named *Petrify*), involving the audacious idea of sailing into Guernsey's St Peter Port harbour with the aim of capturing a German E-Boat. This was later changed to attacking and sinking German shipping in the harbour with limpet mines. The force, in two MTBs, would sail from Portland at dusk, and when off St Peter Port the men of the Small Scale Raiding Force would take to canoes to paddle into the harbour and place the mines on as many ships as they could. *Witticism* was first discussed on 4 December 1942, with the date for the mission being the most suitable between the nights of 7/8 December to 13/14 inclusive.

As was the case with all the raids, a great deal of planning took place. The nature of the port's defences, the berthing arrangements of the vessels in the harbour, the number and type of enemy troops in the area, the nature of the seabed, and the rate and direction of the tides were all taken into consideration.

Bad weather prevented the operation going ahead during the above period, but Mountbatten was 'anxious' to see *Witticism* go ahead, arguing that: 'apart from the actual damage done to enemy shipping at St Peter Port on this operation, we should learn some useful lessons which may open up possibilities of similar raids on other targets on the French, Belgian and Dutch coasts.' He suggested, therefore, that *Witticism* should be remounted as soon as possible.[2]

The dates of 2/3 January to 13/14 January were selected. The attack would be made in two canoes, launched from between a quarter and half a mile from the harbour from MTB 112. On the night of 8 January, the MTB set off from Portland, but the wind steadily increased and the crew were forced to turn back. Though Lieutenant 'Bunny' Warren and his men waited for the weather to improve, they waited in vain and on 14 January, *Witticism* was officially cancelled.

Strangely, the idea of an attack in the Brittany area was reconsidered in November 1942, with Mountbatten being 'very reluctant' to give up the idea. This time under the codename *Lethal*, the same arguments were presented by the Combined Ops planners. Again, comparisons were drawn between an attack on the Brittany/Brest Peninsula and the Cherbourg/Dieppe region. This perhaps demonstrates how desperate Mountbatten was to undertake a major operation.

One of the advantages of a landing in Brittany was the slower reinforcement of that area by the enemy. This was therefore highlighted by Mountbatten. On D-Day, it was estimated that the Germans could transfer just elements of two armoured divisions and one flak brigade to Rennes (at the base of the Brittany Peninsula), compared with elements of two armoured divisions, three motorised divisions, and a complete airborne division which could be amassed at Rouen (centrally placed to the south-east of Le Havre). On D+1 these forces would concentrate in their respective areas with, in both cases, elements of one infantry division engaging the Allies. On D+2, further enemy divisions would arrive at the rate of 1.3 or 1.5 per day at Rennes against at least two per day at Rouen. By D+4 all available reinforcements would have reached Rouen while they would not reach Rennes until D+6.

Mountbatten added to this by declaring that these reinforcements could be delayed in reaching Rennes by bombing a limited number of roads. A considerably greater effort would be required to try to slow the

American and British Chiefs of Staff in discussion at the Anfa Hotel during the Casablanca Conference, 14–24 January 1943. The man with the dark spectacles is Alan Brooke. (*Historic Military Press*)

President Roosevelt, Prime Minister Churchill, and their Combined Chiefs of Staff at the Casablanca Conference in January 1943. Standing (left to right) are: General Brehon B. Somervell; General Henry H. Arnold; Admiral Ernest J. King; unidentified; General George C. Marshall; Admiral Sir Dudley Pound; General Sir Alan Brooke; Sir Gerald Portal; and Vice Admiral Lord Louis Mountbatten. (*Historic Military Press*)

A German bunker and other structures that can be seen to the south of La Corvée, near Cachalière Pier, Alderney. (*Historic Military Press*)

A camouflaged bunker that formed part of *Stützpunkt* (Strongpoint) Biberkopf, which was located at Bibette Head, overlooking the eastern side of Saye Beach on Alderney's north coast. (*Historic Military Press*)

A Tobruk, or Ringstand, bunker, with a concrete-lined entrance trench on Bibette Head, to the east of Saye Beach. These small, circular, reinforced concrete bunkers were designed to shelter a single soldier, usually armed with a machine-gun. This example was part of *Stützpunkt* Biberkopf. (*Historic Military Press*)

A 20P7 *Sechsschartenturm* which, forming part of *Stützpunkt* Biberkopf, can be seen on the very tip of Bibette Head. (*Historic Military Press*)

The Jäger Stand bunker of *Stützpunkt* Biberkopf seen on Bibette Head. (*Historic Military Press*)

Some of the German bunkers and defences on the headland by Fort Albert, overlooking the harbour at Braye, Alderney. (*Historic Military Press*)

German officers inspecting the harbour at Braye, from Fort Albert, in 1942. The heaviest of the three Kriegsmarine batteries on Alderney was Batterie Elsas, which was headquartered in, and centred on, Fort Albert. The three 17 cm SKL/40 guns that comprised the battery were mounted on Fort Albert's ramparts. (*Bundesarchiv, Bild 101II-MW-5152-14A/Järisch/CC-BY-SA 3.0*)

The Luftwaffe command bunker and tower at Les Mouriaux, at St. Anne, Alderney. Of a unique design, the Alderney government notes that this structure 'contained the Luftwaffe HQ and listening post. It was the only significant bunker in the town area apart from personnel shelters and some MG positions.' (*Historic Military Press*)

A machine-gun post is visible in this stretch of the formidable *Panzermauer* 1 anti-tank wall that was built around the sweeping sandy beach at Longis Bay. *Panzermauer* 1 was the largest of the anti-tank walls built on Alderney. (*Historic Military Press*)

This bunker can be seen at the western end of the beach at Longis Bay, providing cover to *Panzermauer* 1. (*Historic Military Press*)

The scale of the *Panzermauer* 1 anti-tank wall can be gauged from this view, taken looking west from roughly its half-way point along Longis Bay. A casemate for a 4.7 cm Festung Pak gun can be seen at the end of the wall. Dates left on the structure by its builders suggest that it was built around June 1943. (*Historic Military Press*)

An emplacement for a 4.7 cm Festung Pak gun that can be seen at the western end of *Panzermauer* 1. (*Historic Military Press*)

The casemate for the 4.7 cm Festung Pak gun at the western end of *Panzermauer* 1, part of which can be seen to the right of the bunker. The steps on the left lead up to a Tobruk position that also covers Longis Beach. (*Historic Military Press*)

A section of *Panzermauer* 12 that was constructed to defend the crescent-shaped, shingle beach at Platte Saline on Alderney's north-west coast. The wall continues behind the photographer. (*Historic Military Press*)

The defences of St Peter Port, Guernsey, in 1945. (*Major Rice*)

German 88 mm flak guns, Guernsey, 1945. (*Major Rice*)

French tanks which constituted the German Armoured Reserve on Guernsey, 1945. (*Major Rice*)

The enormous emplacement of one of the 30.5 cm guns at Batterie Mirus, Guernsey.

View from a command bunker on the high ground overlooking Vazon Bay.

The still impressive Fort Hommet, which flanks Vazon Bay, formed part of Stützpunkt Rotenstein that embraced the whole of the headland. The fort held a 60 cm searchlight.

The entrance to one of the 10.5 cm casemates of *Stützpunkt* Rotenstein showing just how strong such fortifications were. This is open to the public.

A 10.5 cm gun overlooking Vazon Bay.

One of the restored 22 cm guns of Batterie Dolmann.

Looking out from a heavy machine-gun position which covered part of L'Ancresse Common.

A view of L'Ancresse Common with the bay just visible in the distance, showing how relatively flat and open it was and indicating why it had been selected as a parachute drop zone.

Even radar emplacements such as this one on L'Ancreese Common (Marine *Stützpunkt* Großhügel) were built to withstand the heaviest punishment.

A casemate for a 4.7 cm Festung Pak 36 (t) in Vazon Bay. Note the loopholed tower in the distance. This is one of fifteen such towers that were erroneously called Martello Towers by the British planners. They were actually built between 1778 and 1779 during the American War of Independence. One third of these towers were built around L'Ancresse Bay.

The defences of L'Ancresse Bay show how difficult it would have been for the British troops to exit the beach if defended by the Germans.

St Sampson harbour entrance, with Vale Castle in the background. The castle formed part of *Stützpunktgruppe* Talfeste, the defences of which included 5 cm mortars and 10.5 cm field guns, which could have brought heavy fire down on the harbour. The early capture of St Sampson to bring in supplies was a crucial part of the Allied plan. However, the Germans had laid a demolition mine which would have brought down the harbour walls and blocked the entrance.

A fine example of a tank turret (from a FT-17 French Light Tank) used in static defence, this one being at Batterie Dolmann.

One of the two 105mm coastal artillery casemates constructed overlooking the Royal Bay of Grouville on Jersey's east coast. With walls over six feet thick, this casemate covers the northern sections of what the Operation *Condor* planners designated as Landing Area A1. (*Historic Military Press*)

Located behind the beach at Grouville, and today within the grounds of the Royal Jersey Golf Club, is Fort Henry. Built in 1758, this fort, consisting of a square tower and rectangular surrounding defences, was adapted by the Germans to serve as a searchlight and personnel/ammunition shelter. Along with the nearby wartime bunkers, the fort would also have stood in the way of Allied troops landing on D-Day if *Condor* had gone ahead. (*Historic Military Press*)

A view of one of the more isolated *Condor* landing beaches – L7 – which is located at the top of Fliquet Bay on the north-east corner of Jersey. The breakwater that projects out to sea from Verclut Point can be seen in the background. Only a visit to this location can provide a clear illustration of just how big a task the troops landing here would have experienced in attempting to link up with the remainder of the invasion force. (*Historic Military Press*)

Located on the shoreline in the very centre of Fliquet Bay, just to the south of landing beach L7, is Fliquet Tower (also known as Telegraph Tower). Dating back to the 1780s, the tower was one of three built to defend the island's east coast from French forces. It was also put to use by the Germans to defend against a British attack, as part of which the roof and castellations were reinforced with concrete. (*Historic Military Press*)

A 4.7 cm Pak K36 (t) anti-tank gun built into a rocky headland at La Carrière overlooking the wide, open sandy beaches of St Ouen's Bay on the west coast of Jersey. Another of the German coastal fortifications on the bay, the southern sections of which were allocated as Landing Area A2, is home to the Channel Islands Military Museum. (*Historic Military Press*)

Part the anti-tank wall at St Ouen's Bay with a coastal defence gun position incorporated into it. A total of nine such walls, massive structures consuming vast quantities of concrete, were planned for the island. Seven were completed, one almost completed and the last abandoned at an early stage. (*Historic Military Press*)

Much altered by quarrying, this is how the beach at La Houle – landing beach L6 for *Constellation* – appears today. The photograph was taken from Sorel Point. (*Historic Military Press*)

A bunker on Sorel Point which overlooks the small landing beach below, this being designated L6 for *Constellation*. (Historic Military Press)

An open emplacement at Batterie Moltke, Les Landes, on the north-west corner of Jersey. This complex housed four main guns, two heavy machine guns, fourteen defensive flame-throwers, three Renault tank turrets with machine-guns, and a searchlight. This is actually a re-constituted 155mm gun, comprising a carriage retrieved by the Royal Navy from the base of nearby cliffs, a barrel recovered from the same location by a local resident, and replacement trail legs. (*Historic Military Press*)

Of all the German fortifications in Jersey, the most prominent and impressive are the three large naval artillery direction and range-finding towers. Nine were planned, but only the examples at Noirmont Point, La Corbière and Les Landes (pictured here) were built. Of a design that is unique to the Channel Islands, all survive today. The MP3 tower at Les Landes covered the sea passage between Jersey and Guernsey. (*Dronegraphica/Shutterstock*)

A view of Portelet Bay, or L1 as it was known, taken from Noirmont Point, the most southerly headland on Jersey. Not only is the island in the middle of the bay defended, but Noirmont Point was also the site of the Batterie Lothringen. In time, a total of four 15 cm naval guns were emplaced there, along with associated personnel, ammunition and command structures. With a field of fire of nearly 360°, the guns here could have been brought into action against L1. (*Historic Military Press*)

The author looks down on landing beach L4 from the precipitous western heights of Plemont Point on the north-east corner of Jersey. (*Historic Military Press*)

On the opposite side of Plemont Point from L4 was another proposed Landing Beach: L5. The rocky and inhospitable nature of this stretch of coast is evident in this picture. The camouflaged German reinforced field position in the foreground was built on top of an existing 19th-century guardhouse. A variety of machine-gun and mortar emplacements also existed in the area. (*Historic Military Press*)

The house nearest the camera in this picture taken on the harbour front at Gorey was converted into a reinforced concrete gun emplacement; the embrasure can still be seen. The gun emplaced in this position faced south towards the landing area in the Royal Bay of Grouville. (*Historic Military Press*)

One of the buildings from which the German defence of Jersey might have been directed should the order for Operation *Condor* to proceed have been issued. This is the Type 609 command post built at Le Coin Varin and is one of only three such structures built on Jersey during the occupation. Note the fake wooden shutters on what appears to be a blocked-up window. In certain light conditions it is still possible to see the outline of the 'window' that was painted on to help camouflage the structure. (*Historic Military Press*)

A German bunker at *Stützpunkt* Corbière, on the extreme south-western point of Jersey, looks out over the surrounding beaches and coastline. La Corbière lighthouse can be seen in the distance. The formidable array of defences built at this location, all of which are watched over by the MP-2 naval direction and range-finding tower, are a pair of bunkers for a 10.5 cm K331 (f) coastal defence gun, an M-19 automatic fortress mortar bunker, a Type 634 *Sechsschartentürm* (a steel machine-gun turret), and a Type 606 searchlight bunker. (*Shutterstock*)

Operation Constellation: The Retaking of the Channel Islands 123

enemy troops reaching Rouen owing to the larger number of practicable routes available to the Germans.

The same factor which had led to the abandonment of *Arabian* still applied to *Lethal* – the distance from the UK was too great for the RAF to be able to provide adequate fighter cover, and the Chiefs of Staff saw no reason to change their view. So, Mountbatten tried another tack, telling them that: 'especially in view of the new commitment in North Africa [*Torch*] circumstances might arise in which it might become a necessity to secure a base on the Brittany coast from which to operate anti-submarine craft.'[3] This was dismissed by the General Headquarters of the Home Forces, who believed that 'no defensive position in Brittany, even if you are trying to hold only one port, can be held against prepared attacks.' It was quite a preposterous suggestion, but in deference to Mountbatten, they placed his comments 'on record'. *Lethal* was quietly dropped, though not officially cancelled until 9 March 1943.

Mountbatten, therefore, with little alternatives available, focussed his attention on the Channel Islands, but not as a mere raid. He wanted to recapture them. The re-occupation of the Channel Islands, either as a stand-alone endeavour or as part of an attack upon the French coast, would have enormous propaganda value. All he needed to do was convince Brooke and the Chiefs of Staff to back his plans.

One justification for his scheme to invade the Channel Islands was as part of the deception policy for *Husky* adopted at the Casablanca Conference. One of the two main elements of this policy was 'To contain enemy forces in Western Europe'. This would be done by:

i) Exaggerating Allied strength in the UK
ii) Carrying out suitable dispositions of our forces to simulate invasion preparations
iii) Initiating intensive invasion training
iv) Accelerating the physical preparations (both real and by means of decoys and dummies)
v) Indicating to the enemy that every available man and all possible resources are being mobilised for an attack across the Channel in conjunction with an assault on the south coast of France.[4]

If an actual large-scale assault upon the Channel Islands was undertaken in conjunction with these other measures, the Germans were certain to believe that the occupation of Jersey, Guernsey and Alderney was the first stage in the re-invasion of the Continent, thus ensuring existing German troop strength would be maintained in France.

It was under the codenames *Concubine I* (Jersey) and *Concubine II* (Guernsey) in November 1942 that consideration was initially given to the recapture of the Channel Islands. These were studies of the nature of both the main islands and the state of the German defences and garrisons, and especially the places suitable for use as aircraft landing strips.

This first study assumed that Alderney, Guernsey, and Jersey would all be attacked simultaneously and that operations in the Soviet Union and in the Mediterranean theatre would continue to tie down the German Air Force at the levels existing at the time of the study. The view was expressed that although no diversionary measures would be undertaken, surprise would be achieved as no operation against the Channel Islands on such a scale had occurred before.

A very detailed study of the defences, garrisons, and beaches of all three islands was undertaken. This, interestingly, included information on how landmines were sown and was obtained from a German prisoner captured on Sark during Operation *Basalt*, a small-scale raid on the island on the night of 3–4 October 1942, who was an engineer. 'The mines are laid in rows in such a fashion that every mine is five paces away from its neighbour, either vertically or horizontally. The mines are laid just deep enough to be covered with soil, with the contact pins sticking out of the ground. The mine is exploded either by kicking against the contact pin or treading on it.' He also told his interrogators about a safety device which was fitted to each mine.

Despite the very extensively complied study, it does not appear that an actual plan of operations was made for the *Concubine* operations. All we know, is the raids would be limited to a maximum of 48 hours,

However, with the proposal mooted of an operation to seize the Cotentin Peninsula, codenamed *Hadrian*, the prospect of holding the Channel Islands permanently in an even more ambitious combined operation was taken up by Combined Ops Headquarters.

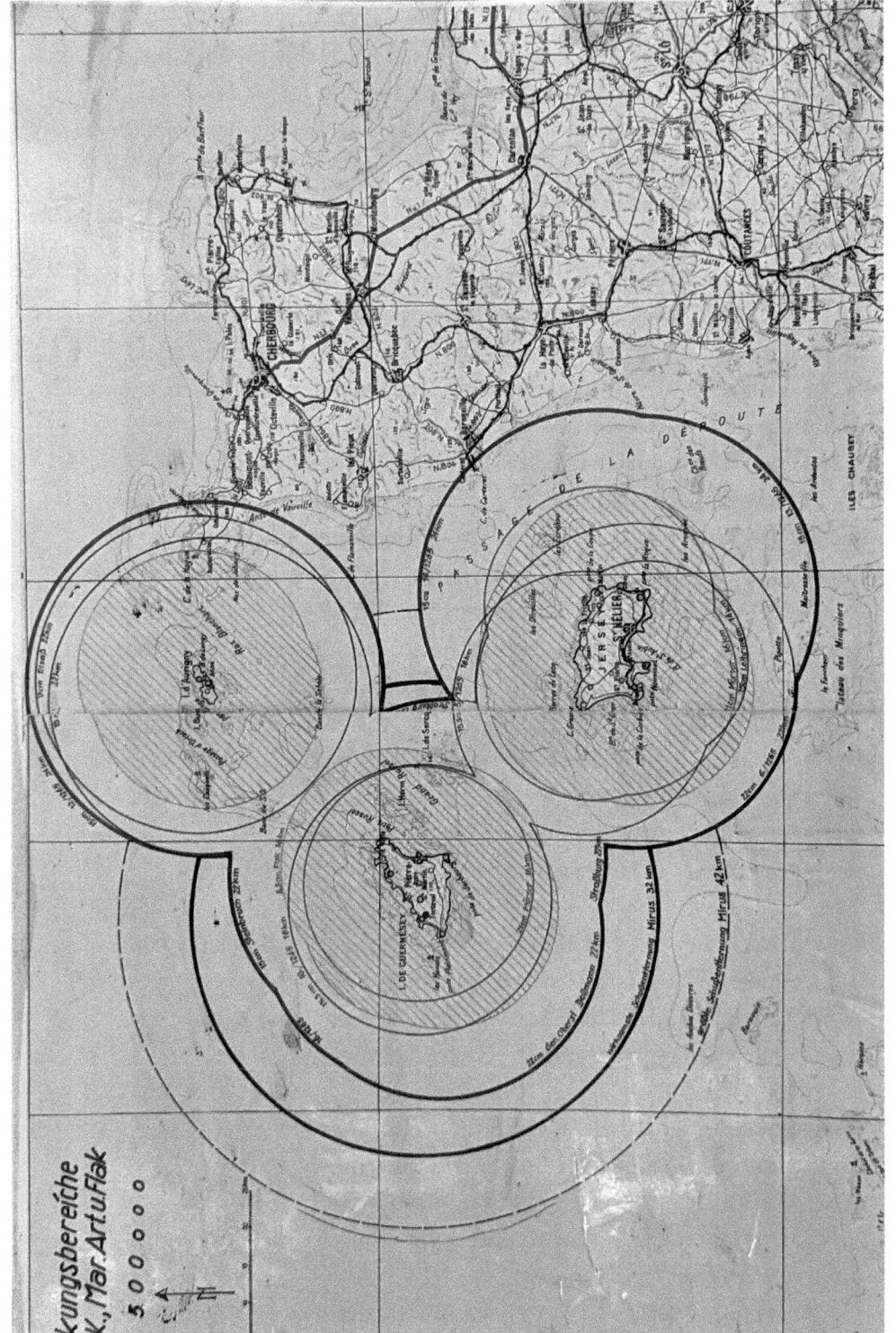

The Cotentin Peninsula was chosen because: '[It] is the only possible objective for offensive operations of which the object is to remain on the Continent, as it is the only area with a short and easily defensible line within reasonable distance of the beaches, and one which, at the same time, permits reasonable air support.'

The capture of the Cotentin Peninsula would be undertaken by eight divisions with some additional infantry, tanks, and Commandos, in cooperation with an airborne force of one airborne division and ten additional parachute battalions. Preliminary air action would be taken against the main communication centres through which enemy reinforcements would pass.

In Allied hands, the Channel Islands would be the ideal springboard for *Hadrian*, which was scheduled for the first week of April. Furthermore, the interlocking nature of the coast defences and dual-purpose anti-aircraft artillery on Guernsey, Alderney, and Cap de la Hague made it 'essential' to find a means of preventing effective fire from these guns before any attempt could be made to pass the assault convoy through to the west coast of the Cotentin Peninsula.

The follow-up convoys approaching the western side of the Cotentin Peninsula in daylight would pass some 12,000 yards from Alderney, well within the range of the big German guns if the ships were to stay out of the range of the coastal batteries on Guernsey. It was calculated that the following number of guns were capable of hitting the convoys:

From Alderney ... ... 4 heavy guns; 7 medium guns; 3 light guns; 12 heavy anti-   aircraft/coastal defence guns.
   From the mainland ... 2 heavy guns; 6 medium guns; 6 heavy anti-aircraft/coastal defence guns.

It was also estimated that 'at least' the following number of guns could cover the channel between Alderney and Guernsey:

From Alderney ... ... 4 heavy guns; 4 medium guns; 8 heavy anti-aircraft/coastal defence guns.
   From Guernsey ... ... 4 heavy guns; 6 medium guns; 3 light guns; 6 heavy anti-aircraft/coastal defence guns.

If, however, the Alderney guns could be neutralised, the Allied shipping would be within range – and extreme range at that – of only one heavy battery in Guernsey. It was also assumed that the four heavy guns on Alderney would have been registered on the Vauville beaches on the west side of the Cotentin Peninsula. which was to be the main Allied landing beach. The silencing of the guns on Alderney was therefore vitally important and became the focus of the study.

In the 'Appreciation' drawn up by the Combined Ops Headquarters planning staff, the defences of Alderney were described as 'formidable'. It stated that the island tends to favour the defender by reason of its commanding features, comparative lack of cover, and good fields of fire and observation. 'The beaches are small, difficult to approach and generally have bad exits for vehicles. On no single beach could more than one battalion be used in the assault.' What the Appreciation did say, though it was not entirely accurate, was that as there were no British subjects on the island (there were a handful) 'no restrictions in the tactics of the assault need be considered'.[5]

While Alderney's terrain was considered suitable for a parachute landing, its small size would make it difficult to find dropping zones at a safe distance from any of the defensive strongpoints. The approaches to the island were covered by heavy concentrations of anti-aircraft artillery and a high rate of casualties both in aircraft and parachutists could therefore be expected.

The same problem, but in an even more acute form, would affect the choice of landing grounds for gliders. The only really suitable area was the airport and the ground immediately to the north of it, but this area was well defended with anti-aircraft batteries. (Another idea was to saturate the town of St Anne with parachutists, where the many gardens would provide open spaces where they could land). It was stated in the 'Appreciation' that the only real hope of successfully using airborne troops was under the cover of darkness or smoke – 'contrary to all previously accepted principles' and, no doubt, quite terrifying for the parachutists unable to see where they were landing.

It was estimated that there were approximately 2,500 Germans on the island, mostly army personnel from 319 Division who also manned the coastal artillery and anti-aircraft batteries, as well as the few light French tanks it was thought were on Alderney. Drawing an imaginary line across the centre of the island from Cachalière Pier in the south to Newtown near Braye Harbour in the north, the defences to the east were regarded as 'heavily organised with tactically wired entrenchments, in which there are prepared positions for some 67 identified machine guns'. A total of twenty-four concrete pillboxes had also been seen on aerial reconnaissance photographs which, it was assumed, also held machine-guns. To the west of the Cachalière Pier -Newtown line, the entrenchments and wire entanglements were less prevalent, but it was noted that the coastal defence and anti-aircraft artillery positions were protected with heavy wired entanglements and defended by machine-guns, some of which were in concrete emplacements. It was further appreciated that mines were being laid 'on a large scale' across the island's beaches, and that weapon pits had been dug along the entire length of Braye Harbour and Corblets Bay. A boom stretched across the outer points of Braye Harbour and a double anti-torpedo net protected the inner harbour. It was also reckoned that 60 per cent of the coastal guns could be trained to fire in any direction.

The conclusion was that: 'The nature of the defences and the strength of the garrison is such that any operation to capture the island would be hazardous and would require unusually great effort.' So rather than risk heavy casualties that would inevitably follow an amphibious assault, a less dangerous means of neutralising the guns on Alderney was considered. It was thought that aerial bombardment would not silence the coastal or anti-aircraft batteries, and cannon or machine-gun fire from fighters was only effective at the time it was undertaken as the gunners would hide during the strafing and return to man their weapons when the aircraft had flown away.

This led the planners to consider instead, disabling the guns' fire control systems by knocking out the German radar installations or the communications from them; extinguishing the searchlights at night; and by the screening of targets by day and by night with smoke. The radar installations on Guernsey would also have to be knocked out. The 'Freya' radar on Guernsey, it was said, could be effectively jammed to prevent the long-range guns on the island interfering with the convoys outside visual range, as well as hindering any indirect fire from Alderney. Searchlights could be taken out by 'intruder' aircraft.

None of these measures, however, would stop the big Alderney guns firing on their presumed pre-set targets on the Vauville beaches. This could be achieved, though, by harassing bombing attacks or by cannon-armed fighters to keep the gunners within their shelters, though it could not be sustained indefinitely.

The problem with all these preventative measures was that it would only be on D-Day – as the assaulting craft full of troops were on their way to the landing beaches – that it would be known if they had been effective, and by then it might be too late. Therefore, the recommendation was that 'plans must be made for the capture of Alderney on the night of D-1/Day-D'.

Having come to that conclusion, three possible courses of action were considered. The first was a purely seaborne assault; the second was an airborne assault; and the third was a combination of the two.

For course one to succeed, both the coast defence and anti-aircraft artillery on the island would have to be neutralised, as well as the very strong beach defences. But it was felt that no amount of shelling or bombing could achieve this. A purely seaborne assault was, therefore, ruled out.

An airborne assault, for the reasons stated above, was equally impracticable. A daylight drop would not succeed in view of the scale of anti-aircraft defences, and a night drop would be highly problematical. So, this was also rejected. Which left just one option – a combined air and sea assualt.

As only the area around St Anne was suitable for a parachute drop, the most paratroops that could be employed was two battalions. Equally, the small size of the beaches meant that only one reinforced infantry regiment – possibly a US regimental combat team – could be landed. As well as these, a US Ranger battalion, three 'tank destroyer' companies and three engineer companies heavily armed with demolition equipment and flame-throwers, would accompany the infantry.

The seaborne assault could be delivered against any or all of the beaches, though the parachutists would only be able to offer support initially to troops going ashore on Saline and Crabby bays. To facilitate these airborne and amphibious landings, diversionary actions would have to be taken elsewhere by small parties. The dropping of the parachute battalions was to be preceded by a heavy aerial bombardment with the object of demoralising the defenders.

It was accepted that after the island had been captured, a much larger force would be needed to garrison and hold the island. Many of these would be flown into the island's emergency landing airfield by 200 C-47 Douglas Skytrain transport planes.

The number of British and American aircraft involved in the operations as whole was colossal. There were to be ninety squadrons of fighters, eight squadrons of fighter-bombers, twenty squadrons of light and medium bombers, five tactical reconnaissance fighter squadrons, twelve night fighter squadrons, 1,116 aircraft for the airborne forces and 518 gliders. In addition to this, every single operational squadron of the RAF's Bomber Command and at least 300 US heavy day bombers were to be employed!

On 18 November 1942, the Chiefs of Staff Committee considered the question of how to find enough landing craft for both *Husky* and *Hadrian*. However, if Alderney had already been recaptured, the force needed to attack the Cotentin Peninsula could be reduced by 6,562 men and 270 vehicles (because of the shorter distance between the island and the Cotentin Peninsula), which translated into a saving of 351 landing craft of varying types.[6] With the availability of landing craft being one of the main constraining factors at that time as we know, this was an important consideration.

At the same meeting, the COS Committee members, General Bernard Paget, Air Chief Marshal Sholto Douglas, and Commodore Clifton Caslon, declared that they considered *Hadrian* practicable, but cautiously stated that they did not know how advantageous such an operation might or might not be. However, they did make one particular claim: '*Hadrian* will bring about a major air battle which might lead to the break-up of the German Air Force, and thus have a decisive effect on the war as a whole. It would also contain a number of German land forces which might otherwise be moved elsewhere. In our opinion, this operation offers the best opportunity for Home Forces and Fighter Command to play an effective part in breaking down German resistance in 1943.'

All of these, and many more subjects, were discussed at Casablanca, and towards the end of January 1943, the Combined Chiefs of Staff laid down their objectives for the coming year under the title 'Conduct of the War in 1943'. This included preparations in and from the United Kingdom, in particular amphibious operations. These were of three types:

(i) Raids with the primary object of provoking air battles and causing enemy losses.
(ii) Operations with the object of seizing and holding a bridgehead and, if the state of German morale and resources permit, of rigorously exploiting successes.
(iii) A return to the Continent to take advantage of German disintegration.

Of these the Chiefs stated that: 'Plans and preparations for (i) above will proceed as at present. An attack on the Channel Islands is an example of the type of operation which we have in mind.'[7]

The United States Chiefs of Staff were not against resources being used against the Chanel Islands, stipulating only that the requirements for the planned invasion of Sicily, such as the provision of landing craft, should not be affected.

Whether an attack on the Channel Islands would be a stand-alone operation or would form part of a larger enterprise, i.e., *Hadrian* or the reinvasion of Europe, it would be the Combined Operations Headquarters which would be responsible for control and command 'on the same lines as the Dieppe raid'. As the Dieppe raid had been an unmitigated disaster caused, in part, by poor planning, one can only assume it was thought that Combined Operations Headquarters would not repeat the errors of the previous year. One of the main reasons the Dieppe raid had failed was because the planners had decided against a preliminary aerial bombardment, being worried, among other reasons, about the damage such a bombardment would have on French civilians and property, as well as the blocking of the roads in Dieppe. While the subject of collateral damage was raised with regard to the attack upon Guernsey, this was not the case with the assault upon Jersey.

Twelve days after the above discussions on the conduct of the war, on 6 February 1943 Mountbatten's staff produced another of their many Appreciations, this time of operations to recapture the Channel Islands.[8] It opened with a topographical outline of the islands of Alderney, Guernsey, and Jersey, followed by comments on the nature of the beaches and the approaches to them. It was recorded that on the whole, the beaches were 'bad' with few of them suitable for amphibious landings or possessing good exits, particularly for vehicles. The approaches to most beaches were rocky with strong cross currents offshore. On Alderney, the beaches were backed by anti-tank walls, and by seawalls in Guernsey and Jersey.

The German garrisons on the islands were estimated to number 8,300 on Jersey, 10,800 on Guernsey, and now 2,750 on Alderney. It was also understood that the number of coastal guns was, respectively, forty, thirty-eight, and sixteen; with ninety-two anti-aircraft guns on Jersey, 116 on Guernsey, and fifty-eight on Alderney.

It was stated for the first time in this Appreciation, and repeated (and contradicted) many times afterwards, that because it would not be possible to achieve any degree of surprise and because the islands were so powerfully fortified, the German defences would have to be neutralised by a preliminary air bombardment before any landings could be attempted. As Alderney was, for its size, the most heavily defended of the islands, the bombardment would 'have to be on such a scale that nearly all personnel on the island will become casualties'.

It was also recognised that during and after the recapture of Guernsey and Jersey, supplies to sustain the civilian populations would be affected. Unless people were evacuated to the UK, living standards would be no better than those experienced under German rule.

Following from this, on 17 February 1943, Mountbatten submitted a 'study' to the Chiefs of Staff Committee under the title 'Operation Constellation' following up on his Appreciation. He admitted that his staff's examinations had not reached the stage where they could definitely say that an attack on Jersey and Guernsey was practicable and it might be found that, of the Channel Islands, only the capture of Alderney was possible with the means at the UK's disposal in 1943. But this was Mountbatten's best chance of mounting a major operation, and he asked the Chiefs of Staff to approve his plans.

In the preamble of his Operation *Constellation* study, Mountbatten wrote: 'In considering the desirability of operations against the Channel Islands or mainland France in 1943, the assumption has been made that, in order to further our Mediterranean strategy, a well-timed offensive in north-west Europe will be required during the summer of 1943.'

The study stated that the geographical position of the Channel Islands was such that prior to an assault on the beaches of the Cherbourg, or Cotentin, Peninsula (which, of course, is exactly where the Allies were to land on D-Day in June 1944) it would be 'essential' to capture Alderney and 'highly desirable' to capture Guernsey. Of the latter, its capture was deemed 'essential' if large forces were to be sent to the Cotentin Peninsula. The occupation of Guernsey would only be practical if Alderney was already in Allied hands. The capture of Jersey was regarded as being 'desirable but by no means essential', but any attempt on Jersey could only be contemplated if Guernsey had already been taken.

Under the heading 'Defences', Mountbatten wrote that the Germans had turned each one of the main Channel Islands into 'a veritable fortress'. An attack on any of them could not be considered unless the German defences had been neutralised or reduced to a very considerable extent by bombing or shelling prior to an amphibious assault.

With regards to the possibility of taking the Germans by surprise, Mountbatten said that the distance between the UK and the Channel Islands and the navigational difficulties of the approach, especially in the case of Alderney and Guernsey, precluded landings in darkness. This meant that there was really no chance of achieving surprise. This was a moot point anyway, as the preliminary bombardment would have been a sure indicator that an assault was imminent.

In his study, Mountbatten next considered the civil populations of the islands. It was estimated that there were still around 35,000 British subjects on both Guernsey and Jersey. With regards to Alderney, it was known that a few civilians had returned and that there were also some 500 Russian prisoners of war. The following is taken verbatim from Mountbatten's study: 'The presence of these civilian populations will require consideration when the question of supporting action such as air and artillery bombardment is examined. There can be no doubt that support of this nature would cause civilian casualties which might be heavy. Nevertheless, the support would be essential.' In other words, regardless of the likelihood of heavy civilian casualties, if the reinvasion was to take place the islands would be heavily bombed. The last two sentences read: 'In these circumstances it is considered that the defenders and their defences must be crushed or almost crushed before the assault is made', and chillingly, 'There can be no finesse.' Meaning, no doubt, that there could be no holding back on the extent of the bombing regardless of whatever consequences there may be for the islanders. This was permitted due to a ruling by Churchill which lifted the ban on 'blind' bombing of areas occupied by the Germans during a coastal assault.[9]

Mountbatten then laid out the findings of the Joint Intelligence Sub-Committee regarding the retaking of the Channel Islands. Firstly, it was thought that an attack on one of the islands would indicate that attacks would follow against the other islands as there would be no advantage to the Allies in taking just one island. Secondly, that after the islands were back in Allied hands, the Germans would not attempt to retake the islands, but would instead undertake every effort to make the Allied hold on them 'sufficiently precarious' by air and naval action, meaning that the islanders who had survived the Allied bombardment would be subjected to further bombing and shelling by the Germans. The Germans were also likely to assume that the seizure of the islands meant further operations against the French coast were imminent, especially the Cherbourg or Brest peninsulas.

The capture of one or more of the Channel Islands would create a belief among the Germans that it was the first step to the Allies obtaining a foothold on the Continent but, the Intelligence Sub-Committee believed, this would only result in a 'minor' redistribution of the forces already available to them in western Europe. Even so, they reckoned that there would be improvements in the defences and an increase in the state of readiness on the Cherbourg and Brest peninsulas. It would also deter Hitler from moving any troops away from France to other theatres. They also believed that no German air forces would be transferred to the Cherbourg/Brest peninsulas from other theatres until the threat of an Allied landing on the mainland had materialised.

Finally, the Sub-Committee stated that, with all the factors taken into account, they considered the re-occupation of one or more of the Channel Islands would lead to air battles 'on a large scale'. As we know, this had been something the Allied air forces had been wishing for for some time. Furthermore, the occupation of the Channel Islands would give the Royal Navy advanced bases from which it could interrupt, and possibly even stop, German coastal convoys to and from the Biscay ports.

The other factor that had to be taken into consideration in all of this was its effect upon Operation *Husky*. Remarkably, the verdict of the Sub-Committee was that: 'the capture of one or more of the Channel Islands would, by further stretching the German Air Force and by implying a threat against the mainland, increase the tension of all German forces in France and in doing so have a direct and beneficial effect on *Husky*.'

As a result, the 'considered' recommendation of the Intelligence Sub-Committee was: 'that the forces required for *Constellation* should be made available, and that action against one or more of the Channel Islands should be taken shortly before *Husky*.' The three phases of *Constellation* were to be an attack upon Alderney – Operation *Concertina*; Guernsey – Operation *Coverlet*; and Jersey – Operation *Condor*. Each one, however, was to be examined, and justified individually.

The last sentence in the Sub-Committee's report read: 'Since it is not considered possible to obtain any appreciable degree of surprise, the extremely strong defences of the islands must be very severely battered before landings are attempted.'

The average circular error of level bombers in 1943 was 1,200 feet, meaning that only 16 per cent of the bombs fell within 1,000 feet of the aiming point.[10] These figures were known[11] at the War Office. Only with the deployment of hundreds of bombers could there be any hope of hitting the German defensive structures – and this is exactly what was proposed in the Outline Plan – but what was absolutely certain was that there would be massive and widespread damage across whichever island was subjected to such a bombardment.

Chapter 10

Operation Concertina: The Re-occupation of Alderney

In his memoires, Hughes-Hallett recalled that Mountbatten's team 'were given astonishing latitude to decide the sequence in which the islands should be attacked', and he and Leigh-Mallory agreed that Alderney should be attacked first. He wrote:

> No great amount of work was involved in the planning of "Concertina" since we were able to make use of the detailed plan that had been prepared for the abortive attack on Alderney in May, 1942. There was, however, one major difference. We now had 12 L.C.I. (L), each capable of carrying 300 troops, which gave a lift for 3,600 Infantry, which was well in excess of the number which it was proposed to land in the assault. The superior speed of these craft (12 knots as against 5 or 6 knots in the case of L.C.A.) was a very great asset, and as we only needed 8 for the assault it was possible to obtain a qualified navigating officer for each one.[1]

On 4 March 1943, another meeting was held to consider an operation against Alderney, in which Mountbatten requested that the Royal Marine Division and the Senior Officer of Force 'J' (largely the forces involved in the Dieppe raid, Operation *Jubilee* – thus Force J) should in future be continually represented by officers who would take part in the planning process. That same day a memorandum was sent to Air Vice Marshal Basil Embury, the head of No. 2 Group Bomber Command, which was to become part of the new Second Tactical Air Force and was to provide the aerial support for the operation. The memorandum told Embury that he had to produce an air plan to fit in with the naval plan, submitted by Hughes-Hallett and the Army Force commander, Royal Marine Major General Robert 'Bob' Grice Sturges. All three plans would be put into a Joint Detail Plan.

Embury was told on 5 March: 'So far as the planning is concerned the only decisions of any importance reached at yesterday's meeting was that the assault should be a night one timed for about 2 hours before first light, and that the bomber effort would probably need to be spread over two or more nights in order to get the requisite tonnage on the island.' He was also told that the Navy would consider the use of 'Flare Droppers' to assist the aircraft in their final pilotage up to the beaches.[2]

The stated aims in taking Alderney by attack and then holding it were to provide a small craft base for cutting the German convoy route along the coast of France, the establishment of a radar station to extend Fighter Command coverage, the establishment of an emergency landing strip, the creation of a diversion which might lead the Germans to withdraw air forces from other fronts (including bombers from Norway), the creation of a diversion which might lead the Germans to withdraw ground forces from other fronts, the creation of an opportunity to bring German air strength to battle under reasonably favourable circumstances, and the provision of a springboard for further combined operations.

As has been repeated, one of the main reasons the Dieppe raid failed was the decision not to precede the assault with an aerial bombardment, with one concern being its effect on the French people. There is no evidence in the files to indicate that there was anything other than passing concerns regarding the inhabitants of the Channel Islands.

The bombing, therefore, was to be on a very heavy scale, and it was estimated that a minimum of 270 tons of bombs would be dropped on the island. Embury was asked if it would be practical for the bombers to be able to destroy the enemy's barbed wire entanglements and tank obstacles. The response was that this was not really known and the only way to find out was by conducting trials. But, after discussions with staff at Bomber Command Headquarters, Embury replied: 'You must realise that the planning of an operation of this kind is an extra commitment superimposed upon the ordinary day to day work which we have to undertake as an operational Group. We, therefore, do not have the time or status to conduct trials.' It was therefore concluded that it would not be possible to select individual targets and the bombing would be 'indiscriminate throughout the island'.

Mountbatten, though, was worried that there would be a 22-minute gap between the end of the bombing and the start of the assault, because

Air Marshal Arthur Harris insisted that his bombers would have to be withdrawn 40 minutes before civil twilight to avoid being spotted and caught by enemy fighters. Mountbatten said that unless this gap could be closed, he did not believe the operation should go ahead.

Alan Brooke also doubted the effectiveness of such bombing on the beach defences. From his experience, he said: 'It would be wrong to rely upon the bombing neutralising the beach defences, particularly as the Germans had developed these very considerably during the last three months.'[3]

Another consideration was whether the occupation of Alderney should be either a land and stay operation or a limited re-occupation followed by a withdrawal. The Combined Ops planners replied on 3 April 1943 that they saw no advantage in the latter.

The first reason why they drew this conclusion was that there would be no less a strain on the necessary naval forces, and it would still need a considerable commitment by the RAF. Indeed, they pointed out that the expedition could not be undertaken in less than three days which would tie up immense forces continually throughout that time to the detriment of other commitments.

The second was that a withdrawal so soon after the occupation of Alderney would hardly fail to be noticed by the enemy. Whereas, the initial assault would take the Germans by surprise (note the contradiction), so much attention would be focussed on the island after its capture every movement by the British would be closely watched. In such circumstances a withdrawal would be extremely difficult – and any armed force is always at its most vulnerable when retreating.

Equally, there could be no certainty about the weather over what would be five days from the start of the assault. Weather predictions that far ahead were far from certain, and the troops and the Navy would be committed to the withdrawal even if the weather turned. Heavy seas would make the embarkation of artillery, tanks, and other vehicles extremely hazardous and prolong the operation at the worst possible time.

Employing all the necessary forces and incurring considerable risks just for the sake of holding the island for a few hours with, therefore, no tangible gain, seemed quite senseless compared with fully reoccupying and permanently retaining Alderney which would involve similar commitments and dangers.

Operation Concertina: The Re-occupation of Alderney

Despite such considerations, Hughes-Hallett had high hopes for *Concertina*:

"J Force" by this time also possessed no less than 18 L.C.F. [Landing Craft, Flak], each of which carried 8 Pom-Poms or twin Bofors Anti-Aircraft guns. Leigh-Mallory had great faith in the efficiency of the L.C.F. as a means of deterring attacks by low flying fighter bombers, which was the form of attack which he found it most difficult to counter with his fighters. On this occasion we planned the heavy saturation bombing which was to proceed the landing with more detail than had been done the year before. It was to take place in three phases with a ten-minute interval between each phase. We thought that this would deter the island's garrison from leaving the shelter of their bomb-proof dug-outs too soon after the bombing had ceased. We also enlisted the help of the famous "Pathfinder" Squadrons by laying lines of coloured flares to mark the ends of each of the landing beaches. On the whole, both Leigh-Mallory and I felt far happier about this modified plan for attacking Alderney, than we had about the original plan. Perhaps I should add that it was intended as far as possible to use nothing but experienced Commandos for the first assault.

Early in April I sent the L.C.I. (L) together with H.M.S. Locust and a number of L.C.P. round Land's End to Milford Haven, and I proceeded there myself by air a few days later. The idea was that Milford Haven area, with its strong tidal streams and numerous small beaches with rocks at either end of them would prove a good place from which to practice the L.C.I.(L) in entering and beaching themselves under conditions not dissimilar from those to be found in the Channel Islands. On my arrival, however, I acted on local advice and moved on to Fishguard. On the short passage there we routed the L.C.I. (L) and indeed the Locust as well, inside, and indeed in between the Bishop Rock. It was evident that the lighthouse keeper thought we were quite mad, and through my binoculars I could see him frantically waving a red flag. Nevertheless, it was a good opening exercise for the somewhat inexperienced R.N.V.R. captains of the L.C.I.(L) to see what was involved in keeping station while passing through narrow channels with cross tides of anything up to eight knots.

> By April 15, I was satisfied that the L.C.I.(L) could be relied upon to carry out the task that would face them at Alderney, and, after a final briefing meeting, I returned to Cowes.'[4]

The following month, May 1943, the planners were told to look again at the value of seizing Alderney as an isolated operation, unrelated either to *Husky* or to a reinvasion of the Continent through Normandy.[5] Before considering the advantages which might accrue from taking and holding the island, the Combined Operations team sought to point out the not inconsiderable, possible disadvantages.

The first, and the most telling, was that the Germans would be likely to infer from the capture of an island so close to the French mainland that this was a preliminary step to the Allies obtaining a foothold on the Continent through Brest or the Cherbourg Peninsula. The Germans would, in that instance, look to rapidly strengthen the defences in those areas – thus defeating all the measures undertaken and planned to deceive Hitler into believing that the re-invasion of Europe would be through the Pas-de-Calais.

That having been stated, the planners did not believe Hitler would draw any men from either Italy or the Eastern Front, instead the additional German troops sent to the area would be taken from the reserve depots. Indeed, it was believed that once Operation *Husky* had commenced, the Germans would see that Italy was the main focus of the Allied effort and that a reinvasion of northern France in 1943 would be beyond Britain's and America's resources. Hitler would, therefore, have been alerted to the likelihood of the invasion being planned against Normandy without accruing any benefit for the other active fronts.

The planners also pointed out that launching an operation to recapture Alderney was one thing but holding it and supporting the troops there in such close proximity to the enemy-held coast would be another matter altogether. Not only would it place a heavy burden on the Navy's already stretched light coastal forces, but the island would also need very considerable air protection in an area where the RAF, at a distance from its UK bases but close to those of the enemy, would be at a distinct disadvantage.

While it might be thought that re-taking Alderney would play well in the press and be a boost to Allied morale, it was considered that it would have quite the opposite effect across Occupied Europe, and in particular France, when it became apparent that it was not the first stage of the re-invasion of the Continent. 'The limited scope of the operation,' ran the assessment, 'would have extensive propaganda value for the Germans in their efforts to strain the relations between this country and Russia.' This is because its limited scope would not be seen as constituting a second front, merely the British selfishly using their resources to take back part of their own territory.

There were, nevertheless, a number of potential advantages that might be derived from re-occupying Alderney, though some of these were the direct opposite of the stated disadvantages which clearly showed that no one had any real idea how it would play out. The most obvious of these contradictions was the statement that 'Air battles over the area of assault, and along our convoy route between this country [the UK] and the island, would strain the G.A.F. to a degree which would depend on the scale of the attempted interference.' The planners had said that the RAF would be placed at a disadvantage operating far from their English bases but then that the operations over Alderney and the Channel would put a heavy strain on the Luftwaffe.

A similar contradiction was made with regards to the Royal Navy's coastal forces which, it was stated under 'disadvantages', would be severely stretched. Then under 'advantages' it claimed, 'The ability to base coastal naval forces in the island would enable us to interrupt the coastwise convoys to the Biscay U-boat ports. Similarly, the island would provide a base from which amphibious raids could be mounted.'

The occupation of Alderney would also give the Allies an emergency landing ground for damaged or malfunctioning aircraft within 10 miles of the Cherbourg Peninsula (though it was pointed out that such a place was likely to be attacked by German bombers from the mainland). Also, RDF equipment could be installed on the island which would considerably extend the range of the Chain Home early warning system 'and enable us more easily to direct and control our aircraft operations over that area.'

Looking ahead to the proposed Normandy landings, the planners considered that the attack upon Alderney would be a good rehearsal for what would become Operation *Overlord*, in that effectiveness of the preliminary bombing on the enemy's fixed defences could be gauged as well as the method of amphibious assault.

What was described as 'available intelligence', presumably aerial reconnaissance, indicated that the Germans were undertaking extensive tunnelling work on Alderney. The planners stated that if this was allowed to continue and *Concertina* delayed, the chances of a successful assault upon Alderney would be considerably reduced as the garrison would be able to sit out the preliminary bombardment in relative safety. These tunnels, it has subsequently been suggested, were not to shelter the garrison but were for the housing of V1 flying bombs which would be launched against the Allied invasion forces assembling in the English south coast ports.[6]

The conclusion drawn was: 'If CONNCERTINA [sic] were carried out as an isolated operation, unrelated either to HUSKY or to a major operation for re-entering the Continent through the North Coast of France, certain limited advantages would be gained.

'Provided the operation did not involve the withholding of forces required for our major effort in the Mediterranean, it is considered that these advantages would outweigh the disadvantages.'

Having concluded, then, that the re-occupation of Alderney would be advantageous to the Allies, the next step was to examine the island's defences and then to draw up a plan of attack.

Under the heading 'General Sequence of Events', the outline plan of attack was laid out as follows:

Preliminary Air Bombardment
1. It is proposed that:-
    (a) On the night of D-2/D-1 the island is attacked by a force of 500 to 600 heavy and medium bombers.
    (b) During D-1day P.R.U. [Photographic Reconnaissance Unit] sorties are flown first and are followed by daylight attacks carried out by heavy American bombers.
    (c) On the night of D-1/D Day the island is again attacked by a force of 500 to 600 heavy and medium bombers.

Preliminary Naval Bombardment
2. As soon as the bombing attack ceases on the morning of D Day a monitor and destroyers will commence to bombard, and will continue

doing so until the last possible moment before the landing of the first flights.

The Landings
3. The first flight landings will be made as early as navigationally possible after a.m. nautical twilight.[7] At the same time a special detachment will attempt to open the boom which covers Brays harbour and the beach adjoining it.
4. The second and remaining waves will be called in immediately the main assault beaches, which would be badly obstructed, have been sufficiently cleared.
5. Over and above the assault force a floating reserve of not less than two battalions will be available for use as required by the Force Commander.

Air Cover during the Landings
6. Maximum cover will be given over the beaches when there are landing craft lying off and fighter escorts will be provided for convoys passing between this country and Alderney.
7. Fighter sweeps will be carried out as and when possible but it is appreciated that Fighter Command will be at full stretch and that it would be preferable to accept considerable gaps rather than to request continuous but weak air cover.

The forces required for the operation were immense. In addition to the heavy and medium bombers for the two nights preceding the assault, six squadrons of medium or light bombers were to be employed for 'diversionary' bombing and sixteen squadrons of USAAF heavy bombers to continue hitting the island. There would also be a requirement for an astonishing forty to fifty squadrons of fighters, one Coastal Command squadron for air-to-surface radar and one squadron of Coastal strike aircraft armed with torpedoes or bombs to deal with any enemy light naval forces. At least two aircraft of the Photographic Reconnaissance Unit to keep the Force Commander fully apprised of the effect of the bombardments and of surviving enemy installations were required. The Naval forces needed were also considerable:

1 Monitor (mounting two 15-inch guns)
1 Anti-aircraft cruiser
Anti-submarine destroyer escort
8 *Hunt*-class destroyers
12 Motor Torpedo Boats
12 Motor Launches
Landing craft as required for the military
6 Minesweeping trawlers
6 Anti-submarine trawlers
1 Boom Defence Vessel

It was hoped that the bulk of the military forces could be drawn from the Royal Marine Division which was, of course, trained in amphibious operations. Where this could not be met by the Marines, the Commander-in-Chief, Home Forces would be expected to allocate the units required. The total military forces were:

One Brigade Group
Two Commandos
One Field Company, Royal Engineers
Two heavy and one light Anti-Aircraft batteries
One battery of 4.5-inch gun-howitzers for coast defence as soon as the island was secured
On squadron of tanks
Ancillary units

Of crucial important in any amphibious operation is the weather. The planners specified a calm sea with wind not exceeding force 4 (13 to 18 miles per hour) and minimal tide conditions i.e., neap tides, and they required no cloud below 8,000 feet. These conditions had to be forecast to prevail for 48 hours.

Once re-taken, it was estimated that maintaining the garrison would, from D + 2 onwards, require supplies totalling 120 tons to be shipped to the island each day. They would have to be landed on Braye Bay beach if Braye Harbour was too severely damaged. This would mean a heavy drain on resources and had to be taken into consideration when assessing the value accruing from seizing Alderney.

Operation Concertina: The Re-occupation of Alderney 145

The entire plan hinged on there being no opposition to the landings. Alderney was a 'fortress' and one that would not be easily stormed if it had a garrison with defences it could man. Hence the enormous scale of the preliminary bombardment. In putting this into meaningful numbers, the USAAF heavy bombers referred to were the Consolidated B-24 Liberator and the Boeing B-17 Flying Fortress. The B-24 normally carried a bomb load of 5,000 pounds (2,250 kg) – though it could carry considerably more on short-distance, low-level missions – and the B-17 had a payload up to 4,800 lb (2,200 kg) of bombs. So, 500 or 600 of these aircraft would be able to deliver around 2,000,000 lb, or more than 900 tons, of bombs. As Alderney is just 3 square miles in extent, this would average out at more than 300 tons per square mile. This was to be repeated a second time, though with the use of medium as well as the heavies, increasing the likely average across the little island to a staggering 500 tons per square mile. The famous, or infamous, bombing of Dresden in February 1945 saw 3,740 tons of bombs and incendiaries hit the German city. It is stated that more than 21 square kilometres (8 square miles) of the city was devastated. This meant 467.5 tons per square mile – Alderney was to be bombed more heavily than Dresden. When coupled with the naval bombardment, it is hard to imagine that any part of Alderney would have escaped being blasted and bombed into ruin – but the German fortifications were immensely strong, as visitors today can see; would they have survived the bombardment?

The German garrison was now estimated at 2,750 men, of whom about 1,000 were workers with the Organization Todt engaged on adding to the island's defences and excavating the tunnels referred to above. These numbers may have been an underestimate as it is now known that the garrison was gradually increased, and by 1944 it totalled 3,200, composed of 890 infantry, 590 navy and 1,050 air force personnel, and there were more than 4,000 OT workers.[8]

The defences built by the Germans on Alderney included five batteries of large calibre guns, three of which were interlinked with heavy guns on Guernsey and the Cotentin Peninsula, making any approach from the sea extremely hazardous. Of these, three were operated by the German Navy Coastal Artillery, one by the Army Coastal Artillery and the fifth one by the 319 Divisional Artillery. It was the German Air Force which manned all the island's anti-aircraft batteries, of which there were eventually twenty-two on the island. In addition, there were thirteen strongpoints (*Stüzpunkt*). These were generally formed around a single casemated 10.5 cm beach defence gun and comprised a number of smaller positions with anti-aircraft or lighter artillery pieces including anti-tank guns along with mortar and machine-gun pits plus infantry communication and fire trenches, the whole being surrounded by mines and barbed wire. There twelve similar, though smaller, Resistance Nests (*Widerstandsnester*), usually with an anti-tank gun and infantry positions placed to secure tactically important locations. Finally, there were three 400-metre-long infantry defence lines and other infantry positions across the island.

So considerable were the German fortifications, the planners repeatedly stressed that unless they were all destroyed, the operation might fail. They were especially worried about what they described as 'the powerful coast defence battery at the centre of the island'. This is, presumably, the one the Germans had named 'Blücher'. Its four 15 cm guns were mounted on turntables in open circular emplacements allowing them to be rotated in any direction. 'Should this battery remain effective,' read the report, 'it will almost certainly result in the failure of the entire plan.'[9]

The planners also produced a report entitled 'Rumour and Deception, Project to Follow "Concertina"'. The object of the project was 'to bring about an air and land battle at a time and place of our own choosing after Operation "Concertina"'.

It was surmised that for three weeks after Alderney was in Allied hands, the British garrison would be hard at work clearing the damage caused by the naval and air bombardments and, where necessary, erecting new defences on the island. The beaches would be mined, barbed wire entanglements would be laid, new fortifications constructed, and infantry positions dug. In the meantime, camouflage coverings on a large scale would be prepared in the UK.

At the end of that three-week period, the British public would be informed that the retention of Alderney might not prove practical nor in the country's interest. At the same time the rumour would be spread abroad that the seizure of Alderney was only undertaken to cover a landing on the beaches of the Cherbourg Peninsula, an operation due to take place in the very near future.

The planners believed that these rumours would have a very good chance of inducing the Germans to move land, and certainly air forces to the Cherbourg area and possibly to contemplate a major attempt at re-taking Alderney. But, as long as no large-scale British shipping movements took place there would be some uncertainty among the Germans about the veracity of the rumours – placing just enough doubt in their minds to strengthen their forces around Cherbourg but holding them back from committing themselves to a costly invasion attempt against the island.

From that point onwards Alderney's fortifications would be camouflaged and one by one the artillery emplacements would disappear from sight, machine-gun positions would no longer be seen, and construction work would seem to come to a halt, though, in reality, work on the defences would be carefully stepped up.

Almost four weeks after the capture of Alderney it would be announced that an evacuation of the island by the British troops might become inevitable at any moment owing to the difficulties in maintaining the troops so far from the UK mainland and because of the heavy bombardment of the island from German batteries on the French coast.

While this was going on, a fleet of small craft would be secretly assembled in a few English south coast ports, the Royal Navy would undertake anti-submarine patrols to keep the Western Approaches and the English Channel clear of enemy vessels, and the RAF would conduct sweeps over the Continent. The fleet would sail for the Cherbourg Peninsula under the cover of darkness. Every vessel would carry nothing but 'dummy' anti-aircraft personnel. Believing that an invasion fleet was heading towards them, the German Air Force would fly off every available aircraft to attack the vessels – but they would be lured into a trap to be pounced on by a mass of RAF fighters.

In the meantime, news would then be leaked out that the evacuation of the island was about to take place. By then, the men of the garrison would have completed camouflaging all their guns and gone to ground. No one would be visible, no fires would be lit, no enemy aircraft or vessels would be engaged, no supply ships would be sent from the UK and there would be strict radio silence. It would look, to all intents and purposes, as if the island had been completely abandoned, with full details and photographs of the successful withdrawal announced in the British press.

The Germans would be likely, in the first instance, to send reconnaissance aircraft over the island. If the camouflage and concealment was well accomplished, the Germans would be deceived into believing the island was no longer occupied. With Hitler so determined to hold onto the Channel Islands, there would, therefore, be every expectation that the Germans would attempt to return to Alderney. The second part of the trap would then be sprung. As the unsuspecting German troops landed and began to move across the seemingly deserted island, the British would uncover their weapons and gun down the hapless enemy soldiers.

The forces stated as available for the battles were given as forty-four fighter squadrons, nine Typhoon squadrons for close support of the ground troops, six Ventura day bomber squadrons to produce smoke, three day bomber squadrons to bomb enemy airfields, five Army Cooperation squadrons for strategic and tactical reconnaissance, and an unspecified number of aircraft from Coastal Command to attack enemy surface vessels. The maximum possible effort was to be expected from Bomber Command and the US Eighth Air Force, with large numbers of enemy aircraft being based so close to the UK.

A highly specific Order of Battle for the land battle was also prepared, with the Royal Marine Division making up the bulk of the total plus one Army commando. There were, in addition, detachments from the Royal Engineers, the Royal Army Service Corps, the Medical Corps, the Pioneer Corps, the Armoured Corps and the standard auxiliary units. Intriguingly, two Special Boat Sections from the Small Scale Raiding Force were to be included.

The naval forces were to comprise the monitor *Albrighton*, which would act as the headquarters ship, and eleven *Hunt*-class destroyers plus thirteen gunboats and enormous flotillas of infantry, personnel, and tank landing craft, plus landing craft support vessels.

As the discussions continued with the practicalities of mounting *Concertina*, there were fears that the operation would not be possible for two reasons. The first of these was the fact that there might be insufficient time for the troops to be trained to allow the operation to be mounted ready for it to be synchronised with *Husky* with the objective of drawing off the Luftwaffe. The second was that *Concertina* would deprive the forces invading Sicily of valuable landing craft.

Mountbatten's team, therefore, came up with a further reason for why the attack on Alderney would be a good idea, so determined were they to mount a signature operation. This was that *Concertina* should be used to investigate the effect of heavy bombing as a prelude to an assault. He declared that owing to its geographical location it was particularly well suited to such an 'experiment' as the 'maximum experience would derive for the British forces, whereas the Germans would not be able to give them any definite information'. Mountbatten made it clear, nevertheless, that he would only 'sponsor' such a devastating assault upon a British Crown territory if General Sturges could state that the occupation of Alderney had a reasonable chance of success.

If the new reason for assaulting Alderney was to test the effects of heavy bombing as a prelude to an assault on the French coast, there appeared no case for holding the island afterwards. Professor Solly Zuckerman, scientific advisor to the Allies on bombing strategy, said that from his experience on a recent tour of North Africa, he was convinced that a considerable reduction of defences and demoralisation of the garrison could be achieved by an uninterrupted heavy bombing programme. According to Hughes-Hallett, Zukerman said that the island 'made a readily identifiable target and was so small that a saturation bombing was easily within our capabilities [and]expressed the opinion that we had asked for too many bombers in our original outline plan.'

Hughes-Hallett and Sturges pointed out that if the bombing went on too long the Germans would have the chance to relieve the garrison and bring in fresh troops, thus the psychological effects of the bombing would be wasted. Embury, on the other hand, said that this was not of great importance as the Force Commanders had agreed to the use of fighter-bombers for 20 minutes after 'Zero' hour, thus there would be no relaxation in the bombing. All aircraft flights would take off from the UK after civil twilight on D-1 to maintain secrecy.

It was suggested by the Vice Chief Combined Operations, Major General Joseph Haydon, that the occupation of the Casquets Lighthouse might aid the flotilla to navigate the approaches to Alderney. Sturges and Hughes-Hallett agreed to this, marking it down for capture on the night of D-1/D-Day.

It was Major N.W. Gray, of the Royal Marines, who outlined the Military Plan. He said that there would be simultaneous landings at several points, timed as close as possible to the end of the bombing. Sturges then asked Mountbatten to state how long the Military Force would be expected to remain on Alderney now that the purpose of the attack was to examine the damage the bombing had done to the German defences? Mountbatten answered that if the troops were on the ground there was no point in them leaving until they had smashed all the enemy's defensive works. Hughes-Hallett added to this the consideration that the troops would either have to evacuate immediately after neutralising the garrison or a period of around 72 hours would have to be allowed to enable the landing craft to return to base to refuel. He also said that a plan which included the evacuation of the Military Force with its equipment would require more landing craft than one which left a holding force on the island. Hughes-Hallett and Sturges were therefore asked to submit their estimations of how many landing craft would be required if the operation was undertaken with the object of holding Alderney compared with simply destroying the defences and withdrawing.

For his part in discussing the Air Plan, Embury said that the bombing would still take place over two consecutive nights with daylight bombing by American forces and intervening air reconnaissance. He agreed to ensure that tactical reconnaissance squadrons were instructed in Kriegsmarine E-boat recognition. With regards to aerial protection during the actual landings, Embury believed that the bomber force would be better employed dropping smoke bombs; leaving the Army Cooperation aircraft to provide close support. If an evacuation was decided upon, Fighter Command would need to be involved to provide cover during the potentially highly dangerous withdrawal period.

The conclusion drawn was that if *Concertina* was to be carried out as an isolated operation, unrelated to either *Husky* or for a major operation for re-entering the Continent through the north coast of France, certain limited advantages would be gained. The decision from the Chief Planner was, therefore, that providing such an operation did not involve holding back any forces required for *Husky*, he believed the advantages of seizing Alderney outweighed the disadvantages.

Despite all this, on 16 April Major General Godfrey Edward Wildman-Lushington, Mountbatten's Chief of Staff, wrote to the various force commanders that: 'Circumstances have made it impossible to carry out this operation this year, either in the form of an occupation or a raid and return.' Those circumstances were that the armoured landing craft Hughes-Hallett and Leigh-Mallory had placed such faith in were to be transferred to the Mediterranean.

Chapter 11

Operation Coverlet: The Re-occupation of Guernsey

A highly detailed plan, or 'Appraisal' for the reinvasion of Guernsey as the second phase of *Constellation* was prepared by Mountbatten's Combined Operations Staff under the codename Operation *Coverlet*. It opened with a description of the island and a presumption (before the cancellation of *Concertina*) that Alderney had already been retaken but that Jersey was still in enemy hands. The stated objective was to capture Guernsey in July 1943.[1]

In the description of the island, the plan explained that Guernsey was extensively covered in glass houses, particularly in the north (for the cultivation of tomatoes – the famous Guernsey 'Toms'), but that there were small areas of open common land immediately inland of the northern coast (L'Ancresse Common) and bordering the cliffs along the south coast and the shore of Portinfer. The island had a few densely wooded areas with the rest being covered by very small fields separated from each other by thick hedges and earthen banks about 4 feet high.

The position of the island in relation to the German-occupied French coast precluded RAF fighter cover during offensive operations being maintained on anything but a light scale for any protracted length of time. Because of all the glass houses and small fields, Guernsey was most unsuited for the deployment of parachute troops apart from one or two areas, neither of which could be considered ideal.

Harbours and Airfields

The two main ports of St Peter Port and St Samson, both on the east coast of the island, were used daily by the Germans, with three or four merchant ships being observed each day in the former and one or two coastal ships seen in the latter. Together, it was estimated, these two ports had the berthing and unloading capacity to maintain the British garrison after Guernsey's recapture. With regards to supplies for the assaulting troops, the report stated that because of the unreliability of the weather and to avoid congestion on the beaches, the seizing of these two ports should be undertaken as swiftly as possible. It was noted, however, that a double boom had been placed across the inside of St Peter Port harbour which, it was assumed, held anti-submarine and anti-torpedo nets.

There was only one airfield on the island, which was just 800 yards long by 800 yards wide (today's Guernsey Airport at Forest). It had been well equipped by the Germans, with good dispersal areas and shelters, and unobstructed approaches. Small numbers of fighters could operate from the airfield, though, being so close to Luftwaffe airfields in France, their effectiveness would be reduced unless supported by fighters on Alderney and Jersey. The airfield would, however, be extremely useful for flying in reinforcements and stores by glider. Eventually, after the completion of *Constellation*, it was thought that two squadrons of fighters could be based in Guernsey.

The western approaches to Guernsey were fringed with precipitous rocks. The north-western and eastern shores were rocky and the approaches to the beaches are narrow and dangerous, the report noted. The most favourable approach for an invading force was from the south-east which, though also rocky, was notably safer. Unfortunately, the best beaches were those in the north and north-west which were difficult to approach, the ones in the east which were more easily approached were poor, and those in the south were very narrow with bad exits.

The other factor the invasion flotilla needed to be conscious of were the tidal streams. These swirl round the island, are variable and strong, and come from all points of the compass.

Guernsey's coastline is ringed with rocks and as it was regarded as essential that the first wave of invading troops landed while it was still dark, the employment of good, local pilots would be essential.

It was also understood, based on information received in November 1942, that all the exits from the beaches were mined except those on the south coast and those at L'Ancresse Common, Vazon Bay and Belle Grève Bay. A report in 1945 revealed that between the end of the war in May and August of that year, a total of 68,550 mines were lifted from the beaches and fields. There were also more than 3,000 beach obstacles removed including many explosive devices.[2]

With all these factors taken into account, it was concluded that despite the difficulties of the approach, the invading force, including tanks and artillery, would have to be landed on the north of the island. In addition, as the beaches on the south were the least heavily defended, this would make them more suitable for infantry scramble landings. If the Military Commander deemed it absolutely necessary to have motor vehicles or tanks landed in the south, then the preparation in advance of portable wooden ramps was highly recommended by Mountbatten's staff, as well as demolition charges to breach the seawalls which were to be found on most of the beaches.

The final consideration with regards to the landing beaches was that those in the north-west of Guernsey, where the land is relatively flat, are overlooked by high ground to the south. The beachhead in the north-west, therefore, had to be extended to include that high ground.

Invasion Points

The Appreciation next looked at which places would be suitable for the landing of the amphibious assault troops and supporting vehicles.

On the east coast, Belle Grève Bay, just to the north of St Peter Port, is about 2,200 yards long, although the beach itself is much broken up with rocks, while reefs and more rocks out to sea also make the approach hazardous. Local knowledge here would be essential. Infantry could exit at almost every point, but motor transport could only exit north of where the marina stands today.

Immediately south of St Peter Port, Havelet Bay is 250 yards long at high water, where it is rocky, and 400 yards at low water where it is firm sand. At half-tide the water still touches the seawall, which was 15 feet high and was replaced by rocky ledges for the last 30 yards or so. The approach to the beach was considered good, with ramps for motor transport at both the north and south sections of the beach.

The next bay to the south is Soldier's Bay, which sits close to Clarence Battery. At around 300 yards long and completely covered at high water, infantry could still land there up to 3/4 tide. It is composed of firm sand with pebbles by the cliffs which surround it, with just one footpath leading up from the beach. This beach is currently – as of 2021 – closed to the public on safety grounds.

Continuing southwards along Guernsey's east coast is Fermain Bay. This lovely, little bay, approximately 280 yards long, was considered suitable for landing at all states of the tide. It is backed by a 12-foot-high seawall and a loophole tower, while a ramp in the seawall could be used by motor transport.

The narrow Petit Point Bay on Guernsey's south-east coast is just 200 yards long. Composed of firm sand, it was considered suitable for a landing, though the beach is completely covered at high water springs. There is just one footpath up from the beach.

Saint's Bay to the west is 300 yards long and is also completely covered at high water springs. Nevertheless, it would be best used for a landing at half tide up to high tide because of a rock in the middle of the approach at high water. There are a number tracks up from the beach and one track which could possibly be used by tanks.

Petit Bot Bay, in almost the middle of the island's south coast, is just 100 yards long. Its firm sand is found between low water and half tide, then stony up to the bay's only exit. The bay is very restricted at high water. As well as obviously infantry, motor transport could exit the beach through the gap in the 15-foot-high sea wall.

There are no other beaches along the south or south-easterly coasts, the next bay which was considered was, therefore, Vazon Bay in approximately the centre of the east coast. The beach here is 1,800 yards long and is composed of sand, shingle, and rock, backed by a seawall 5 to 10 feet high. The approach is good, and infantry could exit the beach more or less anywhere along its length. There were also three ramps which motor vehicles could use.

A little further up the west coast is Cobo Bay. Though 320 yards long, this beach has a very difficult approach narrowed by rocks to just 150 yards and is further hampered by strong cross currents. It was considered suitable for landings at any state of the tide, though at its best at high tide. It is backed by a seawall 5 to 10 feet high. Infantry could exit the beach at most places and motor vehicles could do so via two ramps.

Saline Bay, also known as Grandes Rocques, just north of Cobo Bay on the north-west coast, also suffers from having a difficult approach restricted by rocks to a width of 200 yards and is affected by strong cross currents. The beach itself is 330 yards long and, as with Cobo Bay, was regarded as suitable for landings at all times, but best at high water. It, too, was backed by a 5- to 10-foot seawall, but towards its southern end is backed by a long sandy ridge up which it was thought tracked vehicles might be able to climb. Infantry could exit the beach anywhere and motor transport by two ramps.

Grande Havre beach extends from 900 yards at low tide to 3,000 yards at high water and was practicable for landings all along its length, though rocks in the middle of the bay meant that the approach was best made at half tide to high water. The beach is flat with a few rocks and infantry could exit the beach anywhere and, though not regarded as particularly good for motor transport, it was possible for vehicles to exit at two points.

Finally, the approach to the beach at L'Ancresse Bay, which reaches to the northern tip of the island, is unobstructed, the beach itself stretching from 600 yards long to 900 yards at high water. It allowed for good landings at any state of the tide. It is backed by a long sandy bank which ranges from a few feet in height to 15 feet. The open L'Ancresse Common (part of which is now a golf course) is behind this bank. There were exits everywhere for infantry and at three points for motor transport.

The German Defences and Garrison

With regards to German naval forces, there were E-boats and minesweepers at Cherbourg and St Marlo. These normally escorted coastal convoys. Smaller convoys, escorted by patrol craft, ran almost daily.

The next consideration was the possible extent of the Luftwaffe's potential air effort against the invaders. Working in the worst-case scenario, i.e., that no aircraft had been drawn away by diversionary sorties, it was estimated that the Germans could put into the air:

Long range bombers	200
Reconnaissance bombers	90
Dive bombers and ground attack	30
Single-engine fighters	360
Twin-engine fighters	330
Army Cooperation	–
Coastal	90
Total	<u>1,100</u>

It was estimated that 15 per cent of the single-engine fighters were fitted out as fighter-bombers. This impressive number of aircraft, it must be noted, was considered 'conjectural'.

It was believed that reinforcements of single-engine fighters, as well as the dive bombers and ground attack aircraft based in the north of France, would be sent in some 3 hours after the start of the operation. These would possibly amount to thirty dive bombers and ground attack aircraft, 120 single-engine fighters, and thirty twin-engine fighters, giving a total of 180 aircraft. Such was the detail of the planning appreciation, a table of the scale of the Luftwaffe's likely effort was compiled:

SORTIES	LRB	RB	DB&GA	SEF	TEF	AC	TOTAL
D-Day, first 3 hours	15	5	-	50	5	5	80
D-Day, rest of the day	70	30	45	310	45	20	520
D+1	85	35	55	420	60	25	680

The strength of the German garrison was estimated to number 10,800 troops, not including the Organisation Todt, of which there were thousands of foreign workers and prisoners of war. The troops were believed to be composed as follows:

319 Division	6,000
Coast Defence	1,400
Anti-aircraft	1,600
Tank personnel	400
German Air Force, including Signals	500
German Navy	200
Labour troops	700

It was also said that there was a mixed battalion of tanks, including Mark IV Panzers, based on the island with detachments on Alderney and Jersey.

Guernsey had the largest artillery pieces in the Channel Islands and later figures have shown that by May 1943, the garrison numbered 12,000 troops – approximately one soldier for every two civilians on the island.[3]

In terms of defensive artillery, it was believed there were thirty-two heavy coastal defence guns, nine heavy howitzers, eight field guns, eighty-seven light anti-aircraft guns, seven heavy anti-aircraft guns and twelve dual purpose guns. The Appreciation stated that the majority of the battery positions were protected by barbed wire and encased in concrete, with the heavy howitzers being concentrated in three batteries in the centre of the island from where their fire could be brought to bear on all or any of the beaches.

We now, of course, have more precise information, and Guernsey was indeed powerfully defended. The most important battery was Marine Batterie Mirus, overlooking Rocquaine Bay, the largest in the Channel Islands, with four 30.5 cm former First World War Russian naval guns. These had a potential range of between 32,000 metres and 51,000 metres, depending on the nature of the projectile. The battery was protected by nine 2 cm anti-aircraft guns with 16 machine guns and three 7.5 cm field guns protecting the battery from ground attack.[4]

The other major positions were Batterie Generaloberst Dollmann of four 22 cm guns on the Pleinmont headland and Marine Batterie Strassburg also of four 22 cm guns at Jerbourg Point. In addition, there were nine other army and marine batteries with guns ranging from 22 cm to 15 cm.

The heavy howitzers and field guns were, in fact, 10 cm Czech (Skoda) guns with a range of up to 6 miles of which there were five batteries with four guns in each.

Machine gun posts and pillboxes had also been sited 'in depth' to cover the beaches throughout the island. There were Freya and Würzburg radar stations at three and possibly four locations, two of which were believed to be ship-detecting radar.

The report detailed the following regarding the effective range of the Germans' coastal guns:

> In October 1942, two British destroyers came under fire from the Guernsey batteries. Fire which appeared to come from 6-inch guns continued up to a maximum of about 24,000 yards [13.6 miles], and from 9-inch guns or bigger up to a range of 36,000 yards [20.4 miles]. One battery appeared to range up to 40,000 yards. No illuminate was used. Both ships were straddled with the first salvos and thereafter fire was accurate both for range and line.

A slow-moving invasion flotilla would suffer greatly from these guns and the need to silence them was of paramount importance. Equally, the heavy howitzers would have to be neutralised as far as possible to prevent serious losses on the landing beaches. This might have to involve a preliminary naval bombardment or entail the use of paratroopers to capture these batteries before the main assault. The presence of powerful Panzers on the island necessitated the landing of infantry tanks and/or 6-pounder anti-tank guns early in the assault.

The German garrison could be reinforced both from the air and by sea, but it was felt that by the time the Germans on the Continent had assembled a body of troops large enough to materially affect the Allied landings, they would be too late.

Before considering the timings of the assault landings, reference was made to the civilian population, which was estimated by Mountbatten's men to be around 35,000 (but was in fact closer to 23,000), the report accepting that: 'Owing to the presence of the British population, only limited bombing air attacks on particular objectives have been contemplated.' So that a true estimate of the likely casualties could be made, a request was submitted for an estimate of the number of people living within 1,000 yards of the south coast of the island.[5]

Guernsey is 65 nautical miles from the English south coast and owing to the Germans' powerful coastal defensive armament which, if only limited aerial bombardment was possible, would mean there could be no guarantee these guns would be destroyed, Landing Ships, Infantry (LSI) would have to stop some 15 miles offshore to lower their landing craft. Because of ship detecting radar there was little chance of surprise and so the best chance of limiting casualties was for these ships to stop to unload in darkness.

Landing Craft, Tanks (LCT) travelling from the UK would take 7 or 8 hours to reach Guernsey (their speed was around 8 knots).

Likewise, as the main landings would take place in the north and north-west, where the beaches were more powerfully defended, it was considered essential that the initial landing should take place in darkness and sufficiently early as to enable the troops to capture the high ground inland, mentioned above, before first light.

The timings for the amphibious assault by Commandos delivered by Landing Craft, Infantry (LCI), regardless of the chosen date, were calculated as follows:

Zero Hour -5.5 hours – the landing ships would be 10 miles off the English coast

Zero Hour -2.5 hours – the landing ships would be 15 miles off the Guernsey coast

Zero Hour the troops would land

Zero Hour + 2.5 hours A.M. nautical twilight

The only dates when it would be possible to land the Commandos 2.5 hours before nautical twilight would be possible up to the second half of May and from the second half of July. The shorter nights between those dates would not be long enough for the vessels to move to Guernsey under the cover of darkness.

The other factor for the planners to consider were the tides. We have seen that the tidal races around the island can be very fast, so ideally the assault would have to be planned to avoid spring tides. The first phase of the landings should also be made on a rising tide to prevent the craft grounding. For the paratroopers, at least a half-moon would be necessary for visual identification of drop zones and obstacles.

A forecasted period of 48 hours of good weather needed to be obtained before the operation would be launched. Cloud cover must be no more than 3/10ths to 5/10ths cloud, and the wind speed should not be more than 25 miles per hour on the night of the landings. The sea should be calm with little swell and there should be no fog.

System Of Maintenance

Initially, the maintenance of the invading force was to be through the beaches of Vazon Bay and L'Ancresse Bay which, it was considered, would be adequate for the tonnage envisaged over the course of the first few days. Such a calculation depended entirely on reasonable weather conditions, making the early seizure of St Peter Port and St Samson a priority and an absolute essential requirement by D+5.

The comparatively short distances involved in Guernsey meant that transporting supplies could be carried out by the transport units of the first line troops and so only a small number of Royal Army Service Corps members would be attached to the invasion force.

The projected capacities of the two ports were 500 tons for St Peter Port and 200 tons for St Samson per day on the first day they were back in Allied hands. This rose to 1,000 tons and 400 tons respectively after thirty days, rising to 1,500 and 400 when the new British garrison was fully installed.

In these figures the possibility of some demolition of the ports' facilities had been undertaken by the retreating Germans and of damage inflicted by Allied bombing and shelling was taken into account, but no allowance had been made for interference of the convoys from the UK by German air or coastal craft. Owing to the strong tides around Guernsey, it was assumed that the Germans would not have risked planting sea mines around the ports because of the danger of them breaking free.

Courses Open

A summary of the courses of action available to the Army, Navy and Air Force commanders was given: 'It is considered that an essential part of any course is a preliminary naval and/or air bombardment of selected parts of the island followed by the dropping of a large number of parachute troops to destroy the heavy howitzers in the centre of Guernsey and to capture the main parts of the enemy defences overlooking the beaches. There must also be a number of Commando landings to capture the strong points overlooking the beaches.'

After these objectives had been secured, a number of possible next steps were laid out:

a) A frontal assault on St Peter Port combined with large seaborne landings on the north of the island which would be joined by smaller landings from the east coast.

or

b) The main assault delivered on the north coast with subsidiary landings by infantry only in the south. These would link up for the attack upon St Peter Port.

or

c) Seaborne assaults on the north and north-west coasts, the assaulting forces sweeping south and eastwards to envelope St Peter Port.

or

d) The same as c) but with diversionary landings by infantry alone on the south coast.

The planners stated that while aerial photographs did not show exceptionally heavy defences in the centre of the island, it was thought the majority of the buildings in the vicinity of St Peter Port had been turned into fortified strong points, as had been experienced in the Dieppe raid. Nevertheless, the Combined Operations Headquarters Staff believed that a frontal assault as envisaged in plan a) would have quite a good chance of success, but only if an old battleship was available to ram and breakthrough the boom and lead the assault in.

With regards to b) and c), both had the advantage of preventing the Germans from concentrating their mobile forces to repel one invasion point and would compel them to disperse their troops to counter the attacks from two directions. Of these two alternatives, c) enabled the landing of a more heavily armed force and more armour than b), and it allowed an alternative line of assault in strength if one landing was held up. It also permitted the reinforcement and maintenance of each force through the other's breaches, if necessary, after D-Day.

Course d) was regarded by the planners as being the best of all the courses of action, but they did not believe there would be enough landing craft available to carry it out. The course of action that was advocated, therefore, was c).

Appended to the *Coverlet* study by Combined Ops Headquarters was a document produced by the aforementioned Professor Zuckerman, called 'Appreciation of the effect of one night's bombing, 500 sorties on the Island of Guernsey'. In this paper, Zuckerman examined what he considered were the probable consequences of an attack by 80 Lancasters, 100 Halifaxes, 50 Stirlings and 270 Wellingtons. The combined bomb load he calculated at 3,077,000 lb, which is more than 1,500 tons of bombs. As the whole of Guernsey is only around 25 square miles, if spread evenly across the island it would mean 60 tons of bombs being dropped on each square mile. However, the aiming point for this study (as opposed to the actual *Coverlet* plan) was on the eastern side of Guernsey, meaning most of the bombs would be dropped there, with the aim of demolishing the German defences on the part of the island. In this area Zuckerman said the 'bombing intensity will not drop below 300 tons per square mile'. This is the most densely populated region of Guernsey. It may be recalled that the German attack of 28 June 1940 had caused considerable damage and resulted in almost 150 casualties on Guernsey and Jersey with a total of just 12 tons. What was being proposed was a bombardment more than 100 times greater.

Chapter 12

Coverlet – The Plan of Attack on Guernsey

The Joint Outline Plan for the attack upon Guernsey was to take place in six phases:[1]

(a) Phase I. Night of D-1/D-Day
An aerial bombardment of the north coast of the island would open the operation, followed by parachute and Commando landings at approximately 3 hours before first light. The neutralisation of the heavy howitzer batteries in the centre of the island would be a priority target by air and parachute attack. Further Commando landings, supported by paratroops, would take place in the north-west of the island.

(b) Phase II. Night of D-1/D-Day
The landing of infantry, field artillery, and light anti-aircraft guns would take place in the north of Guernsey at about 2 hours before first light to form a bridgehead. Also, the landing of infantry, field artillery, and light anti-aircraft guns would happen in the north-west of the island.

(c) Phase III. D-Day
Tanks and more artillery would be landed in the north and north-west bridgeheads commencing at first light. The two bridgeheads would push out southwards and eastwards to link up by means of the western coast road. All these operations were to receive close aerial support from fighters and tactical reconnaissance, as well as diversionary raids on the Cotentin and Brest peninsulas.

(d) Phase IV. Night of D-Day/D+1 and D+1
There would be further landings of infantry in the north and north-west and the bridgeheads would be widened and lengthened. Air support would be provided as per Phase III.

(e) Phase V. Night of D+1/D+2 and D+2
During the night the troops would prepare for the assault upon St Peter Port, which would commence at first light on D+2 and would be delivered from the north-west, west and south-west.

(f) Phase VI. D+3 and D+4.
Reduction of the south and west of the island.

Coastal reconnaissance patrols were to be flown at dusk of D-1/D-Day, and anti-surface vessel patrols on the nights of D-1/D-Day and D-Day/D+1. These reconnaissance patrols would possibly include Coastal Command strike aircraft.

Outline Military Plan

During the hours of darkness of D-1/D-Day, a force of 500 heavy and medium bombers would attack the northern end of the island with the object of destroying the defences in the vicinity of Grand Havre Bay and L'Ancresse Bay. No bombs would be intentionally dropped south of a line from the southern end of Baie des Pêqueries in the west to St Sampson Harbour in the east. At the same time as the bombing attack in the north, 'Intruder Aircraft' (most likely meaning Bristol Beaufighters and de Havilland Mosquitos) would attack the heavy howitzer batteries and anti-aircraft batteries in the centre of the island.

After the air attack, the operation would take place in the six phases outlined above.

Phase I

At about 3 hours before civil twilight on D-Day the airborne and seaborne assaults were to be launched as follows:

Northern sector
At the conclusion of the aerial bombardment, one battalion of paratroopers would be dropped on L'Ancresse Common to complete the destruction of the beach defences in the L'Ancresse/Grand Havre areas.

Simultaneously with the dropping of the parachute battalion, two Commandos were to effect landings in the west of Grand Havre Bay and

Creve Coeur respectively to complete the destruction of the batteries at Pulias, on the Chouet headland, and at La Varde on L'Ancresse Common.

North-western sector

At the conclusion of the Intruder attacks on the heavy howitzer batteries in the centre of the island, one parachute battalion was to be dropped as near as possible to the batteries with the object of completing their destruction, or at least neutralising them.

At the same time, a second parachute battalion was to be dropped immediately east of Vazon Bay to secure the beach. A third battalion was to be dropped south of King Mills to secure the high ground overlooking Vazon Bay from the south and to destroy Batterie Scharnhorst (4x15 cm guns) near Les Lohiers, and a fourth parachute battalion was to be dropped to the north-west of Sous L'Eglise to destroy the Batterie Mirus and join the third battalion in securing the high ground overlooking Vazon Bay.

One Commando was also to effect a scramble landing at Fort Richmond or Vazon Bay and destroy the defences flanking the south of Vazon Bay, while another Commando was to land in Cobo Bay and attack the defences flanking Vazon Bay on the northern side.

Yet another Commando was to land in either Port Soif or Port Infer and destroy the defences flanking the north of Saline Bay.

Phase II

At about 2 hours before civil twilight on D-Day the main assault would be launched as follows, on beaches already secured by the paratroopers and the commandos:

Northern sector

One infantry brigade, one field battery, two light anti-aircraft batteries, and one platoon of a field company, Royal Engineers, would land in L'Ancresse Bay; and one infantry battalion would land in Grand Havre Bay. These forces, joined by the two commandos and the parachute battalion landed in Phase I, would form a bridgehead to include Baie des Pêqueries, L'Islet, Solidor and Miellette Bay, by civil twilight.

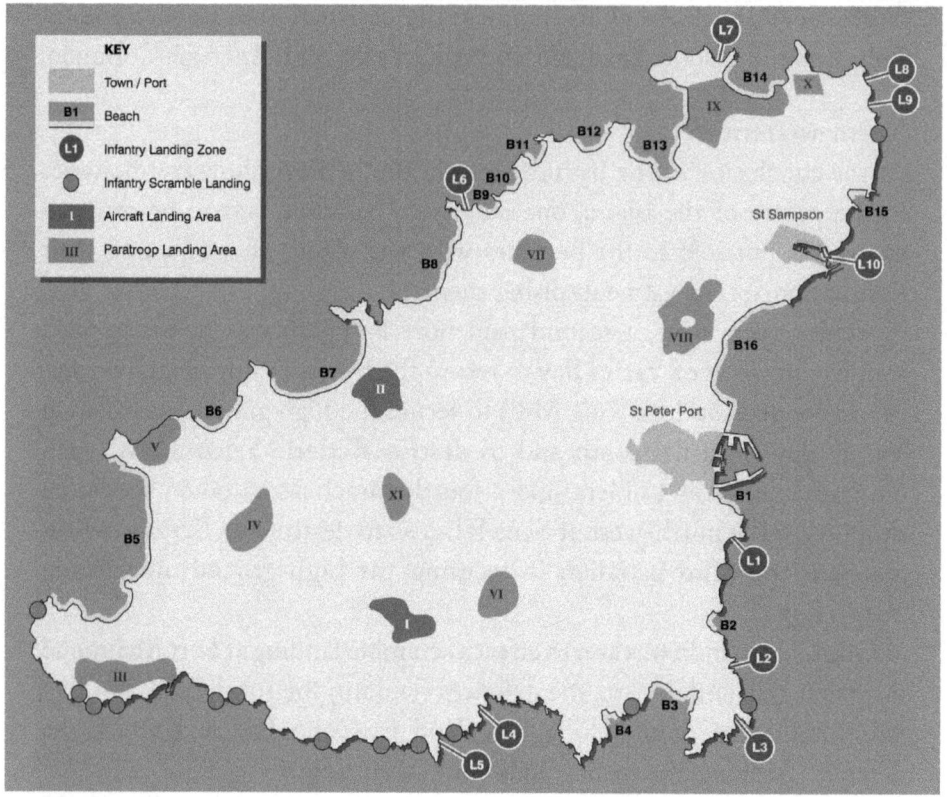

A German map showing the overlapping arcs of fire of the principal guns on the Channel Islands.

North-western sector

One infantry brigade, one field battery, one light anti-aircraft battery, and one field company, Royal Engineers less two sections were to land in Vazon Bay. This force, joined by the two commandos landed in Phase I, would form a bridgehead to include Fort Richmond, Mont Saint, Les Lohiers, King's Mills, Albecq, and the high ground secured by the parachute battalions in Phase I.

One infantry battalion, one light anti-aircraft battery, and two sections of the above field company, Royal Engineers, would land in Saline Bay and join the forces with the commandos landed in Phase I in Port Soif who, by then, would have secured the Grand Rocque Peninsula.

It was also stated that, if possible, a battery of 25-pounders would be landed on the Island of Herm to give artillery support to both the northern and north-western assaults and to support subsequent operations. (A Commando raid, Operation *Huckaback*, was undertaken in February 1943 to assess the practicalities of landing artillery on Herm.)². Its primary task would be to neutralise the heavy howitzer batteries in the centre of the island, though how this would tie in with the paratroopers who were also supposed to be neutralising the batteries was not explained.

Cruisers and destroyers would also be on standby off the coast to provide supporting gunfire if called upon, with Forward Observation Officers being landed to direct their fire.

Phase III

Commencing at civil twilight on D-Day, tanks and supporting artillery would be landed in both sectors:

Northern sector

One tank battalion (fifty-two tanks), one battery of a Royal Artillery field regiment (eight guns), on light anti-aircraft battery, and one field company less one platoon of the Royal Engineers, would land in L'Ancresse Bay. During the day the northern bridgehead would be extended to reach a line running from Pleinheaume in the west, through Saltpans, to St Sampson Harbour in the east.

North-western sector

Two squadrons of tanks (thirty-six tanks) and one battery of a Royal Artillery field regiment would land in Vazon Bay. During the day the north-western bridgehead would be extended to reach a line from Les Effards across to Le Villocq.

During the day the three bridgeheads would be joined so that by the evening of D-Day any forces scheduled to land in either L'Ancresse Bay or Vazon Bay would be able to use whichever was the most suitable both for ease of access and exit and was receiving the least opposition from the enemy. From whichever bay they landed, those forces would move through the secured bridgeheads to their pre-determined positions.

Phase IV

During the night of D-Day/D+1, forces within the bridgehead would be reorganised, plus a further two infantry battalions and one field battery would be landed in both L'Ancresse Bay and Vazon Bay. An additional light anti-aircraft battery would also be landed at Vazon Bay. During daylight on D+1 the bridgehead would be extended to run from Perelle in the west, through Guernsey airport to Richmond Corner on the east coast.

Phase V

During the night of D+1/D+2, the forces would re-organise within the bridgehead and the tanks would be moved forward in preparation for the assault on St Peter Port. At twilight on D+2, the assault on St Peter Port would begin with attacks from Haviland Hall in the south-west, Rohais Manor in the west and Les Cartiers in the north. The operation would be supported by artillery fire directed from the high ground to the south-west of the town.

Phase VI

Commencing on D+3, operations would be carried out against the southern and south-eastern areas of Guernsey. Just how these developed would be determined by the positions taken up by the Germans at this stage of the battle. But, by then, two-thirds of the island would have been recaptured, and it was estimated that the whole island would have been retaken by D+4.

If, continued the planners, there had been insufficient time between the assault on Alderney and that on Guernsey for all operations to have ended on the former, a floating reserve of one infantry brigade group (i.e., a self-sufficient unit with its own artillery and engineers) would be held in Alderney and ferried across to Guernsey in the landing craft used for the follow up forces. If this was to be impracticable due to continuing resistance on Alderney, this reserve brigade group would be kept back in the UK and transported from there directly to Guernsey.

Coverlet – The Plan of Attack on Guernsey

Military Forces Required

Northern sector

	Personnel	*Vehicles*
Assault and follow-up forces		
Force Headquarters	30	6
Tactical Reconnaissance Detachment	4	1
Army Air Support Control 'Tentacle'	3	1
Divisional Signals	250	30
Two Commandos	900	–
Detachment Brigade Signals	20	2
Two infantry brigades	4,363	400
Field company, Royal Engineers	201	14
Tank Battalion	450	75
Field Park Company, Royal Engineers (less bridging section)	100	32
Field Regiment, Royal Artillery	513	121
Light Anti-aircraft Regiment	790	183
Pioneer Company, Royal Engineer (less three sections)	198	1
HQ Company, Royal Army Service Corps	30	6
Brigade Company, Royal Army Service Corps (less one platoon)	254	76
Field Ambulance, Royal Army Medical Corps	245	40
One section, Provost company	16	1
Beach Organisation Units		
2 Beach Signals Sections	160	6
HQ Admin and three beach groups	337	3
Beach Dressing Station, Royal Army Medical Corps	120	12
Pioneer Labour	90	1
Beach Reconnaissance Section	65	8
Royal Navy Beach Party	77	–
Detachment Mechanical Engineers Company (1/2 Section)	31	17
Beach Commander and Staff	20	2

	Personnel	Vehicles
General Transport Platoon, Royal Army Service Corps	61	34
Airborne troops	500	
Total	9,954	1,073

North-western sector

	Personnel	Vehicles
Assault and follow-up forces		
Divisional Headquarters	30	6
Tactical Reconnaissance Detachment	4	1
Army Air Support Control 'Tentacle'	3	1
Detachment Airborne Divisional Signals	40	6
Three Commandos	1,350	–
Detachment Brigade Signals	80	6
Two infantry brigades	4,363	400
Field company, Royal Engineers	201	14
Two squadrons of tanks	280	40
Field Park Company, Royal Engineers (less bridging section)	100	32
Field Regiment, Royal Artillery	513	121
Light Anti-aircraft Regiment	790	183
Pioneer Company, Royal Engineer (less three sections)	198	1
HQ Company, Royal Army Service Corps	30	6
Brigade Company, Royal Army Service Corps (less one platoon)	254	76
Field Ambulance, Royal Army Medical Corps	245	40
One section, Provost company	16	1
Beach Organisation Units		
2 Beach Signals Sections	160	6
HQ Admin and three beach groups	337	3
Beach Dressing Station, Royal Army Medical Corps	120	12
Pioneer Labour	90	1

Beach Reconnaissance Section	65	8
Royal Navy Beach Party	77	–
Detachment Mechanical Engineers Company (1/2 Section)	31	17
Beach Commander and Staff	20	2
General Transport Platoon, Royal Army Service Corps	61	34

Airborne troops

One parachute brigade and Signals Section	1640	
One parachute battalion	500	
Total	11,874	1,048
Total both sectors	21,828	2,121

OUTLINE AIR PLAN

Air Forces Required

1. Bombers
   500 heavy and medium bombers
   16 squadrons USAAF.
   4 squadrons of light bombers for smoke and close support
   290 British parachute aircraft or 145 USAAF aircraft

2. Coastal Forces
   1 squadron of strike aircraft – torpedo-bomber
   1 squadron anti-surface vessel aircraft

3. Fighters
   30 squadrons of single-engine fighters
   6 squadrons of single-engine and twin-engine fighters for close support
   4 squadrons of night fighters-intruders

4. Tactical Reconnaissance
   4 squadrons

5. Intercommunications
   1 Army Air Corps squadron

Sequence of Air Operations

D-1 to D-Day

Coastal reconnaissance of the French coast from Dieppe to Brest on the afternoon of D-1 to locate enemy surface vessels. Similar reconnaissance to also take place ahead and to the east and west of the invasion flotilla.

A concentrated bombing attack by a force of 500 heavy and medium bombers on the L'Ancresse/Grand Havre area to destroy the coastal defence anti-aircraft artillery and the coastal defences. The aiming point for the whole force was to be near Les Mielles by the southern edge of L'Ancresse Common. This point would be illuminated by Pathfinder aircraft. The bomb line, or limit beyond which bombs were not supposed to fall, was drawn from Baie des Pêqueries on the west coast to Port Samson on the east. The devastation in this area would be immense. This attack was not to end more than 15 minutes before the start of the parachute landings so that the Germans would not have time to recover and regroup after the bombing before the paratroopers were on the ground. At the same time as the bombers were hitting the north of the island, the Intruder aircraft were to attack the heavy howitzer batteries and their supporting anti-aircraft batteries in the centre of the island.

About 3 hours before nautical twilight parachute landings would begin. One battalion would land as near as possible to the heavy howitzer batteries in the Les Effards area. Another battalion would land immediately east of Vazon Bay, another south of King's Mills, a fourth would drop northwest of Sous L'Eglise, and the fifth battalion would land on L'Ancresse Common.

Fighter cover would be provided for the convoys leaving the English coast before dark on D-1 and Intruder aircraft would raid German airfields in the Cherbourg and Normandy areas which would include the dropping of delayed action bombs and 'crowsfoot spikes'. The latter, more correctly known as caltrops, are area denial weapons made up of two or more sharp metal spikes arranged in such a manner that one of them always points upwards, hindering the movement of vehicles and personnel until removed.

D-Day

Fighter cover over Guernsey and the naval vessels – both approaching the island and returning to England and/or Alderney – to start at dawn and continue all day as far as aircraft resources permitted. Tactical reconnaissance over the island would be undertaken as requested by the Military Commander.

Bombing attacks, escorted by fighters, would be undertaken against the German airfields in the Cherbourg and Normandy areas. Raids would also be conducted against targets in north-west France and the Low Countries to contain enemy fighters.

Smoke aircraft would deploy a screen over the high ground overlooking Vazon Bay from the south at approximately 30 minutes after nautical twilight.

Night of D-Day to D+1
Anti-surface reconnaissance patrols would be conducted ahead and to the east and west of the naval forces.

D+1 Day
Commencing at dawn and continuing throughout the day fighter cover would be provided over the island and the naval forces. Tactical reconnaissance would again be provided for the Military Commander as requested and close support aircraft would be available on call. Bombing attacks would recommence against German airfields as on D-Day.

D+2 and subsequent days as required
Fighter protection would be provided over Guernsey and the naval forces from dawn until dusk. Tactical reconnaissance would be given as requested by the Military Commander. Close support aircraft would be on call and bombing raids against German airfields would continue.

Outline Naval Plan

Intention
Phase I: To land Commandos at approximately 2.5 hours before nautical twilight at Grand Havre Bay, Creve Coeur, Fort Richmond, or Vazon Bay, Cobo Bay, Port Soif or Port Infer.

Phase II: To land the assault forces about half an hour after the Commandos had been landed at L'Ancresse Bay, Grand Havre Bay, Saline Bay, and

Vazon Bay. During this phase both anti-aircraft and field artillery and detachments of Royal Engineers were to be landed at L'Ancresse Bay, Saline Bay, and Vazon Bay. All of these were to be on the ground by civil twilight.

Phase III: To land armour and more supporting artillery at L'Ancresse Bay and Vazon Bay at twilight on D-Day.

Phase IV: To land additional forces at L'Ancresse Bay and Vazon Bay on the night of D-Day/D+1.

Execution

The main convoy would sail from England to arrive at a position almost due north of Fort Hommet, to the north of Vazon Bay, about 5 hours before nautical twilight. In this convoy would be the Commandos for Phase I and the assault forces for Phase II, and would consist of five Landing Ships, Infantry (Small); and two Landing Ships, Infantry (hand-hoisting), along with numbers of small and large landing craft.

The Landing Craft, Assault, carrying the Commandos would be lowered and would sail for Guernsey to land at about 2.5 hours before nautical twilight. A convoy of Landing Craft, Personnel would be sailed empty from the UK which would go alongside the Landing Ships, Infantry (hand-hoisting) as soon as they had stopped and lowered their Landing Craft, Assault, and would take on troops from the ships.

The first flights of the main assault forces were to be landed on the above-mentioned beaches about half an hour after the Commandos. The remaining flights, or waves, of the assault forces on the four names beaches on small and large landing craft which would have either taken the troops off the Landing Ships or have sailed directly from England.

If the floating reserve was not able to be held in Alderney, landing craft would have to return to England under their own power to pick up the reserve. If the reserve was in Alderney, the landing craft would return to Alderney where they would remain on call.

Approximately thirty-six Landing Craft, Tank, loaded with anti-aircraft and field artillery, and infantry carriers, were to be sailed from England to land their vehicles on L'Ancresse Bay, Saline Bay, and Vazon

Bay at approximately 1.5 hours before nautical twilight. Because of the narrowness of the beaches this part of the operation would have to be undertaken in two waves.

Six Landing Ships (Tank) and twelve Landing Craft (Tank) loaded with tanks, more artillery and more carriers were to be sailed from England so as to be ready to land their vehicles on L'Ancresse Bay, Saline Bay, and Vazon Bay at civil twilight.

There was to be no preliminary naval bombardment before the landings, but once the assault had begun the Army would be able to call on the Navy for harassing or neutralising fire support. A monitor, two cruisers and eight Hunt Class destroyers would be earmarked for this.

Just how formidable the German defences were may not have been fully appreciated by the Combined Ops planners. Some indication of this was revealed in General von Schmettow's post-war interview:

> The geological structure of the islands, which are known to consist of solid rocks reaching 140 meters undersea level, made it possible to build cave-like underground systems on a large scale almost everywhere on the islands.
>
> Thus, especially in the interior parts of the islands, very strong, reinforced underground installations, which were distributed according to tactical viewpoints, could be built for housing or assembling reserves. They offered very strong protection from ship based artillery fire and aerial bombs.
>
> They were frequently lying under 20-30 meters of natural rocks, situated in deep valleys they could not be recognised from the air.
>
> The entrances were prepared for defence.
>
> The spoil obtained by mining made it possible to transport less construction material by sea, needed on very large quantities for fortress construction, road building (approach roads).
>
> Most of the caves were built with a large profile, they had mostly 2–3 entrances permitting close columns eg for ammunition supply, to enter and leave.
>
> Their inside was improved with concrete, light, water pipes and ventilators were laid as well as drainage systems, wherever necessary,

so that dry housing and storing of ammunition and supplies was possible.

The value of underground installations was first recognised on Jersey, there they were began first and perfected to the greatest extent.[3]

This last point is emphasised by considering that 44,000 cubic metres of rock had been extracted collectively from Guernsey, Jersey, and Alderney, while from the rest of the Atlantic Wall from Norway to the Franco-Spanish border just 225,000 cubic metres had been extracted.

Another comparison might also be drawn from the events of D-Day on 6 June 1944. Of the five invasion beaches, the one which proved the most difficult for the Allies forces was Omaha, where casualties have been estimated at more than 6,000 on that beach alone. Yet the 7,800 Germans there possessed comparatively few of the types of heavy weaponry available to the 12,000 defenders of Guernsey.

On Omaha there were four artillery pieces, six heavy mortars, eighteen anti-tank guns, forty-five rocket-launcher sites, eighty-five machine-gun sites, and six tank turrets. This pales into insignificance when compared with the forty-five artillery pieces of between 30.5 cm and 10.5 cm calibre, twenty 10 cm mortars, twenty-nine flak guns, plus sixty-one resistance nests and strongpoints, each of which included several machine-guns, tank turrets, as well as, usually, a casemated anti-tank gun, on Guernsey.

When one also considers that 1,000 British bombers dropped five tons of bombs on the Normandy invasion beaches on 5 June on relatively weakly constructed defences, the effect the 500 bombers would have had against the immense fortifications of Guernsey would have been minimal. The only conclusion that can be drawn is that *Coverlet*, as well as the whole *Constellation* enterprise, would have resulted in a very costly defeat. The destruction of civilian property and loss life the islanders would have suffered would have all been in vain.

Chapter 13

Operation Condor: The Re-Occupation of Jersey

The plans for the retaking of Jersey were extremely detailed and they began as with *Coverlet* and *Concertina*, with an 'Appreciation' of the practicalities involved in the re-taking of the island, which was conducted early in 1943.[1] This report began with an explanation of how the Channel Islands were occupied by the Germans and was followed by an account of the history of the enemy units garrisoning the island. The proposed assault upon Jersey was presumed to have taken place after the capture of Alderney and Guernsey. The aim was to capture Jersey in July 1943.

Jersey lies 100 miles from the nearest port on the English south coast and is the largest and most southerly of the Channel Islands group. It is 15 miles from Guernsey, 30 from Alderney and 12 miles from the nearest point on the French coast. The island has an area of 45 square miles, being 10 miles long and 6.5 miles at its widest.

The nature of the terrain the assaulting troops would encounter was extremely important in the planning of the attack and so was spelt out in the Appreciation. The island, the report stated, consists of a low plateau with a gentle slope towards the north, where heights up to 500 feet are reached, to sea level along the south coast.

The north coast is very broken and presents a series of steep headlands alternating with bays and ravines. The east coast is similar but not so rugged and gives way to low sandy marshland in the south.

The south coast is low-lying, but there is high ground inland of St Aubin's Bay. To the west of this bay on the south coast this high ground reaches down to the sea forming bays and headlands as on the north coast.

The west coastal region consists of low undulating sand dunes, Les Blanches Banques in St Ouen's Bay, which today is a preserved site of special interest. In the 1940s they stretched for about a mile inland and were bound on the north and east by steeply rising ground. The whole coast of Jersey is surrounded with dangerous rocks, few of which are visible above the surface at high tide.

Almost all the island was considered to be heavily cultivated in small fields, with St Helier the only town of any size. There were wooded valleys which ran mainly north to south, as did the main roads except for the two main lateral roads which ran east to west parallel to the north and south coasts.

The Appraisal stated that there were no railways on the island, the Jersey Railways and Tramways Co. Ltd. having ran its last train in 1936, with the rails, locomotives and rolling stock having been sold for scrap. However, the Germans re-opened almost the entire St Helier to La Corbière line to carry construction materials for the building of the bunkers and other fortifications.

As the Appraisal assumed Guernsey, which was only 2.5 hours sailing distance away, would be in Allied hands, it would make an ideal launching pad for the attack upon Jersey. However, it was considered that the difficulty in building up a large convoy due to the limited fighter cover that could be provided, meant that the size of any assaulting force would be restricted. This was because of the long distance from UK airfields which meant that RAF fighters would only have a short period of flying time over the convoy before having to return to England to refuel.

It was considered that there were a few areas suitable for the parachute troops to land, though the general landscape of small, intensively cultivated fields were not idea for parachute drops.

Harbours and Airfields

The main harbour of the island is St Helier, the approach to which is bounded to the west by rocks and the stretch of sand flats on which stands Elizabeth Castle and the Hermitage breakwater, and to the east by rocks and reefs which extend south-south-west of La Collette headland on the La Moye Peninsula. Other small harbours, consisting of just one jetty, were to be found at St Aubin, Gorey, and Ronez Point.

Ships of up to 2,000 tons used St Helier before the war and could berth against Albert Pier for a dredged distance of 1,400 feet; North Pier for a dredged distance of 500 feet; and Victoria Pier for a dredged distance of 450 feet. These three were all served with electronic cranes. The other lengths of these piers dried at low water, as did the berths at three other piers, Old South Pier, Old Quay, and Merchant Wharf. These facilities were regarded as being sufficient to be able support the assaulting forces and maintain a strong garrison after the recapture of the island.

There was one permanent airfield on Jersey, now the site of Jersey airport. It had, at the time, 1,000 yards by 600 yards usable surface, with an estimated capacity of eighteen fighters. It was stated that there was space for the runway to be extended to the north-east to provide a run of 1,200 yards. While the airfield was initially used by the Germans, the 1943 verdict was that this was no longer the case.

There were also six other places considered potentially suitable as aircraft landing grounds. These were Val de la Mare, Ville au Bas, St Peter's Mill, La Falaise and Petit Mourier.

In addition to these landing grounds, aircraft were operated from the beaches of Grouville Bay on the east coast, St Aubin on the south coast, and St Ouen's Bay on the west coast in peacetime. At the time the report was compiled these beaches were without obstructions and it was suggested that troop-carrying aircraft and gliders could use them.

Invasion Points

As with *Coverlet* and *Concertina*, the Appreciation then looked at which places would be suitable for the landing of the amphibious assault troops and supporting vehicles.

The north coast, as we have seen, is mainly rocky with precipitous cliffs, but there are a number of bays and inlets where troops could land. The first of these, looking from west to east, is Grève au Lançon. Except for one 14-foot-high rock at the western edge of the beach, the approach is clear. Being northerly facing, this little bay – 700 yards wide – is exposed to northerly winds which can produce a dangerous surf. Inland from the beach are steep cliffs, 250 feet high. There was just one flight of steps which could be used by infantry, but no vehicles could leave the beach. This is still the case today.

The beach at Petit Plemont is just 180 yards wide. Again, there are precipitous cliffs beyond the beach and a single track suitable only for infantry is the only exit. Infantry landings here, it was considered, would be of 'the nature of scramble landings'.

There is dangerous shallow water and rocks lying off Greve de Lecq. The beach here is 360 yards long, but almost half of this is 'masked' by rocky ledges. There was, and still is, a vertical seawall which was some 6-8 feet high, apart from the central section which was only 3 feet high. Infantry could easily advance inland from here, and a slipway provided, and still provides, a roadway up from the beach.

Devil's Hole and Mourier Valley at Crabbe were suitable only for infantry to scale the steep cliffs. At Ronez Point, also at Crabbe, where a quarry for building materials existed and still exists, was a small harbour with a jetty on which was a crane allowing for light motor transport to be unloaded here.

A 300-foot-long and 27-feet-wide pier created a small harbour at Bonne Nuit Bay, backed by an 8-feet-high sea wall. There is also a beach here, 180 yards long, but this could not be used for landings at low water. Both the harbour and the beach were regarded as difficult to use at any state of tide and there was no access from the beach for vehicles, though today this is a popular spot, and a slipway runs up from the beach.

Further east is Giffard Bay. Due to large and dangerous boulders on the approach to the beach, behind which are steep cliffs, this was considered unusable even by infantry.

The approach to Bouley Bay was clear of obstructions and consists of a small harbour and a 320-yards-long beach. Due to steep cliffs that surround the bay, troops and motor vehicles could exit the beach on a single, narrow road, as is the case today.

The next inlet to the east is Rozel Bay, where a 240-foot-long pier forms a harbour which dries completely at low tide, is easily usable at high water. There is a curving beach, 400 yards long, backed by a seawall and sloping cliffs which rise from 15 feet by the jetty to 304 feet by the little village. It was said that infantry could scramble ashore to the north-west of the jetty where the ground is lower and that motor vehicles could exit the beach via a slipway up the single road which leads inland.

Along the east coast of Jersey, four points were identified as worthy of consideration. The first of these, from north to south, was Fliquet Bay. The approaches to the 100-foot-long beach are clear. It is sheltered from the east and is backed by steep cliffs cut by a sunken road. Infantry could land here and make their way up the road which leads all the way down to the beach, but there are many rocks present which would make this an uncomfortable one for motor transport to use.

St Catherine's Bay presents a slightly different picture, with two exits on slipways from the 2-mile-long beach which could be used by vehicles, including armour. The bay is sheltered by a well-built breakwater, though this had not been used by ships. There were many points where infantry could land and exit the beach.

Petit Portelet to the south was only deemed suitable for infantry scramble landings.

The Royal Bay of Grouville is 2.25 miles long and reaches down to the southern end of the eastern coast. Though there are some off-lying dangers on the approach to the beach, particularly at the southern end, this is a good beach with few obstacles and a low seawall to impede attackers and with easy exits for all types of motor and armoured vehicles.

The conclusion drawn was that the island's beaches were not particularly suitable for amphibious landings and, except for the Royal Bay of Grouville, it was only up narrow ramps or slipways that motor vehicles and AFVs could leave the beaches. The west coast is exposed to the prevailing wind and has only poor exits from its beaches, though it does have the longest beach. The north coast is very precipitous, making only infantry landings possible. The eastern end of the south coast is almost impossible to approach on account of offshore hazards and the western end of the south coast is also precipitous. The centre of the south coast, where the main harbour is situated, has a good beach backed by a continuous seawall and was certain to be strongly defended

The main assault, involving motor transport and tanks, certainly in the initial stages, would have to be delivered on the sheltered east coast. In reality this meant Grouville, which was the only place suitable for landings on the scale necessary to establish a firm foothold. Even in this case, this would only be practicable for Landing Craft, Tanks an hour either side of high tide because of the steep gradient from the beach. The bay along the seawall would obviously also be heavily defended.

The German Defences and Garrison

It was known that there were some 8,300 enemy troops on the island, not counting the workers of Organisation Todt, which was composed of foreign i.e., non-German workers, and prisoners of war. Those troops consisted of:

319 Division	4,000
Coast Defence	1,200
Anti-Aircraft	1,600
Tank personnel	150
German Air Force (including signals)	550
German Navy	200

It was understood that there was a detachment of tanks on the island. The majority of these were known to be light French tanks with the remainder likely to be medium Pz.KW.4, in other words the Panzer IV.

The German naval forces disposed in the Channel ports were very light and would not pose a problem to a well-guarded invasion flotilla. There was a chance, however, that submarines based in the Biscay ports or diverted from operations in the Atlantic could be sent into the Channel to attack the follow-up or replenishment convoys. The naval forces supporting the landing would be exposed and vulnerable to air attack from enemy aircraft based on the French mainland. Heavy warships could only be risked if adequate air cover was guaranteed.

With regards to the latter, a list of the airfields and their respective capacities was given as follows:

RAF Bold Head, Salcombe (95 miles from Jersey) 2 squadrons from No. 10 Group

RAF Exeter (110 miles from Jersey) 4 squadrons from No. 10 Group

RAF Hurn, Dorset (105 miles from Jersey) 4 squadrons from Army Cooperation Command

RAF Ibsley, Hampshire (112 miles from Jersey) 3 squadrons from No. 10 Group

RAF Warmwell, Dorset (95 miles from Jersey) 2 or 3 squadrons from No. 10 Group

The Appraisal stated that, given the above statistics, it would be impossible to keep more than one Wing, i.e., three squadrons, in the air to cover the attack convoy and this Wing would be under a grave disadvantage fighting so close to the Cherbourg Peninsula, where an important Luftwaffe Fighter Directing Station was located.

The potential scale of the German Luftwaffe attack on the convoy would possibly include the greater part of its long-range and reconnaissance bombers based in France and the Low Countries, together with the single-engine fighters and coastal aircraft based in the west of France. The enemy forces immediately available within striking range at the start of operations were estimated as follows:

Long range bombers	140
Reconnaissance bombers	60
Dive bombers and ground attack	30
Single-engine fighters	90
Twin-engine fighters	30
Army Cooperation	–
Coastal	40
Total	360 aircraft

As with the *Coverlet* Appreciation, it was believed that reinforcements of single-engine fighters, as well as the dive bombers and ground attack aircraft based in the north of France would be sent in some 3 hours after the start of the operation. These figures were the same as those estimated for *Coverlet* and were estimated as thirty dive bombers and ground attack aircraft, 120 single-engine fighters, and thirty twin-engine fighters, giving a total of 180 aircraft. Again, as with *Coverlet*, a table of the estimated scale of the Luftwaffe's effort was compiled:

SORTIES	LRB	RB	DB&GA	SEF	TEF	AC	TOTAL
D-Day, first 3 hours	15	5	–	50	5	5	80
D-Day, rest of the day	70	30	45	310	45	20	520
D+1	85	35	55	420	60	25	680

Against such opposition one Wing of RAF fighters would be unable to provide any serious protection to naval or land forces taking part in the assault.

If an invasion of Jersey was to become a practical reality, very large numbers of aircraft would have to be drawn from No. 11 Group and Bomber Command to carry out diversionary sweeps large enough, and important enough, to demobilise the enemy fighters from northern France and the Low Countries, attacking them at their own bases thus preventing from interfering with *Condor*. If, as expected, Alderney and Guernsey were already in Allied hands then these islands could be used as advanced airfields which would greatly increase Fighter Command's ability to provide aerial protection, not by making any more aircraft available, but by a decrease in the turn-round time of the aircraft and increase the extended time they would have over the battle area.

Over the centuries, a considerable number of forts and towers had been built around Jersey's coastline. To these the Germans added two batteries and large numbers of casemates, loopholed turrets, and resistance nests.

Batterie Moltke, on a headland to the north of St Ouen's Bay, housed four captured French 15.5 cm cannon (Canon de 155 Grande Puissance Filloux (GPF) modèle 1917). These could fire at a rate of two rounds a minute to a maximum range of 21,325 yards, or a little over 12 miles. They could do enormous damage to an attacking flotilla and were housed in open emplacements and could be rotated in any direction.

The battery was protected from infantry attack by a number of Tobruk rings, or *Ringstände*, also with 360-degree fields of fire, on which were mounted either machine guns or a turret from an otherwise obsolete Renault FT French tank.

Batterie Lothringen, near Portelet, is on the Noirmont Point headland which forms the western headland of St Aubin's Bay. Its main armament was four 15 cm SK L/45 German naval guns. These had a range of 20,000 yards, or 11.3 miles. The battery was defended by a personnel bunker.

There were also a large number of tunnels at points around the island, of which seven were fortified defensive posts. Of these there were two at St Ouen (a casemate complex at L'Etacq, and a personnel bunker at Mont Matthieu); two at St Brede (Batterie Derfflinger at Le Mont de la Rocque, and Batterie Seydlitz at Le Mont du Coin); and two at Grouville which were Batterie Schliefen at Verclut and another casemate complex at Verclut Point; and a *stützpunkt*, or strongpoint, at La Corbiere.

In terms of weaponry, the German garrison had at least sixty-four light and eight heavy anti-aircraft guns plus twenty-two coastal defence anti-aircraft guns. There were also forty light, medium and heavy coastal defence pieces plus four field guns. There were eight searchlight positions.

The majority of the battery positions were surrounded by barbed wired and were within concrete emplacements. Machine gun posts and pillboxes had been sited to cover most of the likely landing beaches. The south and west coasts were the most strongly defended, while the north coast is the least well protected. Owing to the small size of Jersey, the coast defence guns situated anywhere on the island could probably bring their fire to bear on most of the western, eastern, and southern approaches. It was also thought probable that the houses along the front of St Aubin's Bay and St Helier had been fortified and garrisoned, though there was no direct intelligence to confirm this.

Reports had also been received indicating that all the beaches had been mined, with particular emphasis on St Ouen's Bay. The presumption had to be made that every potential landing place had been mined, not necessarily on the beaches themselves, but on the exits from the beaches and the ground immediately inland. Strongpoints found on the coast and inland were also likely to be surrounded by minefields.

Having considered the island's defences, the Appraisal then drew a further conclusion:

a) Infantry landings can be made on the north coast where the defences are weakest, but the east and west coasts of the island, being less well defended than the south, are probably the best for the main assaults. Obstacles on the west coast, however, limit the assault to mainly infantry.
b) The presence of enemy armour on the island will necessitate the landing of tanks and/or 6-pounder anti-tank guns early in the assault.
c) Unless heavy casualties to landing craft are to be accepted, the coast defence batteries which bear directly on the approaches selected for landing must be destroyed or neutralised as early as possible.

Because of the numerous obstacles on the approaches to the Jersey coastline, the employment of pilots at night with local knowledge was regarded as being imperative for any operations against the island. The large number of landing craft that would be required in the assault would mean the troops would have to be landed in waves and the navigational difficulties and strong tides and currents might affect some waves more than others.

For the purposes of planning the operation it was assumed the invasion would take place in July. But it was pointed out that should the attack take place in August or September, the longer nights would give added cover for any convoy with the assaulting forces sailing from the UK to the jumping off point in Guernsey and expose it to a much shorter period of passage in daylight.

The distance between both Plymouth and Portland and the most south-westerly of Guernsey's ports, was roughly the same, at 75 nautical miles. From there to the western beaches of Jersey is 26 miles and to the eastern beaches is 45 miles. From Guernsey's St Peter Port to Jersey's eastern beaches is 20 miles; to the western beaches is 30 miles.

To reach the west coast of Jersey from Guernsey was 3 hours' journey time for slow-moving craft such as Landing Craft, Assault and slightly longer for the larger Landing Craft, Tanks. Forces landing from these craft would therefore only be able to go ashore 2 hours before daylight, at the earliest. If part of the invasion force had to sail directly from the UK, troops carried in Landing Ships, Infantry would arrive at Jersey approximately 8 hours after leaving port. Those troops carried in Landing Craft, Tanks would reach Jersey approximately 14 hours after leaving port, and those in Landing Craft, Infantry, 7 hours after leaving port. If some of the forces coming from the UK were required in the initial assault, the Landing Craft, Infantry convoy would have to depart 5 hours before dark.

The east coast of Jersey is a further 2 hours sailing time for the assault landing craft from Guernsey.

If the landing were to be made on the west coast of Jersey at first light, the Assault Force from Guernsey must leave 3 hours before first light and the force from the UK must leave 3 hours before dusk; while those landing on the east coast must leave Guernsey 5 hours before first light, and those from the UK 5 hours before dark.

In the case of the craft leaving the UK, sailing for a few hours during daylight could mean that they would be spotted by German aircraft and thus the element of surprise would be lost. However, as *Condor* would most likely only go ahead after Alderney and Guernsey had been captured, the garrison in Jersey would be on high alert fully expecting to be attacked. Whether surprise could be achieved at all was questionable.

A further consideration was that if tanks were to be taken on the first waves it would be advisable for the tanks and the Landing Ships, Tank to leave from Guernsey rather than expose them to a long period of travel from the UK during daylight hours.

All of the above depended upon the weather and tide. At least a half-moon was considered necessary to help with pilotage, while a calm sea was required with no more than a slight swell. Though infantry could be landed in any tidal state, the ideal tide conditions would be to land the infantry at half tide and the tanks near high water.

Courses Open

Under this heading, all the factors discussed above were taken into account to enable the military and naval commanders to choose their course of action. As it was presumed the seafront buildings in St Helier had been turned into strongpoints, an assault there would most likely result in very heavy casualties, as per Dieppe, and so this was discounted by the planners. This left them with two options which they described as follows:

a) An assault by seaborne forces supported by paratroops on the East coast with simultaneous scramble landings on the North coast by Commando troops followed by infantry. An armoured force would be put through the Eastern bridgehead to move North, join up the Commando troops and Infantry, subsequently turn South and, supported by the Infantry, assault St Helier from the North. This assault to be synchronised with an attack from the Eastern bridgehead.

b) An assault by seaborne forces supported by paratroops on both the West and East coasts of the island with scramble landings by Commando troops on the S.W. point overlooking St Aubin's Bay (Noirmont Point). Bulk of artillery and armour would subsequently be landed under cover of the Eastern bridgehead, from which forces would move North to secure the whole of the East coast and West to assault St Helier. Force moving North would swing West along the North coast of the island, then South along the axis of the valleys debouching on St Aubin's and attack St Helier from the North. The Western bridgehead to be extended to meet attacking force North of St Helier.

The planners stated that they believed plan b) offered the best prospects of success. It had the advantage of preventing the enemy from concentrating his mobile forces to repel an attack on the eastern beaches, and it would compel the Germans to disperse their troops to meet the threat from the west. The planners also thought this option was more flexible in that the reinforcements could be landed at whichever point was best suited to the state of the battle at the time.

Plan b) was therefore adopted for the development of the Joint Outline Plan, even though as this meant a wider front this would involve the use of more landing craft than plan a).

The Appraisal raised one chilling factor: of the peacetime population of 50,000, there were still half of that number on Jersey. Casualties among those people could not be avoided. While every other statistic had been considered and detailed, this one was figure none of the planners dared to discuss.

Chapter 14

Condor – The Plan of Attack on Jersey

A 'Summary of the Joint Outline Plan' was produced which set out the operation in five stages, or phases, as follows:

(a) *Phase 1.* Night of D-1/D-Day
Aerial bombardment of the east and west coasts, followed by parachute and infantry landings. Scramble landings by Commando troops in the south-west of the island.

(b) *Phase 2.* D-Day and night of D/D+1
Landing of artillery and more infantry in the eastern beachhead and extension of this beachhead to take the high ground overlooking the Royal Bay of Grouville. The joining of the western beachhead to the Noirmont Point beachhead secured by Commandos.

(c) *Phase 3.* D+1.
Landing of armour in eastern beachhead which will move north to take the whole of the eastern coast. The extension of the western beachhead to high ground north of St Aubin's Bay and the pinching out of the La Moye Peninsula.

(d) *Phase 4.* Night of D+1/D+2 and D+2.
Assault on St Helier from the east by infantry from the eastern beachhead, from the west by infantry of the western beachhead, and from the north by armour supported by infantry.

(e) *Phase 5.* D+3 and subsequent days.
Joining of east and west beachheads to the final reduction of the remainder of the island.

The Joint Plan also called for coastal reconnaissance to be carried out at dusk of D-1/D-Day, and anti-submarine patrols to be conducted on the night of D-1/D-Day and D-Day/D+1. The latter to be undertaken by Coastal Command strike forces.

190 The Allied Assault on Hitler's Channel Island Fortress

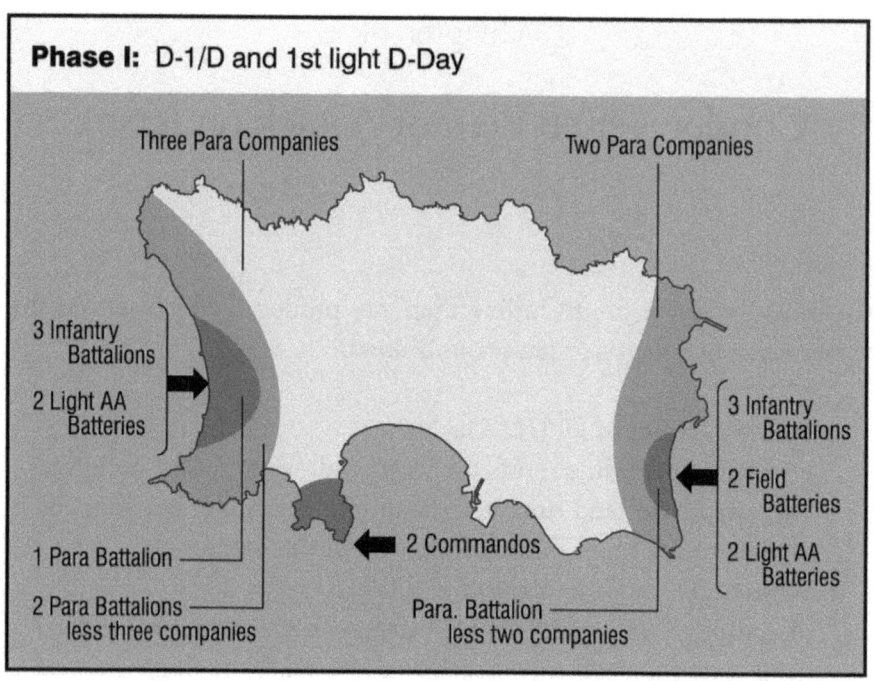

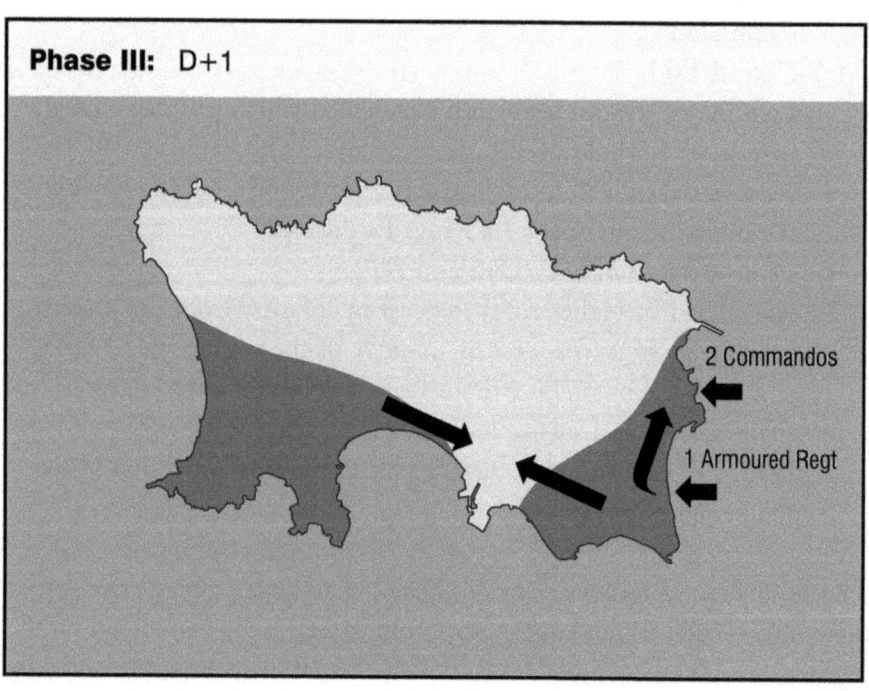

Condor – The Plan of Attack on Jersey 191

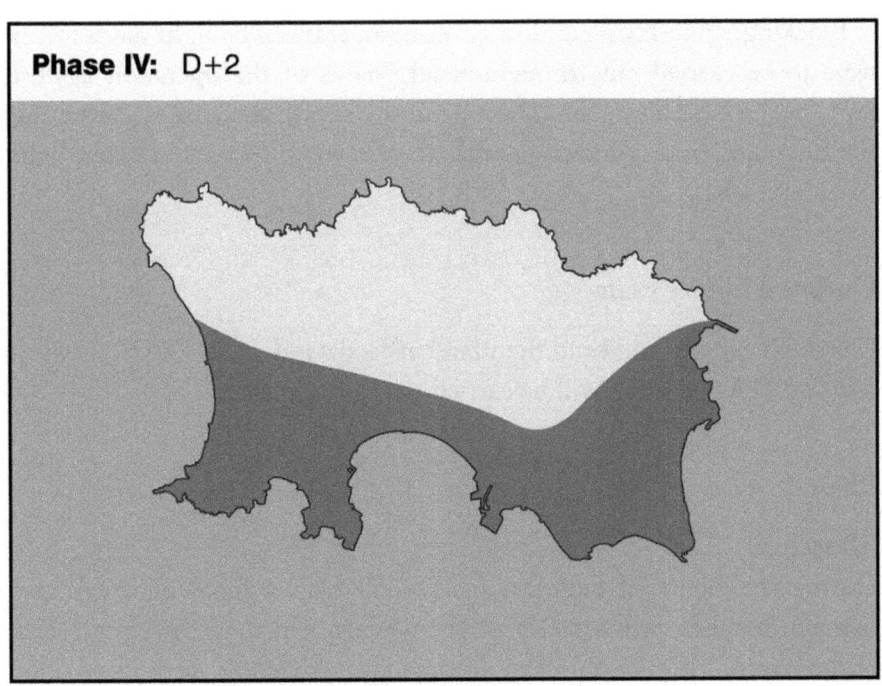

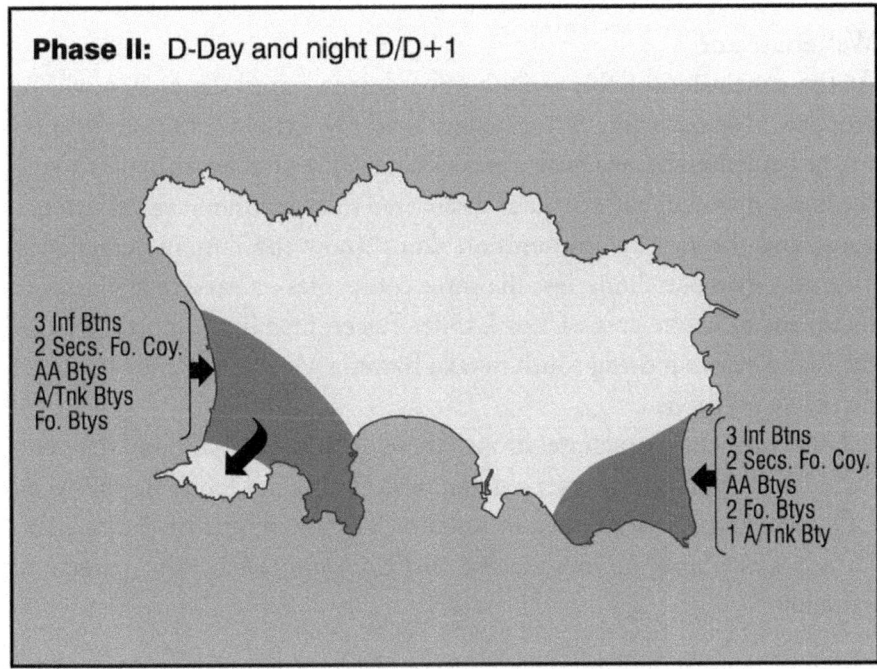

How it was expected the first four stages of *Condor* would play out.

Blocking, mine-laying and/or covering operations by light naval forces were to be carried out throughout all phases of the operation against ports of the Cherbourg and Brest peninsulas, with the aim of preventing the Germans from interfering with *Condor* with E-boats or other light coastal vessels.

Outline Military Plan

Object: To capture and hold the island of Jersey in July 1943.
Method: The operation will be carried out in five phases.

Phase 1

All sectors
During the hours of darkness on D-1/D-Day, a force of heavy and medium bombers will attack first the western and then the eastern end of the island, with the object of destroying the defences in the area of St Ouen's Bay and the Royal Bay of Grouville, and of lowering the enemy's morale.

Western sector
At the conclusion of the aerial bombardment, parachute troops will be dropped. One battalion will seize and hold the airfield. Three companies will be landed in the area by St Peter's Windmill with the task of destroying the heavy howitzer battery (later discovered to be medium coastal defence guns) and the nearby ammunition dump (now the famous Jersey War Tunnels). Two battalions, less the three companies referred to above, were to be landed in the area of Les Landes Racecourse in the north-west of the island before moving south to take Batterie Moltke and the associated defensive positions.

Following the parachute drops, three infantry battalions with two batteries of light anti-aircraft guns were to land at St Ouen's Bay between L'Ouziere and Le Braye, i.e., in more or less the middle of the bay, and form a beachhead to include the airfield captured by the parachute battalion.

Southern sector

At the same time as the parachute drop, two Commandos were to make scramble landings at Portelet Bay and the eastern end of St Brelades Bay, with the object of destroying Batterie Lothringen and of securing a bridgehead stretching from Mont Sohier across to St Aubin, i.e., the whole of the Noirmont Peninsula. By this time, it was expected they would be able to dominate the coastal road which runs from St Helier around St Aubin's Bay (effectively today's A2 and A1) with small arms fire.

Eastern sector

Immediately following the end of the aerial bombardment, a battalion of parachutists, less two companies, was to land on the golf links (now the Royal Jersey Golf Club) to attack and destroy Batterie Schliefen and the strongpoint at La Corbière and attack the beach defences covering the Royal Bay of Grouville from the rear.

The remaining two companies of parachutists were to drop around Maufant in the St Saviour district to attack and destroy a heavy howitzer battery (again discovered to be a medium coastal defence battery) by Clos du Buisson (now the Maison du Buisson) farm.

After the parachute drop, three infantry battalions, plus batteries of light anti-aircraft guns and two batteries of field guns, would be landed, under the cover of smoke, if necessary, in the Royal Bay of Grouville.

Phase 2

Western and southern sectors

During the daylight hours of D-Day all the parachute troops were to withdraw into the infantry beachhead, which would then be extended to join the Commandos on the Noirmont Peninsula. This would isolate any German troops left on the La Moye Peninsula who had not already been disposed of by the parachutists.

Also under the cover of smoke, there would be a further landing of three battalions of infantry and two sections of a Royal Engineers' Field Company. The engineers were to prepare exits from the beach for field, anti-tank and anti-aircraft guns, which were to be landed during the hours of darkness of D/D+1. Just in case the exits from the beaches had not been prepared by the time the artillery batteries arrived, the airfield would have been made ready to receive artillery of the Airborne Division.

Eastern sector
As soon as the eastern beachhead had been extended to include the high ground overlooking the Royal Bay of Grouville, and the Germans therefore denied observation of the beach, whether that happened during D-Day or the night of D/D+1, three more infantry battalions, a further two sections of engineers and a battery of a Royal Artillery field regiment and one anti-tank battery would be landed, again under the cover of a smoke screen if necessary.

Phase 3

Western and southern sectors
During D+1 the western beachhead would be extended to include the high ground to the north of St Aubin's Bay.

Eastern sector
At first light on D+1 one armoured regiment was to land at Grouville, while at the same time there were to be scramble landings by two Commandos at St Catherine's Bay. The armoured regiment would push north to link up with the Commandos in the area of St Martin.

Pgase 4

Western and southern sectors
At first light on D+2 an infantry assault by two battalions on St Helier was to be launched from the western bridgehead

Eastern sector
At first light on D+2, the armoured regiment, supported by the two Commandos, were to move on St Helier from the north, while two battalions of infantry would launch an assault St Helier from the western bridgehead.

Phase 5

The reduction of the remainder of the island would be carried out on a plan drawn up by the Military Commander according to the situation that presented itself at the time.

Military Forces Required

Eastern sector

Force Headquarters

Tactical Reconnaissance Detachment

One parachute battalion

One Light Aid Detachment

One armoured regiment

One field battery, Royal Artillery

One field company, Royal Engineers

One field ambulance

One section, Provost company

Divisional Signals less one Infantry Brigade Section

Army Air Support Control 'Tentacle'

Two infantry brigades

Two Commandos

One field regiment, Royal Artillery

One anti-aircraft regiment, less one battery

One anti-tank battery

½ Infantry Brigade, Royal Army Service Corps

Southern sector

Two Commandos

Western sector

Infantry Division Headquarters

Tactical Reconnaissance Detachment

One parachute brigade signals detachment

Two infantry brigades

One field regiment, R. A., less one battery

One light anti-aircraft battery

One section, Provost company

½ Infantry Brigade, Royal Army Service Corps Company

Divisional Signals less one Infantry Brigade Section

One parachute brigade

Detachment of Airborne Division Signals

One Light Aid Detachment

One light anti-aircraft regiment

One field company, R. E., less one section

One field ambulance

Outline Air Plan

Air Forces Required
1. Bombers
   17 squadrons of RAF heavy bombers
   14 squadrons USAAF heavy bombers
   2 squadrons light bombers – smoke
   2 squadrons light bombers – close support
   4 squadrons light bombers – diversion
   192 British parachute aircraft or 96 USAAF aircraft
2. Coastal Forces
   1 squadron of strike aircraft – torpedo and bomb
3. Fighters
   18 squadrons of day fighters for air cover
   12 squadrons of day fighters for diversions, escort, and naval escort
   2 squadrons of day fighters for close support
4. Tactical Reconnaissance
   4 squadrons
5. Intercommunications
   1 Army Air Corps squadron

Sequence of Air Operations

D-1 Day
Since it was likely that anti-submarine patrols covering Guernsey would be flown in routine defence of that island, it was not considered necessary to fly any special patrols for the attack on Jersey. The only additional support was a coastal patrol to be flown along the French coast between Cherbourg and Brest inclusive, to locate enemy surface vessels.

Fighter cover for the follow up convoy would be provided according to the normal scale for the routine convoys which sailed to Guernsey from the UK.

Night of D-1/D-Day
A concentrated bombing attack was to commence at Zero Hour-2 hours until Zero-1 hour by a force of 100 heavy bombers in a western area of the island, with the bombing centre to be the crossroads at La Croix au Bion.

Though this author had been unable to find this location, it would seem from the coordinates to be in the St Mary's district. The object of this was to 'soften' the German defences and to 'make enemy troops go to ground'. Immediately on the cessation of this bombing attack, the parachute troops were to be dropped at St Peter's Mill and the racecourse as detailed above.

A second concentrated bombing attack was to begin at Zero Hour until Zero+1 by another force of 100 heavy bombers in the eastern area of Jersey, with the bombing centre being what the planners called the village of Hambeye, today's Clos Du Hambye, which is situated to the north-west of the Royal Bay of Grouville. This, again, was to soften the German defences and to make enemy troops go to ground. Immediately after the cessation of this bombing attack at Z+1, the two companies of parachutists would land at Maison du Buisson.

D-Day and subsequent days until completion
Three fighter squadrons (one Wing) based on Guernsey were to provide fighter cover over Jersey. After completing their sorties, they would be relieved by three squadrons flown out from the UK which would have refuelled at Guernsey. Of the first Wing, one squadron would return to Guernsey to provide local defence, and the remaining two squadrons would return to the UK. Further fighter cover would be maintained via the Advanced Landing Ground on Guernsey, thus enabling the fighters to remain in the air longer over Jersey.

One additional Wing would remain at readiness in the UK to 'thicken up' fighter cover if the Luftwaffe increased its attacks on Jersey. There would also be bomber attacks, with fighter escorts, on German airfields in Normandy as well as diversionary raids on selected targets in northern France and the Low Countries.

Aircraft would also be used to deploy 'Smoke Curtain Installations' or to drop smoke bombs to screen the daylight landings on the eastern and western coasts.

Also, on call in the UK if requested by the Military Commander, would be four tactical reconnaissance squadrons and two smoke squadrons, two squadrons of close support fighters, two squadrons of close support medium bombers, and Coastal Command strike forces.

Until an Air Support Command was put ashore, requests for close support or smoke by the Military Commander were to be passed to the UK via the Headquarters Ship.

The above plan was submitted to the Chairman of the Planning Syndicate on 20 January 1943, with the following appended observations. The author of the Joint Plan said that he had asked for additional topographical information on the beaches on the eastern and western shores of Jersey, including the gradients of the beaches. His concern in this regard was the practicality of motor transport being able to climb up off the beaches, particularly the tanks. He said that the reason he had scheduled the tanks to be put ashore as late as the night of D-Day/D+1 was because he did not think the exits from the beaches would be made ready for the tanks any earlier. He said that until the tanks were ashore, the troops would have to protect themselves with their own 2-pounder and 6-pounder anti-tank guns and field artillery, and anti-aircraft guns in a dual role.

Nevertheless, he stated that because beaches on both the east and the west of the island were going to be used, this gave the plan a degree of flexibility in that if the weather conditions were not suitable for the landing of vehicles on one side of Jersey, then they could all be unloaded on the other side.

He also pointed out that he had advised the use of cruiser tanks as opposed to infantry tanks because the beaches on Jersey were mostly of shingle and soft sand and therefore cruiser tanks would have less difficulty moving across them than the heavier infantry tanks. This clearly reflected what had been learned though the difficulties the Churchill tanks experienced at Dieppe.

He reinforced his point in taking the airfield at an early stage in the operation just in case the field artillery could not get off the beaches, in which case glider-borne artillery could be quickly landed on the airfield.

The battles that would inevitably take place on Jersey and Guernsey would, in terms of firepower, be the largest ever seen on British soil.

Chapter 15

Constelation Cancelled

Back in January 1943, Mountbatten had warned the Chiefs of Staff that the armoured landing craft for *Husky* had been allocated from the British Channel Assault Force which threatened to jeopardise *Constellation*, and he asked the Admiralty to double the manufacturing output of such vessels. But that was simply not possible.

Consequently, despite all the time and effort put into planning his attack on the Channel Islands, on 19 February Mountbatten attended a Chiefs of Staff Committee meeting in which he had to concede that he was unable to mount *Constellation*. At the meeting, he said that he had come to the conclusion that of the three proposals, only the attack on Alderney, being the smallest of the group, was practicable because of the limited number of landing craft that remained after those allocated to *Husky* had been taken.[1]

The Committee members therefore focussed their discussion on the wisdom of mounting an attack on Alderney only. Sir Charles Portal 'doubted whether the capture of this island would, in fact, bring about the desired air battle. He pointed out that Alderney lay within range of field batteries mounted on the western tip of the Cherbourg Peninsula, and that the Germans would be unlikely, therefore, to risk aircraft in an attempt to accomplish what could be more easily achieved by the use of artillery.'

In response to this, Mountbatten stated that 'if, owing to the [German] bombardment from the [French] mainland, it proved impossible [for British troops] to remain on the island, the assaulting forces could be withdrawn after demolishing the extremely strong defences.' The advantage of this would be that, 'the approach to the western shore of the Cotentin Peninsula would thus have been opened.'

Alan Brooke said that:

the present plan was unsound. The proposed scale of the air bombardment, even allowing for the peculiar granite formation of the island, was most unlikely to destroy the defences. A far heavier scale of bombardment would be needed, but he considered that a better chance lay in a surprise attack.

He was opposed to any conception of this plan as an isolated operation. He foresaw that, sometime during the summer, a landing would have to be made against the French mainland in order to test the strength of the enemy defences; an assault on Alderney should be regarded as a complement to an operation of this nature.

Mountbatten, still hoping to keep the Alderney element of *Constellation* alive, said: 'The forces involved, namely the Royal Marine Division and J Force, were available, and that it would be easy to cancel the operation if required once preparations had started. But, he stressed, it would be most difficult, if not impossible, to prepare an operation of this nature at short notice.'

He asked if his staff could 'examine by other means of carrying out *Constellation*', and he requested permission to consult the other force commanders concerned 'where necessary'.

The Chiefs of Staff refused to give Mountbatten their approval, doubting 'if it should ever be undertaken'. Instead, Mountbatten was advised to examine and report on an attack against Lorient, or of a raid similar to *Aflame*, which was a planned naval demonstration off the French coast near Berck-sur-Mer in the Pas-de-Calais region of France in conjunction with the drop of dummy paratroopers and the landing of a small party of No. 12 Commando. The aim of this was to persuade the Germans that a major landing was about to be made, in the hope of drawing the Luftwaffe into major combat. This, though, was another operation which failed to be realised.

In his diary for 19 February, Brooke wrote the following: 'A long COS meeting at which Dickie Mountbatten gave me a heap of trouble with a proposed attack on the Channel Islands which was not in its proper strategical setting and tactically quite adrift.'[2] And that, thankfully, put an end to Mountbatten's outrageous scheme, though in the official record of this compiled by Combined Ops Headquarters, it is stated that the reason *Constellation* did not take place was mainly on account of the strength of the enemy's defences. It would seem, then, that Hitler's massive fortification of the Channel Islands did the islanders a huge favour for, as the historian of *Festung Alderney* observed: 'If the islands had been *less* heavily defended, then military operations to recapture one or more of them would have gone ahead. Even if they had succeeded, with great cost to attacker and defender alike, the subsequent loss of life to the civilian population does not bear thinking about.'[3]

At the end of the war, a note was prepared for Brooke, though the originator was not referenced, with the title 'Operations Against the Channel Islands 1940-1945'.[4] It is worth repeating the most salient points of this document as it lays out the reasons why *Constellation* and the other enterprises were not undertaken. It states that even if the islands were captured 'with considerable casualties to ourselves', the project would be impracticable since:

(a) It would be too difficult to supply the liberating garrison in face of the air attack that could be brought against it
(b) The necessary air and anti-aircraft defences which would be required to defend the islands would result in a far greater drain on our own resources than those of the enemy.
(c) As the war proceeded and the risk of enemy invasion lessened, the strategic importance of the Channel Islands diminished … In consequence … attacks on the Channel Islands were not considered further and their eventual liberation was planned solely in the form of an undertaking to re-occupy the islands when the surrender of the German forces was seen to be inevitable.

There is, however, an interesting postscript to this story. In June 1944, the Allies finally launched their re-invasion of Europe with the D-Day landings in Normandy and the Cotentin Peninsula. During the drive on Cherbourg, and after its subsequent liberation, the Allied units and supply routes on the Cotentin Peninsula came under fire from the German 15 cm K18 guns emplaced at Batterie Blücher. With Alderney just 9 or 10 miles from this part of the French coast, a number of Allied positions on the Cherbourg Peninsula were within range of the guns. This was similar to the situation which had been envisaged when *Hadrian* was discussed.

The task of removing this threat to Allied forces fell to the Nelson-class battleship HMS *Rodney*. Her initial approach to the island was made on the 8/9 August. As a result of the good visibility surrounding the island at the time, it was considered too hazardous, in view of the extensive anti-aircraft defences believed to exist on Alderney, to allow the RAF spotter aircraft to operate in the skies overhead. The aircraft were duly turned back.

For three days HMS *Rodney* waited on station off the Cherbourg Peninsula, approximately 20 miles from the island. At last, at 14.11 hours on 12 August 1944, the conditions were considered appropriate, and the battleship opened fire. For 2.5 hours, her 16-inch guns unleashed a barrage of some seventy-five 1-ton shells, at a rate of fire of one shot every two or three minutes, at this one small part of British sovereign territory.

Just before the first salvo was fired, the *Rodney*'s captain had announced to the ship's crew, through her tannoy system, what was about to happen. He added that it would be quite likely that they were about to destroy the home of the battleship's paymaster who, before the war, lived on the island!

On board the *Rodney* was the War Correspondent John Moroso: 'Our first shot landed 300 yards from the target, we corrected the range, and on the fifth, sixth, seventh and eighth shots made direct hits on the Nazi guns ... Especial care was taken to avoid hitting the town of St Anne roughly 600 yards behind the target ... The spotting planes reported so many hits that on the 21st shot Captain Fitzroy ... remarked, "That gun bears a charmed life".'[5]

On board *Rodney* at the time was Corporal James Mitcheson – one of her complement of Royal Marines. Recalling that the battleship did not approach the island any closer by virtue of the German 9-inch guns, he also remembers: '*Rodney* was blessed with having one of the finest gunnery officers in the Navy ... a Lieutenant-Commander Peter Larkin ... we were delighted when we were told that we had hit our target with our second salvo and had caught the German gun crews napping as they sunbathed around their gun turrets ... there must have been a general pandemonium as they could have had no idea from where the shelling was coming.'

There can be little doubt that *Rodney*'s barrage must have looked both formidable and impressive. A Guernseyman who was a rear-gunner in one of the spotter aircraft would remark that that Alderney 'seemed to be a mass of flames'. It was even reported that the explosions could be felt in Guernsey.

Even though the first round had fallen wide, destroying Ronde Mare – a farmhouse belonging to Mr J.P. Renier on the Longy Road, opposite Balmoral House – the rest of the shoot was regarded as accurate. According to von Schmettow in his post-war interview, while a few men were injured, only one man was killed.[6] Despite Mountbatten's various schemes to annihilate the garrison, these were the only battle casualties the Germans suffered on Alderney. Regardless of this, and the fact that the spotter aircraft stated that hits had been seen on three of the four guns (a claim widely reported in the Allied press at the time), only one of the four had actually been damaged, even though the battery was in an open emplacement.

German reports on the effects of the bombardment, found after the war, suggest that the cradle and recoil mechanism of this one gun had been damaged. It was later repaired, even though a spare part had to be flown from Germany to the Channel Islands across newly liberated France.

This is a good indication of what might have happened had *Constellation* gone ahead. Despite the 'accuracy' of the Navy's guns, civilian property had suffered similar damage to that of the Germans. This stated accuracy was that forty out of the seventy-five shells that were fired fell within a 200-yard radius,[7] meaning thirty-five of the shells fell more than 200 yards away from the battery. On the more densely populated islands of Jersey and Guernsey, such accuracy would have proven devastating.

Similarly, somewhat earlier, on 2 and 5 June 1944, immediately before the D-Day landings, attempts were made by Allied aircraft to destroy the Luftwaffe radar early warning station based in Guernsey's Fort George, the German *Stützpunkt Georgefest*. Not only did the raid fail to knock out the German devices, but aircraft were also shot down.

If fact, the islands were the subject of twenty-one other minor air attacks, which resulted in ninety-three people being killed and 250 being injured. The main targets were the harbours and airports of the islands. Thirteen Allied air crew were lost in these operations.

The RAF conducted its last raids on a number of nights from 30/31 August 1944 onwards, when thousands of propaganda leaflets were dropped on the islands at the points where German troops were thought to be stationed; Fort Richmond in Guernsey, St Ouen's Manor in Jersey, and St Anne in Alderney. These leaflets made it clear that the military situation was such that there was no point in the garrison holding out any longer. Altogether, 218 air burst leaflet 'bombs' were dropped – it was the heaviest aerial bombardment the islands suffered since 28 June 1940. How different it might have been if Mountbatten's plans had been put into effect.

The final words must be left to Montgomery's biographer mentioned earlier, Nigel Hamilton. In referring to Mountbatten's and Churchill's penchant for wildly ambitious schemes, he wrote: 'the historian may well wonder that so few of their dramatic concoctions ever saw action. For this it is Alan Brooke who must surely be commended – the only Chief of Staff with the courage, integrity, and unimpeachable authority to curb Churchill in his wildest excesses.' The people of the Channel Islands, perhaps unwittingly, owe much to Brooke for his 'hard relentless military logic'.[8]

As for Mountbatten, he is recorded as having claimed: 'It is a curious thing, but a fact, that I have been right in everything I have done and said in my life.'[9]

Epilogue

The German Defences of the Channel Islands Today

As the only British territory occupied by the Germans during the Second World War, the Channel Islands hold a particular fascination not just for the British people, but visitors from across mainland Europe, particularly Germany. Because of the enormous amount of effort put into making each of the main islands into a *Festung*, a fortress, much of the defences built by the Germans still stand as stoutly as they did more than seventy years ago, and many are freely open to the general public. Equally, the bays and beaches where the Allied amphibious assaults would have taken place have changed little since the 1940s.

There are a variety of history tours available in Jersey, Guernsey, and Alderney, most of which focus on the Occupation period, but the islands are not large and it is quite easy for visitors to drive to the main sites unaccompanied. With regards to the places that would have seen parachute landings or bombing targets, many of these are unlikely to be featured on any organised tour and would have to be visited independently.

Jersey's Batterie Lothringen at Noirmont Point, which overlooks St Aubin' Bay and the port of St Helier, is an extensive site which, apart from one of its original 15 cm gun barrels on display, includes an underground command bunker and an artillery direction and range-finding tower (Marine Peilstand 3 or MP3), and searchlight platforms. The exterior is open all year round and there are no admission charges. Some of the interiors are open occasionally during the summer and there is an adjacent car park. In St Aubin's Bay itself, set some distance inland, is Batterie Defflinger (which formerly held four 8 cm guns). This has not been maintained and is on private land.

It is only a short drive from Noirmont Point to La Corbière, where a powerful strongpoint dominates the headland with its memorable views towards its lighthouse. This is another large site which includes another artillery direction and range-finding tower and bunker for the 10.5 cm coastal defence guns, a fortress mortar bunker, a searchlight bunker, and machine gun positions built into the rocks. Again, the outside areas can be visited at any time and there is a car park.

The strongpoint at the southern end of St Ouen's Bay and Batterie Moltke at the northern end, coupled with the bunkers along St Ouen's Bay, and the tall concrete seawall, would have made a landing in the bay extremely costly. As a result, in Operation *Condor* the plan was for Commandos in conjunction with paratroopers to land and take these fortifications ahead of the main landings.

A bunker in the St Ouen's Bay now houses Damien Horn's Channel Islands Military Museum, which holds a highly diverse collection of mainly German artifacts and photographs of the Occupation.

Batterie Moltke is another impressive site and has one of the original 15.5 cm guns in excellent condition in situ. There are also two other gun barrels on display, as well as the third of the three artillery observation towers. Again, the battery is open freely to the public.

The Royal Bay of Grouville is referred to frequently in the *Condor* plans and this long, sweeping bay is an obvious landing point, and while there are no big-gun batteries flanking the bay, there are powerful resistance nests on the La Rocque headland that forms the southern arm of the bay and stand along the shoreline at Fort Henry and Fort William, as well as some fortifications added to Mont Orgueil Castle which forms the northern arm of the bay. Little remains of the Fort William structure, which is on private land, but the Fort Henry resistance nest can be freely examined. Mont Orgueil Castle is open from Friday to Monday throughout most of the year. To give some idea of how formidable these fortifications were, the list of weaponry at Fort Henry was recorded as two 10.5 cm artillery pieces, two 5 cm mortars, six machine guns and ten flamethrowers.

To the north of Jersey, the next fortifications are around the Rozel headland. From Rozel Fort, travelling along the island's northern coast, the visitor can see the Bouley Harbour complex, the most obvious of which is Fort Leicester which has been converted into very unusual holiday accommodation.

Probably the most visited of Jersey's wartime structures are the War Tunnels, Hohlgangsanlage 8. This large complex, situated quite centrally, was built as protection for the German troops from the Allied bombardment which, as we know, would have preceded an invasion. This perhaps indicates that a large part of the garrison would have survived the bombardment. There were many other strongpoints and resistance nests inland from the coast and some of the eighteenth and nineteenth century defences, including the Martello towers around the coastline, were used by the Germans.

Guernsey's Batterie Mirus was the largest battery in the Channel Islands, holding four 30.5 cm guns, none of which are still present, but one of the emplacements is still intact and largely restored. As with the main batteries on Jersey, this is a big site (almost a kilometre square) situated on high ground above L'Eree, on the west coast.

Flakbatterie Dolmen, which was armed with six 8.8 cm Flak 36 guns, still stands but access is possible to only one of the bunkers.

The area around L'Ancresse Bay, which we know had been identified as a key landing ground by the Combined Ops planners, was quite heavily fortified, though not all of the defensive structures are easily found today.

Fort Hommet's 10.5 cm Gun Casemate Bunker, which flanks Vazon Bay, has been fully restored and is open to the public. It formed part of *Stutzpunkt* Rostenstein and is a good example of just how powerful such strongpoints were. The fort seen today originally consisted of a Martello tower in which the Germans built two bunkers housing a 60 cm and 150 cm searchlight. Facing north are two casemates, both of which housed a 10.5 cm gun. Two similar casemates face south across Vazon Beach, one of which is now a museum. A Tobruk pit and a casemate for a 4.7 cm anti-tank gun complete the beach-facing defences, while in the centre of the headland is a bunker that housed a 5 cm mortar. In addition to all this was a personnel bunker and an armoured machine-gun cupola bunker. The whole site was covered with infantry trenches, machine-gun pits, flamethrowers, and was surrounded by barbed wire and mines.

In the middle of Cobo Bay is a highly visible *Widerstandsnest*, resistance nest, the main armament of which were two 4.7 cm Pak 36 fortress guns. Though the bunkers are closed, the whole site is fully accessible and is rarely seen without crowds of people on and around it.

The headquarters of the German Naval Commander of the Channel Islands, which handled all the important radio signals traffic for the German forces in the Channel Islands, has been nicely restored and is now a museum. Open every day, the site is just a 20-minute walk from St Peter Port harbour.

Until recently, few of the fortifications on **Alderney** had been restored and some, particularly the extensive nineteenth century military buildings, lay abandoned. However, recently considerable effort has gone into clearing many of the sites which can now be visited safely – though the wise visitor would carry a torch. This includes part of the northern defences of Fort Tourgis, which were converted by the Germans into a *Stützpunkt*.

Five batteries were established by the Germans on Alderney, including Batterie Dollmann at Pleinmont, which is open to the public, and where one of the four 22 cm gun pits and a number of trenches have been restored. It features accommodation and ammunition bunkers linked by deep, concrete-lined trenches. There is also a command and an observation bunker.

The open concrete emplacements of the four 15 cm guns of Batterie Annes on the south-west coast are still largely intact, as are the sites' ammunition and generator bunkers.

Saline Bay, which as we know was an identified landing point, is still surrounded by its seawall that would have proved a serious impediment to the attackers, as would the Coastal Gun emplacement overlooking Clonque Bay. An 8.8 cm flak battery and a naval range finding MP3 tower are to be seen at Mannez Garenne, both in good condition. The seawall Longis Bay, Panzermauer 1, is a formidable structure, with machine gun positions in and on top of the wall.

Possibly the most intriguing of all the German structures on the Channel Islands are the network of tunnels not far from St Anne, the island's only town, dug into the hillside along a valley called Le Val Reuters. Long assumed to be nothing more than ammunition storage shelters or possibly electricity generating stations, the true purpose of the complex was unknown. That was until former military men, John Weigold and Colonel Richard Kemp, after intensive investigations and explorations, came up with a startling conclusion – that the configuration of the tunnels corresponded precisely with V-1 flying bomb launch sites found in France. Even more disturbing is that they believe they have uncovered evidence pointing to the possibility that the V-1s would be used to deliver chemical weapons, with their likely target, as mentioned earlier, the assembly ports for the D-Day landings along the English south coast. Fortunately, Operation *Overlord* took place before the Alderney site could be brought into use, being abandoned in June 1944. Access to the tunnels is difficult and entry is not recommended.

Alderney has the unwished-for distinction of being where the only German concentration camp on British soil was built. This is Lager Sylt, situated to the south-west of the island. It has been suggested that it was prisoners from Sylt who helped excavate the mysterious Le Val Reuters tunnels. All that now remains of the camp are a few concrete bases and its ominous-looking concrete gate posts.

As with Jersey's Fort Leicester, it is possible to stay in one of the fortifications on Alderney, Fort Clonque, which has been converted into self-catering accommodation.

Notes

Chapter 2
1. Winston S. Churchill, *The Second World War, Volume II, Their Finest Hour* (Cassell, London, 1949), p.214.
2. John Grehan, *Combined Operations: An Official History of Amphibious Warfare Against Hitler's Third Reich, 1940-1945* (Frontline, Barnsley, 2022).
3. Charles Messenger, *The Commandos 1940-1946* (William Kimber, London, 1985), p.26.
4. Brian Loring Villa, *Unauthorized Action, Mountbatten and the Dieppe Raid* (Oxford University Press, 1994), p.65.
5. Nicholas Rankin, *A Genius for Deception: How Cunning Helped the British Win Two World Wars* (Oxford University Press, 2009), p.250.
6. TNA PREM 3/330/9.
7. Messenger, p.37.
8. Courtvriend, V.V., *Isolated Island* (Guernsey Star and Gazette Limited, 1947), pp.100-1.
9. TNA PREM 3/103/1.
10. Jon E. Lewis [Ed.], *SAS and Special Forces: True Stories of the Fighting Elite Behind Enemy Lines* (Robinson, London, 2004), p.209.
11. TNA CAB 80-57-1.
12. TNA WO 106/3017.
13. Hughes-Hallett's memoir is scheduled to be published by Frontline Books in 2023.
14. TNA CAB 121/364.
15. TNA CAB 84/41/39.
16. TNA DEFE 2/106.
17. TNA AIR 8/868.
18. Patrick Bishop, *Operation Jubilee, Dieppe, 1942: The Folly and the Sacrifice* (Viking, London, 2021), p.62.
19. Imperial War Museum, Department of Sound, oral history catalogue No.6708.
20. Ibid.
21. Nigel Hamilton, *Monty: The Making of a General 1887-1942* (McGraw-Hill, London, 1981), p.547.
22. Arthur Bryant, *The Turn of the Tide 1939-1943* (Collins, London, 1957), p.371.
23. Alex Danchev and Dan Todman [eds.] *War Diaries 1939-1945: Field Marshall Lord Alanbrooke* (Weidenfeld & Nicolson, London, 2002), p.552.
24. Ibid., p.236.
25. Fergusson, Bernard, [Ed.], *The Business of War: The War Narrative of Major-General Sir John Kennedy* (Hutchinson, New York, 1858), pp.174-5.
26. Villa, p.250.
27. Danchev and Todman, pp.255-7.

Chapter 3
1. Gallup Vault: US Opinion and the Start of World War II.
2. Chicago Tribune, 4 December 1941.
3. Charles E. Kirkpatrick, *An Unknown Future and a Doubtful Present: Writing the Victory Plan of 1941* (Center of Military History, United States Army, Washington, D. C., 1992), p.35.
4. S.W.C. Pack, *Operation Husky, The Allied Invasion of Sicily* (David & Charles, London, 1977), p.15.
5. Proceedings of the American-British Joint Chiefs of staff Conferences (Washington, D.C., 24 December 1941–14 January 1942), Annex I.
6. Danchev and Todman, p.250.
7. Proceedings of the American-British Joint Chiefs of staff Conferences, ibid.
8. Grehan, Combined Operations.
9. Bryant, p.357.
10. TNA CAB 79-56-34/4.
11. Hughes-Hallett memoir.
12. Maurice Matloff and Edwin M. Snell, *Strategic Planning for Coalition Warfare, 1941-1942* (Center of Military History, United States Army, Washington, 1999.), p.188.
13. Combined Operations, ibid.
14. Churchill, Vol. IV, Hinge of Fate, p.289.
15. Danchev and Todman, pp.248-9.
16. Ibid., p.249.
17. Taken directly from Charles E. Kirkpatrick, *Joint Planning for Operation Torch* (U.S. Army War College, 1991), pp.2-3.
18. Robert E. Sherwood, *The White House Papers of Harry L. Hopkins, Vol. II, January 1942 - July 1945* (Eyre and Spottiswoode, London, 1949), p.558.
19. Matloff and Snell, p.193.
20. See John Grehan, *Churchill's Secret Invasion: Britain's First Large Scale Combined Operations Offensive 1942* (Pen & Sword, Barnsley, 2013).

Chapter 4
1. Villa, p.166.
2. TNA DEFE 2/306.
3. TNA ADM 358/3100.
4. TNA CAB-79-56-45; DEFE 2/306.
5. TNA CAB 79/56/45; CAB 80/62 series 1-5.
6. Earl of Avon, *The Eden Memoirs: The Reckoning* (Cassel, London, 1965), p.141.
7. Brian Loring Villa, *Mountbatten and the Dieppe Raid* (Oxford University Press, 1994), p.67.
8. Jeremy Black, *Strategy and the Second World War* (Robinson, London, 2021), pp.240-1.
9. Matloff and Snell, p.234.
10. Foreign relations of the United States. The Conferences at Washington, 1941-1942, and Casablanca, 1943 1941/1943, The Second Washington Conference, June 19-25, 1942.
11. Matloff and Snell, p.239.
12. Ibid., pp.249-50.
13. Ibid., pp.243-4.

Chapter 5
1. Churchill, Vol. IV, pp.402-3.
2. Marloff and Snell, pp.279-80.
3. Ibid., p.283.
4. Villa, Unauthorized Action, pp.69-72.
5. *Combined Operations 1940-1942* (H.M.S.O., London 1943), p.106.
6. *The Dieppe Raid, The Combined Operations Assault on Hitler's European Fortress, August 1942* (Frontline, Barnsley, 2019), p.8.
7. 21-26 June, 4-9 July, 20-25 July, 3-8 August.
8. TNA CAB 79/22 COS (42) 211th Meeting.
9. TNA WO 106/4196; DEFE 2/542 & 550.
10. Messenger, p.134.
11. Ibid., p.153.
12. In the 'Blazing' and 'Aimwell' file DEFE 2/106, there are two different numbers given for the assaulting force. The figures here are my best assessment of what the action plan called for against the two different numbers given.
13. John P. Campbell, *Dieppe Revisited: A Documentary Investigation* (Routledge, Abingdon, 2013), p.65-6.
14. Field Marshal Sir B. L. Montgomery, *Memoirs of Field-Marshal Montgomery* (London, 1958), p.76.
15. See Loring Villa, op. cit. and Robin Neilands, *The Dieppe Raid, The Story of the Disastrous 1942 Expedition* (Aurum, London, 2005).
16. Churchill, Vol. IV, p.458.
17. Hughes-Hallett papers, Imperial War Museum.
18. TNA CAB 120/684.
19. Colonel C.P. Stacey, *Official History of the Canadian Army In the Second World War, Volume I, Six Years of War, The Army in Canada, Britain and the Pacific* (Department of National Defense, 1956), p.341.
20. Danchev and Todman, p.275.
21. All of the above is drawn from Churchill, Vol. IV, pp.430-5.
22. Library of Congress, "Memorandum in Russian from Joseph Stalin about opening a second front in Europe during World War II, with English translation of same."
23. Churchill, Vol. IV, pp.441-2.
24. TNA PREM 3/76A/12, Records of the Cairo and Moscow Conferences.

Chapter 6
1. Report No.90, Historical Officer, Canadian Military Headquarters, 18 Feb 1943.
2. Brereton Greenhous, "Operation Flodden: The sea fight off Berneval and the suppression of the Goebbels Battery, 19 August 1942", Canadian Military Journal (Autumn, 2003), p.50.
3. Peter Young, *Storm From The Sea* (William Kimber, London, 1958), p. 65.
4. Brereton Greenhous, op.cit.
5. TNA ADM 234/355, Naval Staff History, Raid on Dieppe, Naval Operations 19 August 1942 Battle Summary No.33. Captain Hughes-Hallett's address, Conference on Landing Assaults, Vol. I, p. 21.
6. Capt. G.A. Browne, "Report on the Operation at Dieppe, 19 Aug 42", Directorate of History, National Defence Headquarters, Ottawa. Canada, Report No. 89, July 1986.

7. Reginald W. Thompson, Dieppe at Dawn: The Story of the Dieppe Raid (London, Hutchinson, 1956), p.191.
8. "Les leçons de Dieppe," La Patrie, 16 septembre 1942, p.10, in Béatrice Richard, "Dieppe The Making of a Myth", Canadian Military History, Volume 21, Issue 4, 2015.

Chapter 7
1. Ken Ford, *Assault on Sicily, Monty and Patton at War* (Sutton, Stroud, 2007), p.12.
2. Villa, Unauthorized Action, pp.78-9.
3. All quotations from the Casablanca Conference are drawn from Foreign Relations of the United States, The Conferences at Washington, 1941–1942, and Casablanca, 1943, op. cit.
4. Danchev and Todman, pp.360-1.
5. DEFE 2/98.

Chapter 8
1. TNA CAB 66//8/27.
2. Will Fowler, *The Last Raid, The Commandos, Channel Islands and Final Nazi Raid* (History Press, Stroud, 2016), p.18.
3. William M. Bell, *Guernsey Green: Life and Times of Guernseyman Bill Green* (Guernsey Press, 1992), p.91.
4. J.P. Sinel, *German Occupation of Jersey: A Diary of Events from June 1940 to June 1945* (Jersey, 1945), p.12.
5. Roy McLoughlin, *Living With the Enemy, An Outline of the German Occupation of the Channel Islands with First-Hand Accounts by People who Remember the Years 1940 to 1945* (Starlight Publishing, Jersey, 19995), p.21.
6. jerseybunkertours.com/german-air-raid.
7. Winston G. Ramsey, *The War in the Channel Islands: Then and Now* (After the Battle, 1981), p.56.
8. See Michael Ginns, *Jersey Occupied: The German Armed Forces in Jersey 1940–1945* (Channel Island Publishing, St John, Jersey, 2009); also, conversations with Michael in May 2008. Michael, along with his family, were deported to Germany.
9. Charles Cruikshank, The German Occupation of the Channel Islands (Sutton, 1990), p.199.
10. Charles Stephenson and Chris Taylor, *The Channel Islands 1941–45: Hitler's Impregnable Fortress* (Osprey, Oxford,2013), p.12.
11. *Hitler's Table Talk 1941-1944, His Private Conversations* (Enigma Books, New York, 2000), p.584.
12. McLoughlin, p.201.

Chapter 9
1. TNA CAB 80/68.
2. AIR 9/257.
3. DEFE 2/347.
4. TNA CAB 80/67.
5. DEFE 2/235.
6. TNA CAB 80/66.
7. TNA CAB 80/67.
8. TNA DEFE 2/650A.

9. Combined Operations Headquarters, op. cit.
10. John T. Correll, 'Daylight Precision Bombing', *Air Force Magazine* Oct. 1, 2008.
11. See the Butt Report, TNA AIR 14/1218.

Chapter 10
1. Hughes-Hallett, op. cit.
2. TNA DEFE 2/137.
3. TNA CAB 79/56/37.
4. Hughes-Hallett, op. cit.
5. CONCERTINA as an Isolated Operation, TNA DEFE 2/137.
6. John Grehan, 'Britain's V1 Site' *Hitler's V Weapons, The Terror Campaign* (Key Publishing), pp.82-6.
7. Nautical twilight is when the sky is still quite dark with bright planets visible. This is different from civil twilight when the sky is light all over though the sun is not visible.
8. Trevor Davenport, *Festung Alderney, The German Defences of Alderney* (Barnes Publishing, 2003), p.7.
9. TNA DEFE 2/650A.

Chapter 11
1. All that follows in this chapter, except where otherwise indicated, is drawn from TNA ADM 223/288.
2. Guernsey Archives, from the papers of Howard Baker.
3. Cruickshank, p.204.
4. The details of this battery and other armaments are taken from Ernie Gavey, *A Guide to German Fortifications on Guernsey* (Guernsey Armouries, 2001).
5. TNA DEFE 2/254.

Chapter 12
1. As with the previous chapter, all that follows is drawn from TNA ADM 223/288.
2. See Simon Hamon and John Grehan, *Storming Hitler's British Fortress* to be published by Frontline Books in 2023.
3. https://www.jerseybunkertours.com/graf-von-schmettow-interview   ttps://www.jerseybunkertours.com/graf-von-schmettow-interview

Chapter 13
1. All that follows in this chapter is drawn from TNA DEFE 2/137.

Chapter 15
1. CAB 79/59/24.
2. Danchev and Todman, p.383.
3. Davenport, p.176.
4. TNA WO 106/3017.
5. *The Daily Telegraph*, 16 August 1944.
6. jerseybunkertours.com/graf-von-schmettow-interview.
7. Fowler, p.138.
8. Hamilton, p.547.
9. Richard Alexander Hough, *Mountbatten: Hero of Our Time* (Weidenfeld and Nicolson, London, 1980), p.157.

Source Information

The National Archives

ADM 223/288, Operation 'Coverlet'.
ADM 234/355, Naval Staff History, Raid on Dieppe, Naval Operations 19 August 1942 Battle Summary No.33.
ADM 358/3100, Operation 'Bristle': ML 137, 293 and 324, 4 June 1942, sunk by enemy action; reconnaissance raid on France.
AIR 8/868, Operation 'Blazing'.
AIR 9/257, Channel Islands: re-occupation.
AIR 14/1218, Operational research, Butt Report.
CAB 66//8/27, Strategic importance of the Channel Islands.
CAB 79/56/37, Operation 'Blazing'.
CAB 79/59/24, Operation 'Constellation'.
CAB 79/22, COS (42) 211th Meeting.
CAB 79-56-34, Chiefs of Staff Committee memoranda.
CAB-79-56-45, Command and Planning for Operations on the Continent; Operations 'Sledgehammer' and 'Imperator'.
CAB 80-57-1, Operation 'Attaboy'.
CAB 80/62, series 1-5, Chiefs of Staff Committee, memoranda.
CAB 80/66, Chiefs of Staff Committee, 18 November to 31 December 1942.
CAB 80/67, Chiefs of Staff Committee, 4 January to 5 March 1943.
CAB 80/68, Chiefs of Staff Committee, 4 March to 18 April 1943.
CAB 84/41/39, Operation 'Roundup'.
CAB 120/684, Russia: staff conversations with M. Molotov in London.
CAB 121/364, Raiding operations against the French coast.
DEFE 2/98, 'Basalt', 'Bunbury', 'Bowery' and 'Blarneystone'.
DEFE 2/106, Combined Operations Headquarters, 'Blazing' and 'Aimwell'.
DEFE 2/137, 'Chess', 'Cobblestone', 'Concertina' and 'Condor'.
DEFE 2/158, 'Concubine'.
DEFE 2/306, 'Imperator'.
DEFE 2/235, Operation 'Hadrian'.
DEFE 2/347, Operation 'Lethal'.
DEFE 2/542, 'Rutter' (planned attack on Dieppe) 1A.
DEFE 2/550, 'Rutter' (planned attack on Dieppe) 2A.
DEFE 2/650A, Operations cancelled.
DEFE 2/1375, 'Anteroom': Channel Islands and adjacent French coast.
PREM 3/76A/12, Records of the Cairo and Moscow Conferences.
PREM 3/103/1, Commandos and Special Companies, organisation and equipment.
PREM 3/330/9, Offensive operations (Combined Operations).
WO 106/3017, Operations against the Channel Islands 1940-1945.

WO 106/4125, 'Sesame': study of projected raids on the Continent.
WO 106/4196,   'Jubilee' raid on Dieppe.

Imperial War Museum
Michael Stephen Hancock, Department of Sound, oral history catalogue No.6708.
Private Papers of Vice Admiral J. Hughes-Hallett CB DSO, Catalogue number 14370.

Published books
Avon, Earl of, *The Eden Memoirs: The Reckoning* (Cassel, London, 1965).
Bell, William M., *Guernsey Green: Life and Times of Guernseyman Bill Green* (Guernsey Press, 1992).
Bell, William M., *The Commando Who Came Home to Spy* (Guernsey, 1998).
Bishop, Patrick, *Operation Jubilee, Dieppe, 1942: The Folly and the Sacrifice* (Viking, London, 2021).
Black, Jeremy, *Strategy and the Second World War* (Robinson, London, 2021).
Bryant, Arthur, *The Turn of the Tide 1939-1943* (Collins, London, 1957), p.357.
Campbell, John P., *Dieppe Revisited: A Documentary Investigation* (Routledge, Abingdon, 2013).
Churchill, Winston S. *The Second World War, Volume II, Their Finest Hour* (Cassell, London, 1949).
Churchill, Winston S. *The Second World War, Volume IV, Hinge of Fate* (Cassell, London, 1951).
Combined Operations 1940-1942 (H.M.S.O., London 1943).
Courtvriend, V.V., *Isolated Island, A History and Personal Reminiscences of the German Occupation of the Island of Guernsey, June 1940—May 1945* (Guernsey Star and Gazette Limited, 1947).
Cruikshank, Charles, *The German Occupation of the Channel Islands* (Sutton, 1990).
Danchev, Alex and Todman, Dan [eds.] *War Diaries 1939-1945: Field Marshall Lord Alanbrooke* (Weidenfeld & Nicolson, London, 2002).
Davenport, Trevor, *Festung Alderney, The German Defences of Alderney* (Barnes Publishing, 2003).
Fergusson, Bernard [Ed.], *The Business of War: The War Narrative of Major-General Sir John Kennedy* (Hutchinson, New York, 1858).
Ford, Ken, *Assault on Sicily, Monty and Patton at War* (Sutton, Stroud, 2007).
Fowler, Will, *The Last Raid, The Commandos, Channel Islands and Final Nazi Raid* (History Press, Stroud, 2016).
Gavey, Ernie, *A Guide to German Fortifications on Guernsey* (Guernsey Armouries, 2001).
Ginns, Michael, *Jersey Occupied: The German Armed Forces in Jersey 1940–1945* (Channel Island Publishing, St John, Jersey, 2009).
Grehan, John, *Churchill's Secret Invasion: Britain's First Large Scale Combined Operations Offensive 1942* (Pen & Sword, Barnsley, 2013).
Grehan, John, 'Britain's V1 Site' *Hitler's V Weapons, The Terror Campaign* (magazine special by Key Publishing).
Grehan, John, *Combined Operations: An Official History of Amphibious Warfare Against Hitler's Third Reich, 1940-1945* (Frontline, Barnsley, 2022).
Hamilton, Nigel, *Monty: The Making of a General 1887-1942* (McGraw-Hill, London, 1981).
Hamon, Simon and Grehan, John, *Storming Hitler's British Fortress* (Frontline, Barnsley, 2023).

Hitler, Adolf, *Hitler's Table Talk 1941-1944, His Private Conversations* (Enigma Books, New York, 2000).

Hough, Richard Alexander, *Mountbatten: Hero of Our Time* (Weidenfeld and Nicolson, London, 1980).

Kirkpatrick Charles E., *Joint Planning for Operation Torch* (U.S. Army War College, 1991).

Kirkpatrick, Charles E., *An Unknown Future and a Doubtful Present: Writing the Victory Plan of 1941* (Center of Military History, United States Army, Washington, D. C., 1992).

Lewis, Jon E., [Ed.], *SAS and Special Forces: True Stories of the Fighting Elite Behind Enemy Lines* (Robinson, London, 2004).

Matloff, Maurice and Snell, Edwin M., *Strategic Planning for Coalition Warfare, 1941-1942* (Centre of Military History, United States Army, Washington, 1999).

McLoughlin, Roy, *Living with the Enemy, An Outline of the German Occupation of the Channel Islands with First-Hand Accounts by People who Remember the Years 1940 to 1945* (Channel Island Publishing, St John, Jersey, 1995).

Messenger, Charles, *The Commandos 1940-1946* (William Kimber, London, 1985).

Montgomery, Field Marshal Sir B. L., *Memoirs of Field-Marshal Montgomery* (London 1958).

Neilands, Robin, *The Dieppe Raid, The Story of the Disastrous 1942 Expedition* (Aurum, London, 2005).

Pack, S.W.C., *Operation Husky, The Allied Invasion of Sicily* (David & Charles, London, 1977).

Ramsey, Winston G., *The War in the Channel Islands: Then and Now* (After the Battle, 1981).

Rankin, Nicholas, *A Genius for Deception: How Cunning Helped the British Win Two World Wars* (Oxford University Press, 2009).

Sinel, J.P., *German Occupation of Jersey: A Diary of Events from June 1940 to June 1945* (Jersey, 1945).

Sherwood, Robert E., *The White House Papers of Harry L. Hopkins, Vol. II, January 1942 - July 1945*, (Eyre and Spottiswoode, London, 1949).

Stacey, Colonel C.P., *Official History of the Canadian Army In the Second World War, Volume I, Six Years of War, The Army in Canada, Britain and the Pacific* (Department of National Defense, 1956).

Stephenson, Charles and Taylor, Chris, *The Channel Islands 1941–45: Hitler's Impregnable Fortress* (Osprey, Oxford, 2013).

The Dieppe Raid, The Combined Operations Assault on Hitler's European Fortress, August 1942 (Frontline, Barnsley, 2019).

Thompson, Reginald W. *Dieppe at Dawn: The Story of the Dieppe Raid* (Hutchinson, London. 1956).

Villa, Brian Loring, *Mountbatten and the Dieppe Raid* (Oxford University Press, 1994).

Villa, Brian Loring, *Unauthorized Action, Mountbatten and the Dieppe Raid* (Oxford University Press, 1994).

Young, Peter, *Storm from the Sea* (William Kimber, London, 1958).

Newspapers & Periodicals
Chicago Tribune, 4 December 1941.
Correll, John T., 'Daylight Precision Bombing', *Air Force Magazine* 1 Oct., 2008.

Daily Telegraph, 16 August 1944.

Greenhous, Brereton, "Operation Flodden: The sea fight off Berneval and the suppression of the Goebbels Battery, 19 August 1942", *Canadian Military Journal* (Autumn, 2003).

Internet

Capt. G.A. Browne, "Report on the Operation at Dieppe, 19 Aug 42", Directorate of History, National Defence Headquarters, Ottawa. Canada, Report No. 89, July 1986.

Foreign Relations of the United States, The Conferences at Washington, 1941–1942, and Casablanca,

1943 (Washington: Government Printing Office, Document 336).

Gallup Vault: U.S. Opinion and the Start of World War II.

jerseybunkertours.com.

Proceedings of the American-British Joint Chiefs of staff Conferences (Washington, D.C., 24 December 1941–14 January 1942), Annex I.

Library of Congress, "Memorandum in Russian from Joseph Stalin about opening a second front in Europe during World War II, with English translation of same".

Index of People and Places

Abbeville, 67, 71
Adour Estuary, 44, 70
Alderney, 1-2, 16, 19-21, 23, 25, 71-2, 105, 106, 113-4, 116, 124, 126-135, 136-150, 151, 152, 156, 168, 172, 174, 176, 177, 184, 186, 199-205, 208-9
Alexander, General, later Field Marshal Harold, 102
Alexandria, 51
Algeria, 39, 95, 114
Ambleteuse, 11
Antwerp, 120
Arabian Gulf, 101
Australia, 34, 42, 44

Baille-Grohman, Rear Admiral Harold, 74
Balkans, 31, 93, 97
Balmoral House, 203
Baie des Pêqueries, 164, 165, 172
Barfleur, 71
Bayonne, 44
Beachy Head, 82
Beaverbrook, William Maxwell Aitken, Lord, 31
Belle Grève Bay, 152-3
Berck-sur-Mer, 200
Berneval, 66, 77, 83-4
Biscay, 36, 71, 119, 134, 141, 182
Bletchley Park, 68
Bonne Nuit Bay, 180
Bordeaux, 55, 120
Buisson, Clos or Maison du, 193, 197
Bouley Bay, 180
Boulogne, 7, 8, 11, 33, 45, 48-50, 54, 67, 70, 71, 82, 97, 120, 121, 134, 140, 163
Bourne, Lieutenant General Sir Alan, 6, 8
Braye Harbour, 128, 144

Brest, 13, 54-5, 57, 58, 97, 101, 103, 109, 119, 122, 172, 192, 196
Brittany, 118-123
Brooke, Field Marshal Alan Francis, 12, 13, 25-6, 31, 33-7, 39-41, 44, 48, 50, 52, 54, 56-65, 74-6, 78, 80-1, 93-8, 100-2, 123, 138, 199-201, 202
Browne, Captain G.A., 87
Browning, Major General Frederick, 16, 18
Bruneval, 15, 20, 70
Burma, 30, 36, 42, 95

Cadogan, Alexander, 80
Calais, 11, 32, 45, 46, 48, 50, 53-5, 57, 71, 97, 2120, 140, 200
Cachalière Pier, 128
Cairo, 42, 74-6, 78
Canada, 87, 91
Canary Islands, 11
Cap de la Hague, 126
Cap Gris Nez, 71
Casablanca, 93, 95, 103, 123, 130
Caslon, Commodore Clifton, 130
Ceylon, 36
Cherbourg (Cotentin) Peninsula, 11, 54, 62, 71, 80, 97, 103, 104, 109, 120-2, 132, 134, 140, 141, 146-7, 155, 172, 173, 183, 192, 196, 199, 201-2
Chouet headland, 165
Churchill, Winston S., 3, 5-13, 19, 24-6, 29, 30, 32, 38-40, 42, 44, 50, 52, 53, 56-62, 64-5, 69, 70, 74-6, 77-81, 89, 91, 93, 102, 105, 109, 118, 133, 198, 204
Clarence Battery, 153
Clarke, General Mark, 96
Clos Du Hambye, 197
Cobo Bay, 154, 165, 173, 207
Corblets Bay, 73, 128

Corregidor, 42
Crabbe, 180
Crabby Bay, 129
Craig, Colonel Howard A., 37
Crécy, 67
Crete, 30, 97, 102
Creve Coeur, 165, 173
Cunningham, Admiral Andrew, 102
Cyprus, 51

Darwin, 42
Devil's Hole, 180
Dieppe, 5-37, 46, 47, 60, 82-92, 95, 105, 118, 121, 122, 131, 136, 137, 161, 172, 187, 198
Dill, Field Marshal Sir John, 6, 102
Dodecanese, 97, 102
Dover, 5
Dresden, 145
Dunkirk, 5, 33, 48, 54, 71, 105
Durnford-Slater, Lieutenant Colonel John, 83, 86

Eden, Robert Anthony, 51
Egypt, 30, 42, 52, 58, 74
Eisenhower, General Dwight D., 42, 58, 92, 99, 102
Elizabeth Castle, 178
Embury, Air Vice Marshal Basil, 136-7, 149-50, 178
Etaples, 49

Fermain Bay, 154
Fliquet Bay, 180
Fort Albert, 19, 23, 72-3
Fort Hommet, 174, 207
Fort Richmond, 165, 173, 204
Fort Tourgis, 72, 208
France, 11, 13, 14, 21, 31-3, 37-8, 40, 44, 45, 51, 54, 57, 61, 66, 70, 78, 79, 85, 90, 94, 97-102, 105, 106, 108, 110, 114, 119, 120, 123-4, 132, 2134, 137, 140, 142, 150, 152, 156, 173, 183-4, 197, 200, 203, 208
French North Africa, 30, 39, 40, 42, 51-3, 55, 61-3, 79, 91, 93, 94, 96, 97, 99, 102, 123, 149

Germany, 1-3, 6-7, 9-12, 14-15, 19-21, 27, 29, 30, 32-6, 38, 44-6, 48, 49, 53, 54, 57, 58, 62, 63, 67, 68-72, 74, 78, 80, 82-9, 91, 94, 95-7, 100, 101-4, 107-8, 110-3, 116, 119, 121, 124, 126, 128, 130-2, 133-5, 137, 140, 141, 145, 146-8, 150, 151, 155-6, 158, 160, 162, 168, 172, 173, 175, 181-4, 186, 193, 197, 199, 201-3, 205-9
Gibraltar, 15, 51, 98
Giffard Bay, 189
Gorey, 178
Grand Havre Bay, 155, 164-5, 172-3
Gray, Major N.W., 149
Greenland, 28
Greece, 93, 97, 100
Grève au Lançon, 179
Greve de Lecq, 180
Guernsey, 1, 3, 7-9, 17, 21, 24, 105-8, 110-14, 116-7, 121, 124, 126-8, 131-3, 135, 151-62, 163-76, 177, 178, 184, 186-7, 196-8, 202-4, 205, 207

Hancock, Major General Michael Stephen, 22
Hardelot, 70
Harriman, Averell, 78-9
Harris, Air Marshal Sir Arthur, 138
Hasse, Generalmajor William, 91
Haviland Hall, 168
Havelet Bay, 153
Haydon, Major General Joseph, 149
Herm, 106, 166-7, 178
Hitler, Adolf, 3, 5, 7, 27-8, 30, 35, 40, 58, 79, 80, 95, 98, 112, 113, 114, 116, 134, 140, 148, 201
Home, Vice Admiral Frederick J., 41
Hopkins, Harry Lloyd, 31, 51, 59, 61
Hong Kong, 30
Houlgate, 12
Hughes-Hallett, Captain John, 37-8, 65, 70, 75, 76, 82, 87, 90, 136, 139, 149-50

India, 30, 34, 36-7, 42, 44, 49
Isle of Wight, 22-3, 67, 69
Ismay, Lieutenant General Hastings Lionel, 5, 6, 9, 52, 57, 59
Italy, 29, 51, 79, 93-4, 95, 97-100, 140

Index of People and Places   221

James, Admiral Sir William, 70, 82
Japan, 27-30, 34, 36, 37, 42, 44, 58, 101, 102
Jersey, 1, 3, 9, 21, 24, 105-8, 110-4, 116, 124, 131-3, 135, 151, 152, 156, 162, 176, 177-88, 189-98, 203, 205, 205, 206, 207

Kennedy, Major General Sir John, 25
Kennedy, Joseph P., 111
Keyes, Admiral of the Fleet Roger John Brownlow, 8-13
King's Mills, 166, 172
King, Fleet Admiral Ernest Joseph, 55, 61, 65, 98, 99, 101
King George VI, 110
King, William Lyon Mackenzie, 30

La Collette, 178
La Corbiere, 178, 184, 13, 205
La Croix au Bion, 196
La Falaise, 179
La Moye, 178, 189, 193
L'Ancresse Common and Bay, 2-3, 151-2, 155, 159, 164-5, 167-8, 172-5, 207
La Varde, 165
Les Clotures Road, 3
Le Braye, 192
Le Havre, 15, 33, 49, 71, 120, 122
Leigh-Mallory, Air Chief Marshal Sir Trafford, 48, 67, 74, 75, 136, 139, 150
Le Mont du Coin, 184
Le Mont de la Rocque, 184
Les Blanches Banques, 177
Les Effards, 2, 167, 172
Les Landes, 192
Les Lohiers, 165, 166
Lewis, Sub-Lieutenant D.J., 83
L'Etacq, 184
Le Touquet, 7, 45, 49
Le Villocq, 167
L'Islet, 165
Littlehampton, 77
Lofoten Islands, 8, 9, 13
London, 25, 40, 60, 61, 64, 76, 98, 103, 108, 110, 111
Longy Bay, 72
Lorient, 119, 200

L'Ouziere, 192
Loustalot, Second Lieutenant Edward, 85
Lovat, Lieutenant Colonel Simon Lord, 70, 86

Maaloy, 12
Madagascar, 42
Malaya, 30, 42
Malta, 51
Manila, 42
Manly, Chesly, 28, 29
Marshall, General George Catlett, 33-5, 37-41, 43, 44, 52-3, 55, 57-60, 61-3, 96-101
Maufant, 193
McCool, Major Brian, 91
McMullen, Lieutenant-Commander, 89
McNaughton, General Andrew, 76
Mediterranean, 11, 31, 36, 40, 42, 51, 52, 58, 79, 93-102, 124, 132, 142, 150
Miellette Bay, 165
Mitcheson, Corporal James, 202
Molotov, Vyacheslav Mikhaylovich, 60, 76
Montgomery, Lieutenant General (later Field Marshal Bernard), 66, 74, 76, 204
Mont Matthieu, 184
Mont Saint, 166
Mont Sohier, 193
Mountbatten, Lord Louis Francis Albert Victor Nicholas, 12-16, 24-5, 34, 37, 38, 43-4, 46, 49-52, 53, 59, 64, 65, 67, 7-2, 74-6, 81, 87, 90, 92, 96, 101-4, 118-23, 131-4, 136-8, 148-50, 151, 153, 158, 199-200, 203-4
Mourier Valley, 189
Morocco, 39, 93, 95
Moroso, John, 202
Moscow, 74, 78, 79, 81

Nantes, 119
Netherlands East Indies, 42
Newhaven, 77
Newtown, 128
Noirmont Point, 184, 187, 189, 193, 205
Norman, Group Captain Sir Nigel, 20-1
Normandy, 12, 13, 140, 141, 172-3, 176, 197, 201
Northern Ireland, 28

Norway, 7, 8, 9, 10, 13, 17, 30, 36, 39, 54, 58, 116, 137, 176

Ostend, 70

Paget, General Sir Bernard, 13, 130
Papua New Guinea, 42
Paris, 46, 47, 48, 50, 110, 120-2, 176
Pearl Harbor, 27-8, 34
Persian Gulf, 99
Petit Mourier, 179
Petit Point Bay, 154
Petit Portelet, 181
Petit Plemont, 179
Philippines, 42
Pleinheaume, 167
Pleinmont, 157, 208
Port Albert, 19
Portal, Air Chief Marshal Sir Charles, 37, 95, 96, 98, 199
Portelet Bay, 181, 184, 193
Port Infer, 165, 173
Port Soif, 165, 166, 173
Pointe de Harbanc, 7
Pulias, 165
Pound, Admiral Sir Dudley, 99, 101
Pourville, 66, 88
Puys (Puits), 87

Rennes, 54, 120, 122
Roberts, Major-General J.H., 67, 74, 75, 83, 90
Rocquaine Bay, 157
Rocque Balan Lane, 3
Rohais Manor, 168
Rommel, Field Marshal Erwin, 30, 74
Ronez Point, 178, 180
Roosevelt, Franklin D., 27-34, 40-1, 44, 50-3, 56, 58, 61-3, 78, 79, 93, 96, 97, 103
Rouen, 46, 47, 120, 122-3
Royal Bay of Grouville, 179, 181, 184, 189, 192-4, 197, 206
Royal, Lieutenant F., 82
Rozel Bay, 180
Russia (Soviet Union), 1, 11, 13, 30-2, 35-9, 40, 45, 48, 49, 51-4, 56-8, 60, 62-4, 68, 76, 78-80, 94, 97, 98, 99, 100, 102, 112, 115, 124, 133, 141, 157
Ruxton, Lieutenant Anthony, 86

Sainte-Cécile, 45
Saint-Nazaire, 14
Saint-Valery-en-Caux, 109
Saline Bay (Alderney), 73
Saline Bay (Grandes Rocques), 154, 165, 166, 173-5, 208
Saltpans, 167
Sardinia, 97, 102
Sark, 7, 103-4, 106, 116, 124
Saye Bay, 72
Scotland, 12, 28, 52
Sinel, Leslie P., 111
Singapore, 30
Soldier's Bay, 153
Solent, 69, 77
Somervell, General Brehon B., 41
Somme, 46-7
Stalingrad, 30
Stalin, Joseph Vissarionovich, 30, 58, 64, 76, 78-80
St Anne, 72, 127, 129, 202, 204, 208
St Aubin, 177, 178, 179, 184, 185, 187, 189, 193, 194, 205
St Brede, 184
St Brelades Bay, 193
St Catherine's Bay, 181, 194
St Helier, 111, 178, 185, 187-8, 189, 193, 194, 205
St Laurent-sur-mer, 45
St Marlo, 155
St Martin, 74, 194
St Mary, 197
St Omer, 50
St Ouen's Bay, 177, 179, 184, 185, 192, 204, 206
St Peter Port, 111, 121, 122, 151-3, 159-61, 164, 168, 186, 208
St Peter's Mill, 179, 197
Spitsbergen, 11
Stimson, Henry Lewis, 33
St Samson, 151, 159, 160
St Saviour, 193
Sturges, Major General Robert 'Bob' Grice, 136, 149-50

Todt, Dr Fritz, 113
Tunisia, 39, 95, 96
Turkey, 31, 51, 98

Index of People and Places

United States of America, 3, 10, 26, 27, 28, 29, 30, 31, 33-42, 44, 50, 52, 53, 55, 56, 58, 59, 61-3, 78, 80, 85, 88, 93, 96, 98, 100, 101, 111, 112, 118, 130, 131, 142, 150

Vaagso, 12
Val de la Mare, 179
Varengeville-sur-Mer, 66, 77, 86
Vauville, 127, 129
Vazon Bay, 152, 154, 159, 165-8, 172-5, 207
Verclut, 184
Ville au Bas, 179
Walch, Lieutenant Colonel A.G., 16
Warren, Lieutenant 'Bunny', 122
Washington, 28, 29, 34, 40, 44, 50, 52, 57, 59, 102
Wedemeyer, Colonel Albert C., 37
Wildman-Lushington, Major General Godfrey Edward, 150
Wilson, President Woodrow, 93
Wybud, Commodore, 83
Young, Major Peter, 84, 86
Yugoslavia, 93, 100